THE GRIT IN
THE PEARL

THE GRIT IN THE PEARL

THE SCANDALOUS LIFE OF MARGARET, DUCHESS OF ARGYLL

LYNDSY SPENCE

First published 2019, 2020

The History Press
97 St George's Place, Cheltenham,
Gloucestershire, GL50 3QB
www.thehistorypress.co.uk

British Library Cataloguing in Publication Data.
A catalogue record for this book is available from the British Library.

ISBN 978 0 7509 9325 8

Typesetting and origination by The History Press
Printed and bound in Great Britain by TJ International Ltd.

'She was an absolute demon; knockout green eyes, mesmeric –
you could not but stare into her eyes.'

Vanity Fair's obituary of Margaret, Duchess of Argyll

Contents

Acknowledgements

Although the scandal surrounding Margaret, Duchess of Argyll, occurred half a century ago, it continues to haunt those who were involved. Many people were reluctant to speak of Margaret, hardly surprising given the themes of libel and slander that were common in her life. On that note, I should like to thank those who helped me by sharing their anecdotes of Margaret, candidly and confidentially, for offering an insight into her character, and also to those who granted me permission to reproduce photographs: April Ashley; Janet Bowler at Tiree Historical Centre; Steve Chibnall; Lord Gowrie; John Halsey; Beverley Jackson; Danny Johnson; Colin Jones; Nicholas Maxwell; Keith McIntyre at *Scottish Field*; David Niven Jr; Michael Thomas; Michael Thornton; Allan Warren; Kim Booth; Julia Camoys Stonor, and Professor Sally Wheeler. I also extend my gratitude to Lady Violet Manners for her early enthusiasm in the project.

Careless People

Before Margaret existed, her mother Helen thought babies were a luxury; something to be anticipated, a rarity.[1] She waited for seven years before conceiving Margaret, her first and only child, and until the birth harboured a romantic notion of babies. Motherhood, however, was not what Helen had imagined and she thought her child a disappointment. 'The top was what I was supposed to be,'[2] Margaret later wrote. But Helen was intent on exposing Margaret's shortcomings – instilling insecurity within her and reminding her that, despite her father's adoration, she was nothing special. The child was a competitor, a usurper in what had become a female-dominated household. Margaret knew her place: 'There was nothing very dazzling about me. I had no high rank, nor indeed any rank at all. Far from being the possessor of great beauty, my photographs show me to have been rather a plain little girl.'[3]

She was born Ethel Margaret Whigham on 1 December 1912 at The Broom,[4] a house on her maternal grandparents' 30-acre estate in Newton Mearns, Scotland, 7 miles outside of Glasgow. Then a small village, it smacked of ordinariness, even dreariness; the several big houses and the railways and roads leading to Glasgow and Ayrshire provided employment for the working classes, and the area was popular with the middle classes who commuted to their jobs in the city. Given the lifestyle Margaret was born into, and the woman she was to become, the place of her birth was symbolic of herself; a girl from a family of mixed fortunes who, albeit briefly, rose to one of the highest ranks of the aristocracy.

Margaret's father, George Hay Whigham, was an industrious man and a self-made millionaire. This ingenuity was perhaps the result of his forefathers' precarious fortunes, beginning in the twelfth century when they were given the lands of Dundas by King David I of Scotland and ending with his father, David Dundas Whigham, who had lost his inheritance of almost £1 million in the City of Glasgow Bank collapse of 1878.[5] Therefore David, who had read law at St Andrew's University, could not afford to study for the bar and instead entered the wine trade, working for Oliphant and Company of Ayr, and later forming his own wine merchant firm, D.D. Whigham and Fergusson.[6] George's mother Ellen (née Murray-Campbell) came from a rich family who owned the Ayr Racecourse; however, her sister inherited it all and gave it to a dogs' home to spite her family for the lack of attention they paid her. Thus in 1879 George, the youngest of ten children (six sons[7] and four daughters) was born to parents who had known wealth and who, at the time of his birth, were grappling with the economics of raising a large family. Stories of their hardship might have been exaggerated, for the 1881 census listed the Whigham family as living at Dunearn, a spacious cottage, with a parlour maid, a cook, a governess, and a nursery maid. At the age of 17, George left school and worked for 30s a week as an apprentice civil engineer at Forman & McCall, a Glasgow firm which headed the commercial development of western Scotland. Having served his time of five years, George was appointed resident engineer on the Lanarkshire and Ayrshire Railway. He also attended night classes to study accountancy, and, by the age of 25, he was not only a qualified civil engineer but also a chartered accountant. George was tall, dark and handsome; his clever brain saw him ascend the corporate ladder, but it was his looks that caught the attention of society women.

One woman in particular stood out; her name was Helen Marion Hannay, the daughter of Margaret (née Richardson) and Douglas Mann Hannay, a rich cotton merchant. Helen was beautiful, capricious and spoilt; her parents had given her every-thing she wanted but they were not prepared to let her marry a penniless man. Thus after a conference with Douglas, George was given an ultimatum: he could marry Helen if he were to earn £500 a year,[8] a daunting task for any young man. In January 1905 George left for Egypt, determined to earn the figure set, but he must have detoured and travelled to New York, as the Civil Engineer List of 1905 recorded him as working for the Cuban Railroad Company at their offices on Broadway.

Given the privileged circumstances in which George's parents were born, it came as a surprise when they, too, discouraged marriage between their son and Helen. They doubted a rich man's daughter could make George happy. And they were also sceptical when George wrote from Khataba, where he was engaged as manager of the Wardan Estate Company, to say he expected an increase in his salary. 'A little too strongly *couleur de rose*,' his mother remarked. Eighteen months later, on 8 August 1905, George and Helen were married, after which she became estranged from her parents and was cut off financially. The couple lived in genteel poverty in Egypt, and Helen recalled those years, childless and living off George's modest salary, as the happiest of her life.

In the spring of 1912, Helen and George moved to New York, where he was to assist Sir William Van Horne with the design and construction of the Canadian Pacific Railway. They stayed with George's brother, Jim, the editor of *Town and Country* magazine, at the apartment on Park Avenue that he shared with his wife, Frances, and newborn daughter, Sybil. Soon after their arrival,

Helen became pregnant, an untimely discovery, as George was planning to leave for Cuba[9] to work for the Cuban Railroad, and his scheduled departure would coincide with the latter stages of her pregnancy. Thus Helen had little choice but to return to her parents' home in Newton Mearns to await the birth of her baby.[10] The homecoming was far from the enthusiastic event Helen had anticipated during the lonely, homesick days in New York, confined to her brother-in-law's apartment while George worked long hours. It soon became apparent that she had come home not to see her parents and restore their relationship, but to take advantage of their hospitality. The Hannays knew they were being used, and they continued to resent Helen for eloping with George, whom they thought not good enough and after the family's money. Their appraisal was not only snobbish but hypocritical, as for several generations the Hannays had been merchants in Glasgow, and Douglas's mother Marion (née Paterson Scott) was born in the Gorbals,[11] which had a reputation for being a dangerous slum.[12]

A baby did not signal a new beginning for the two families, and neither did Helen's gesture of naming her child Ethel Margaret, after her sister and mother, for Margaret Hannay was to remain a distant figure in both her daughter's and granddaughter's lives. Perhaps relieving Helen of the conflict surrounding her child's birth was her superstitious nature,[13] as she believed Margaret, born on a Sunday, was destined to be 'bonnie and blithe, and good and gay'. Six weeks later, on 1 February 1913, Helen and her baby sailed from Liverpool to New York on board the RMS *Mauretania*.[14] As with the dilemma surrounding Margaret's birth, the place of her childhood was undecided. George remained in Havana, and Helen in New York, though she planned to join him there.[15] However, he returned to New York, where he wanted to stay indefinitely, as by then he was a rich man, having merged his interests of engineering and accountancy.[16] It was in America that Margaret's childhood began, and a part of Helen's life ended.

★

The first home Margaret would recall was a fourteenth-floor duplex apartment at 1155 Park Avenue, Carnegie Hill, named after the mansion Andrew Carnegie had built on 5th Avenue and 91st Street. The opposite of the sleepy life led at Newton Mearns, of riding and hunting, and the grey industrial sprawl of Glasgow, this American city suited Helen and George's temperaments: cold, ambitious, modern. Its aesthetic was forever changing, adapting to trends rather than tradition; in 1913, the Armory Exhibition opened, puzzling aesthetes accustomed to the fanciful art from La Belle Époque, with its abstract nude paintings and Cubist Surrealist styles. Unlike British society, a lack of title or high birth did not limit the Whighams' social standing in Manhattan, and George's money opened doors that would have otherwise remained closed. They were listed in the Social Register – it was not quite Burke's Peerage but it carried a certain exclusivity for those who were rich and, preferably, 'WASP' (white Anglo-Saxon Protestant).

During those early years in New York, in the shadow of the First World War, Margaret had become Americanised; she spoke with an American accent – although Helen would attempt to rid her of this – and she played in Central Park. Her earliest memory of the city was not of its tall buildings, dominated by the Woolworth Tower (the Chrysler and Empire State buildings were yet to be constructed), and the wide tree-lined avenues of the Upper East Side, but of the deafening noise. Night after night Margaret lay awake in her brass bed, listening to ships' horns as they navigated the Hudson and East rivers, the haunting sound evoking thoughts of dying and death. This morbid curiosity with death and the sorrowful thoughts Margaret had did not strike her as strange. She was never sheltered from the adult world of her parents, and although only 2 years old when war was declared, she became a spectator to the effect it had on them, her father in particular. It forced George and Helen to decide whether or not they would remain in New York rather than uproot Margaret and return to Scotland; the latter, George felt, was in the best interests of his own patriotism. His brother, Walter, had gone to France with the 51st Highland Division and was gassed at Ypres and invalided out. During this period, his brother Jim was writing and editing *Metropolitan Magazine*, a left-leaning publication[17] accused by highbrow writers of having no standards, and he used his articles to promote the message of war and to convince Americans to join the cause. An article entitled 'Is America Honest?' prompted a response from President Woodrow Wilson, and he attempted to suppress Jim's journalism under the Espionage Act. Margaret, as young as she was, recalled the excitement that a world war brought; she listened to 'Over There', a patriotic song played on her parents' phonograph, its rousing lyrics warning of the 'Yanks' taking up arms. Finally, after much deliberation, Helen and George decided to remain in New York, and he was relieved when his adopted country entered the war on 6 April 1917, even if he did not enlist to fight, as the idea of living in peace while his countrymen died inspired feelings of guilt.

Throughout Margaret's childhood, she was a loner, though she preferred the term independent. The latter could hardly sum up her abilities, for she was never taught to fend for herself – all her life she could not boil a kettle, prepare a basic meal, and she never made her own bed. But she was solitary, and this isolation nurtured a stubborn and rebellious character. This streak of rebellion was apparent early on, when at the age of 2 she chose her own name, insisting on being known as Margaret instead of Ethel, despite its origins as an Old English word for noble. She achieved what she had wanted, and perhaps Helen thought the name Margaret (Greek for 'pearl') the nicer of the two, for 'Ethel … must have been chosen in a moment of madness'. She had no friends, for she disliked other children; they touched her toys and made a mess of the nursery. She liked things to be neat, orderly.

This transferred on to her clothes, and from a young age she was drawn to pretty dresses; her childhood ambition was to wear a pair of high-heeled shoes and Helen's taffeta petticoat. She was particularly fond of a trio of teddy bears (she disliked dolls), and they had their own knitted clothes and sets of bedroom furniture.

There was nothing unusual about Margaret's childish fixation with the bears, whose fur was bald from her kisses, but it established a love for inanimate objects, placing far greater importance on material things. On one occasion, when the family was setting sail for England, Margaret insisted the bears come too, along with trunks of their clothes and their pram. George put his foot down and refused to bow to Margaret's demands concerning the bears. 'If my teddies don't go, then neither do I,' she told her father, and he relented when faced with a tantrum on the gangplank. It was a universal response from a spoilt child, but the lesson was greater: Margaret had won. The only rule imposed on Margaret was punctuality, especially at meal times. If she were late she would be criticised for being inconsiderate not only to her parents but also to the servants, who were, as Helen said, of far greater importance to the household than she was.

Margaret's identity as her parents' only child was so strong that she dreaded the intrusion of a sibling, and as punishment, Helen often threatened her with a brother or sister. Those words, although frivolous, had a devastating impact on Margaret, and she grew more possessive of the world she inhabited between the walls of 1155 Park Avenue. Helen was outspoken and possessed a critical eye which caught the minutest of details, and Margaret came to dread her mother's candour. 'Nothing was sacred,' Margaret later said. 'Rome would be dismissed as very cold and a boring pile of old stones.' The atmosphere within the household was dependent on Helen's moods, and Margaret entered her mother's bedroom each morning to greet her, not knowing if she would be 'bright and loving' or 'complaining and bad-tempered'. If Helen had a difficult night, Margaret and the servants were expected to be quiet, and if she awoke in a pleasant frame of mind, they knew her mood could change in an instant.

Many dismissed Helen as emotionally unstable. However, Margaret thought her 'fey', as Helen could be whimsical and at times was 'easily impressed by anyone or anything' – a contrast to the hardness she applied to motherhood. A jealous streak ran through Helen, the result of having sacrificed so much to marry George, and despite the happiness she felt in Egypt during those first years of marriage, the arrival of Margaret changed their dynamic and she was no longer the star of his life. As with her toys, Margaret did not wish to share her father, and he did not discourage her possessiveness. The love and devotion he gave to Margaret were gradually taken from Helen, and Margaret herself did not think her mother deserving of it. George appeared to exist only for Margaret, his prized possession, and Helen felt excluded from their private world. 'I absorbed a great deal from being with grown-ups. That's how I learnt,' Margaret recalled. 'I heard them talking and I used to listen quite hard.'[18] It did not help Helen's plight when George taught Margaret how to argue without raising her voice, a concept foreign to her, for her chief emotions ran the gamut of moody silences to hysterical outrage. Margaret thought her father reliable and kind; he rarely lost his temper, but when he did it was wicked and volatile, though never directed at her.

As Margaret grew older Helen sought to improve her physical appearance – 'She always wanted me to look my prettiest' – and aged 6 she was given a permanent wave, as Helen disliked her straight hair. This obsession with Margaret's looks was enforced early on, as Helen, considered the 'ugly duckling' of the Hannay family, never felt attractive compared to her brother and sister, who were both praised for their good looks and athletic abilities. And Margaret became, by her own admission, 'a self-confessed vain little girl'. Helen's fixation with Margaret's outward appearance satisfied her sense of control, but she was frustrated that her child spoke with a stammer which had developed after Margaret was forced to write with her right hand instead of her left. As with most things, Helen thought it curable, and she consulted a specialist who suggested immobilising Margaret's right arm, therefore forcing her to resume writing with her left hand. For unknown reasons it was never attempted, perhaps thought of as a gimmick by the Whighams despite being a popular treatment.[19] The market for peddling goods and cures to those with speech impediments was filled with empty promises and fraudulent practices. Booklets released in 1917, the year in which Margaret began treatment for her stammer, ranged from *Straight Talking Stammerers* to a correspondence course between the stammerer and a speech therapist. As with any abnormality in speech (widely thought of as a 'masculine weakness',[20] or a flaw in Margaret's character) it was the topic of much shame (often referred to as a 'handicap') and was a popular theme of entertainment among music-hall performers and comedians. In the light of the First World War, and with stammering being a chief affliction in those suffering from shell shock, a warning was issued in the press: 'Those who entertain wounded soldiers should be careful to avoid certain forms of entertainment which are regarded in ordinary circles as harmless and mirthful.'[21]

Margaret was taken to London and placed under the care of Lionel Logue, a speech therapist in Harley Street who, although he had no formal training,[22] would later treat King George VI. The sessions were unsuccessful, and the reason behind this is unclear, but owing to Margaret's reputation of 'never [appreciating] the true value of anything in life',[23] it can be assumed she did not apply herself to Logue's exercises. The doctor who almost cured her was Sir John Weir, the Physician Royal to four British monarchs who, at the time of Margaret's treatment, had recently become interested in homeopathy. She went to see him at the London Homeopathic Hospital, where he was a consultant physician, and he prescribed her two types of white powder, to be taken twice daily.[24] The medical world remained unconvinced of his remedy, and George and Helen thought they were placebos. But Margaret claimed it worked and her stammer did improve. However, Sir John changed the powders without telling her, and her stammer became worse. She then decided to give up on finding a cure and accepted that she was a stammerer. Helen, though, was far from understanding and her only response was impatience.

Not only did Margaret have a speech impediment, but Helen also thought she lacked a sense of humour. A psychiatrist was consulted and it was suggested Margaret be taken to the cinema to watch Charlie Chaplin comedies while her parents observed her small, unsmiling face. Books were her preferred recreation, though Helen worried that the strain on Margaret's eyes was too great and she would have to wear spectacles if her reading habit continued. The latter would be another physical flaw,[25] from Helen's point of view, and Margaret's reading time was rationed, which, to her, was the 'worst punishment'. From Helen's perspective the 'worst punishment' might have been having a child with whom she shared so little in common. It was said that Helen liked to laugh at herself and others, using humour to emphasise her own and other people's shortcomings. Margaret credited her mother with being witty – even if she did not find her jokes funny – and thought it a cruel and intimidating character trait. For Helen, whose relationship with her parents made her something of an outcast within the Hannay family and who was often ignored by her husband, this non-existent familiarity with Margaret must have inspired a lack of maternal warmth and enforced the emotional distance between them.

Whether or not Helen attempted to bond with Margaret remains unclear, though for the first six and a half years she cared for her child herself[26] before going to London in 1919 and hiring a governess, a Miss Jean Scott,[27] to accompany her back to New York. Miss Scott would remain with Margaret until she was old enough to attend a suitable day school; she was briefly enrolled in the Brearley School and was withdrawn as the curriculum was too challenging. In many ways the Whigham household was a solitary world, with the exception of a nurse[28] for Margaret during her babyhood and a maid for Helen,[29] who was accustomed to staff as before she married she had a nanny, a governess[30] and a lady's maid who had been engaged to care for her clothes. The census for this period listed George, Helen and Margaret as travelling often without any mention of servants – although living in hotel suites for months at a time while they were in England and Europe put staff at their disposal.

It was during a trip to London in 1920 and staying at the Ritz Hotel for the summer that Helen interviewed potential nannies, as English nannies in American households carried a certain cachet.[31] Margaret hid behind a curtain, watching the women come and go, until Miss Winifred Randall entered the room and she was immediately charmed by her sweet face, blue eyes, and youth. 'She's the one, mummy,' Margaret cried, 'please take her.' Miss Randall would become Margaret's friend, confidante, and mother figure; 'I felt that at least I had a real friend who understood me and upon whom I could depend.'[32]

During the summer of 1920, George left his family in London and returned to New York to investigate a new process, invented by the Dreyfuss brothers, for producing artificial fibres. The brothers, who began working from their father's shed in their native Switzerland, first attracted attention for inventing cellulose acetate, which became a staple in the motion-picture and photography industries, and the product was later sold to the expanding aircraft industry. Within a few years they turned their scientific research to refining viscose-acetate, a form of artificial silk, which came out of a tube. George realised the potential for the product within the garment industry, and after several meetings, he sensed that the Dreyfusses were not businessmen and later extracted the Swiss patent at the cost of their original work, from which he profited. Over the next six years, George gambled his money on the product, by then named Celanese, and appointed himself as president of the Celanese Corporations of Britain, America and Canada. He earned millions overnight when its shares on the stock market increased from 6s to £6.

The arrival of Miss Randall and George's interest in the Celanese Corporation changed the dynamic within the Whigham household. Helen became jealous and irritable, feelings that were provoked by Margaret's love for Miss Randall and George's devotion to his new business venture, which saw him neglect her more than before. There were times Margaret feared Miss Randall would pack her bags and leave, particularly when Helen's mood became too much to bear and she had to act as a buffer between mother and daughter. Margaret's only escape was Miss Robinson's dance class at the Plaza Hotel, where, at the age of 10, she met her first boyfriend, Bruce Bossom. They played the Ouija board for fun, asking the mystical device if they would marry; Ouija said 'yes', but when Margaret danced with another boy, Bruce struck him and knocked out two of his teeth.

Regardless of this false start, Margaret learned to enjoy the company of children. As a birthday treat, she was permitted to invite her friends to the New Amsterdam theatre to see *Sally*, a Broadway musical starring Marilyn Miller. Sitting in a private box, she was transfixed by the golden-haired Miller, dressed in a diamond-studded gown and singing 'Look for the Silver Lining', and she elbowed her friends out of the way for a better view. Helen brought Margaret down to earth when she told her Miller's hair was dyed, then a scandalous thing for a woman to do, and perhaps a nod to her lowly origins as a chorus girl and reputation for being 'a foul-mouthed harridan'.[33] As well as her friends at her dance class, Margaret also befriended a young girl with blonde hair, dark eyes and a mournful expression. Her name was Barbara Hutton, the Woolworth heiress, whose mother Edna Woolworth

Hutton had recently died under strange circumstances; she was believed to have suffocated due to mastoiditis, but rumours persisted that she committed suicide by jumping from the window of her suite at the Plaza Hotel. Miss Randall thought Barbara a peculiar little girl – following the death of Edna (whose body she had discovered), she lived with her grandfather Frank Winfield Woolworth at his mansion on Long Island, and after his death in 1919 she would live at a series of boarding schools – and not a good influence on Margaret. The attempt to discourage Margaret from forming a friendship with Barbara was to be in vain, for she was drawn to her pathos. Both were lonely children, the product of troubled mothers, and conditioned to believe that money made everything better.

Friends, however, could not distract Margaret from the tension at home. It had become clear to Helen that George was having affairs with several women, prompting screaming rows, and there was no attempt to conceal their fighting from Margaret, who had become highly strung and sensitive, and as a result, her stammer grew worse. After a particularly volatile fight during a holiday in St Moritz, Helen packed her things and left with Margaret. Aside from wanting to protect Margaret from any hint of scandal, Helen must have known that taking her away would punish George. It appeared to work, for he went after Helen and brought her and Margaret home, though his promise to remain faithful was an empty one for he continued his extramarital affairs, and in 1924 he was listed as co-respondent in a divorce case.[34] The frustration Helen felt from George's philandering and by Margaret's hero worship of him must have inspired a deeper feeling of bitterness and resentment. Margaret accused her mother of being 'very selfish', and George thought his wife difficult; but neither considered Helen's stance as being that of self-preservation. Either way, it must have prompted her latest remark to Margaret, which occurred around this period. 'No matter how pretty you are,

Margaret,' Helen said, 'and however many lovely clothes we give you, you will get nowhere in life if you stammer.'[35]

By then Margaret was attending the Hewitt School, founded by Miss Caroline D. Hewitt, an Englishwoman who had worked as a governess for a prominent New York family and taught private classes in a townhouse on the Upper East Side. In 1923 Miss Hewitt opened an exclusive day school for girls at 68 East 79th Street, a venture that was partly funded by George. In spite of George's faults as a husband he was determined that Margaret would be offered the chances he did not have, and that she would want for nothing. He told her of the early experiences which shaped his outlook and parenting approach; the shame of being sent to boarding school wearing his elder sister's hand-me-down boots, and of his father's wedding present to his new wife: material for her to make curtains for their bedroom.

As Helen had not received a formal education[36] she failed to match George's enthusiasm for the Hewitt School, and according to Margaret she was 'almost illiterate'.[37] What Helen missed in academia she made up for with her shrewd brain for business and her perceptiveness of people, something both George and Margaret lacked and they were therefore dismissed by her as gullible. 'Don't touch him. I don't like him. He's a crook,'[38] Helen would say when George consulted her on a business deal. She also had a talent for encouraging people to confide in her, which she used against them or to promote George's business interests, and she was credited with helping to build his empire. Perhaps this justified Helen's flippancy toward Margaret and the reason for dismissing her due to her speech impediment and lack of a sense of humour. 'I can't bear you when you're not amusing,'[39] might have summed up Helen's approach to the female sex. She felt proud when Margaret was praised for her appearance, as her looks and how she dressed were something which Helen controlled. As for everything else, Helen simply could not muster the energy to make an effort to understand her daughter.

Despite Margaret's nervous temperament and the personality flaws which Helen pointed out, her academic career showed promise; she had won the first prize two years running for her albums on exotic subjects, such as Egyptian and Greek history. The albums, accompanied by essays, were illustrated with clippings from newspapers and magazines. Determined to win the first prize for a third year, Margaret chose to make an album on medieval history. She went to the school library and selected a leather-bound book on the subject, and carefully snipped the illustrations and pasted them into her jotter. The result was not what Margaret had anticipated and, summoned to Miss Hewitt's office, she was greeted by Helen, who sat stony-faced. Not only had Margaret cheated but she had committed vandalism: the book was a rare edition and irreplaceable. As with most things in her young life she failed to grasp the severity of her actions, and with a shrug, she said: '*Ça va.*' When they returned home, Helen locked herself away in her bedroom, unable to look at Margaret or address the shameful act her daughter had committed. After several days of ignoring her, Helen re-emerged and set sail for Europe.

★

The beginning of the 1920s coincided with Margaret's adolescence; it was the era of Prohibition and the sale of alcohol was forbidden in America. This inspired an underworld of organised crime, and American cities became overrun with bootleggers who smuggled alcohol from Canada and the West Indies. There were substitutes: bathtub gin, moonshine, far more lethal than the real thing, and speakeasies run by gangsters, which were illegal drinking dens disguised in hidden rooms and often raided by police. There was Chumley's on Bedford Street, the Stork Club on 58th Street (later 53rd Street) and the Cotton Club in Harlem, popular with writers, actors, and high society alumni.

The speed at which society was changing troubled Helen, and she voiced her disapproval at the scenes unfolding at smart parties. Her rung of society was being infiltrated by gangsters who had become rich overnight, and it was a familiar sight to see debutantes passed out drunk in cloakrooms. She used it as an excuse to leave New York, appealing to George's sensibilities regarding Margaret and how she was at an impressionable age. Things were not much better in London; drugs were rife among high society and on the nightclub scene, and while gangsters largely supplied alcohol in Prohibition America, in London drug dealers came in the guises of waiters and hostesses. The most prominent, Brilliant Chang, known as Billy to his clients, ran a Chinese restaurant and employed a number of drug dealers before his deportation in 1926,[40] and another dealer, a Jamaican named Eddie Mann, was referred to as 'the most wicked man in London'. However, when Margaret was of age to partake in the nightclub scene, the popularity of cocaine, known as 'snow', had declined.

Given the bad influences which existed in both New York and London, perhaps Helen's wanting to leave was due to George and a new generation of American women known as flappers who, in terms of their loose morals and pleasure-seeking ways, were the biggest temptation of all. Whatever Helen's motives were, she achieved her own way. On a summer's day in 1926, the Whighams sailed to England, and Margaret watched as the skyline that had been her home for almost fourteen years slipped out of sight.

2

An English Girlhood

Margaret was 13 years old when she came to live in England. By then she had crossed the Atlantic fourteen times, an underwhelming experience for a child so worldly, and she dismissed ocean liners as the equivalent of taking a train to Glasgow: 'It was absolute peanuts'. The Whighams had left Prohibition behind in New York, and in London the twenties were beginning to roar. It was a summer of political upheaval; their arrival coincided with the General Strike of 1926, in which the General Council of the Trades Union Congress (TUC) called a strike to force the British Government to prevent the reduction of wages and worsening conditions for coal miners. For nine days London came to a halt: trains and buses were driven by undergraduates, society women operated telephone switchboards, and debutantes ran canteens for strike-breaking lorry drivers. It is doubtful the Whighams felt the fallout between the TUC and the government, but, as in New York, change was in the air.

The family moved into a house on Charles Street, Mayfair, which George planned to lease until he found a permanent address. As Margaret had known from her summer holidays in London, the social season began in May and reached its peak in June and July, with the smart set departing for the Continent in

August. She was too young to partake in this rite of passage for girls from her background, but her parents still wanted to adhere to the traditions of the British upper classes, which would be a steppingstone for when Margaret came of age. She was therefore enrolled in Miss Wolff's classes, which catered to girls from wealthy families, and her classmates included Cecil Beaton's sisters, Nancy and Baba; and Lord Birkenhead's daughter, Pamela Smith. The establishment, founded by Helen Wolff and her brother, occupied two upper floors on South Audley Street, off Park Lane, above a saddler's shop. Miss Wolff, an eccentric who carried lorgnettes to hone in on her girls, had a 'tongue as sharp as her nose', and despite being an 'excellent, though exacting, teacher' she was 'impatient of slowness and a little too openly delighted with originality'.[1] Although the establishment was considered a finishing school for young ladies, the curriculum was formal: English, mathematics, geography, art, languages, and elocution. The girls were unruly, and Pamela Smith disrupted lessons by asking to go to the lavatory every half an hour; each time, she spent twenty minutes sliding down the bannisters. In her memoirs, Margaret wrote that she was 'very happy' during her term at the school, even if she did not shine as a pupil. She excelled, however, at dance lessons with Madame Vacani, who was London's most prominent dancing teacher in those days – her future pupils included Princesses Elizabeth and Margaret Rose, and a young Elizabeth Taylor. There, Margaret was taught ballroom dancing (her favourite) and social etiquette. In 1929 she performed in Miss Vacani's matinee at the London Pavilion, in a segment entitled 'lawn tennis girls of the 1880s', and the photograph appeared in *The Sketch*.

After a period of living in London George moved his family to Ascot, a stark contrast to the hustle and bustle Margaret was accustomed to. 'They tried to keep me out of London,' Margaret recalled, though George's favourite pastime of golf was his main reason for leaving. He bought Queen's Hill, a mansion surrounded by 30 acres of land, overlooking the Ascot racecourse and within close proximity to the golf course. There, George played the part of a landed gentleman, perhaps hoping to emulate the aristocratic families Margaret would become acquainted with, or so Helen had hoped. Rich as he was, his money was not an attractive feature on the social scene: extreme wealth – or rather, overt displays of wealth – was deemed 'New York-ish, ill-mannered, and ill-bred'.[2] It could open doors for Margaret; it afforded her world travel, reservations at the finest establishments, fashionable clothes ('it went without saying that well-dressed children had common mothers'),[3] but it would not endear the Whigham family to what the British considered 'old money'. However, working in Margaret's favour was the shift in social sensibilities, which had changed after the First World War. It was the era of the Bright Young Things, and class barriers were becoming ambiguous, often for shock value: royalty mixed with film stars, and actresses married aristocrats. And so, while George's own generation looked down on his vast wealth and self-made origins, Margaret was being launched into an entirely different sphere.

By this time Margaret's personality was firmly established. She respected nobody except her parents, a stance that was enforced by George and Helen, who expressed little to no regard for authority – ironic, as George's paternal grandfather was a Justice of the Peace. From George's perspective the term 'no' did not exist and Margaret decided that she, too, would trample over such restrictions. In Margaret's world, anything could be bought, most things were replaceable, and everything was taken for granted. As she grew older, and when the excuse of immaturity could no longer be applied, she was accused of being rude (years later she befriended J. Paul Getty and told him he was a bad father), deceitful, and lacking a moral compass. Such things were learned in the nursery, for the fundamental traits of Margaret's character were always there: a lack of a sense of humour, her cheating at the Hewitt School, the hold she had over her father, and the affection she inspired in Miss Randall. She also harboured a phobia of becoming bored – surely all the money in the world could not keep her occupied – and cynicism has the ability to dim even the brightest of jewels.

In an attempt to cure Margaret's boredom in the countryside and to answer her whims, George bought her three puppies. She loved the dogs, and all her life she had a passion for animals and was kind to them. 'I wondered sometimes,' her friend Brodrick Haldane wrote, 'if she ever trusted or truly loved anybody other than her father and her dogs.'[4] Helen thought them a nuisance and forbade the dogs to bark when she was taking her afternoon nap, which Margaret thought an impossible demand. 'So I used to practically *sit* on them while she was having this nap,' she recalled.[5] Appealing to her father to go against Helen and side with the dogs did not work and he advised Margaret to comply with her mother's wishes, as it would mean an easier life for them all. Their new surroundings meant mother and daughter were in one another's company, albeit in a large house, for long periods throughout the day. There were few distractions on their doorstep, unlike in London and New York. And, realising she could not reason with Helen, Margaret began to write letters to her, which she showed to George when he came home from the office. He read the letters and told Margaret to wait three days before sending them, and she knew her attempts to argue with Helen using the written word would only intensify her moods. The letters remained unsent and Margaret's resentment unresolved.

Margaret could have been forgiven for being self-centred and unsympathetic toward her mother. Not only did her youth allow for such churlishness, but it was Helen's decision which had uprooted her from New York and then London. There is no evidence to suggest Helen was a social being; sometimes she attended parties, but she preferred to remain at home and in bed. Her mood swings might explain why she experienced periods of solitude, and she seemed to lack a circle of female friends. There was to be no companionship with her daughter, not even as Margaret grew older, and she was tormented by the fact that her husband was seeing other women. Divorce meant social exclusion, but it would have been impossible for Helen to obtain one even if she wanted to, as until 1937 women could not divorce their husbands on the grounds of their infidelity, and only a man could use such evidence against his wife. Therefore Helen would have needed a viable reason such as bigamy, incest, sodomy or cruelty, and none of those applied to George. But if divorce had been an option for Helen it would have threatened to diminish her life. She had given up so much for him and her stubborn nature would not admit defeat, and alimony was not the same as having access to his millions – which she had helped him make – and it would have blighted Margaret's chances in society. The latter was a rare motherly gesture on Helen's part, but still a small element in a list of reasons not to divorce him. 'My life is so hard to live and such an empty place,'[6] could have easily described Helen's existence. However the gift of hindsight was a useful tool, and as with Margaret, Helen's behaviour did not inspire affection or understanding in others. She was simply her own worst enemy.

Meanwhile, Margaret remained in an emotional limbo between childhood and adolescence. Her appearance was that of an older girl, with her permanent-waved hair and sophisticated clothes, but she continued to dote on the teddy bears from her youth. Then one day she forgot to bring the bears inside and they spent an evening on the lawn, and were discovered the next morning soaked with dew and completely destroyed. This, Margaret would recall, signalled the end of her childhood. Helen must have thought so too, for she approached Margaret and 'did the awful thing' of telling her about sex. Margaret could not fathom why her mother had done this, and she did not want to hear about it.[7] 'It's this awful thing we women have to put up with. We close our eyes and bear it,' Helen said.[8] As she had done with her warning about Margaret's stammer ('you will get nowhere in life ...'), there was a motive behind Helen's information. Was she trying to make Margaret understand the sacrifices she made for her, that she merely put up with this side of married life to ensure they had nice things? Or was it a ruse to change Margaret's perception of her father, in that he would enforce something so 'awful' on to Helen? Either way, the information troubled Margaret and it would remain with her for a long time.

During this period the Whighams thought Margaret was growing up too fast, and to remedy this they took her away from Ascot and London for fresh air in the German countryside. George and Helen took the cure at Baden Baden, a popular destination for the rich and famous who sought to restore their health and fix their ailments at the many spa hotels and sanatoriums. It marked a period of Helen and George taking 'pleasure and health' trips, and as the years progressed Helen opted for warmer climates. 'I was told it would be sweltering in Perth,' Helen said of an Australian jaunt.[9] 'I am chasing the sun, and the more heat-waves I encounter during my visit the more I will like it.'[10] While her parents were taking their exercise and drinking the prescribed tonics, Margaret took solitary walks in the Black Forest before breakfast and in the afternoons she joined her parents for sightseeing excursions. Sometimes George would take her to the opera, as they both loved music, and Helen would remain behind at the hotel. On another occasion, Margaret recalled motoring to Nuremberg, where a large crowd forced the car to stop, allowing her to catch a glimpse of Adolf Hitler as he delivered a speech at one of his first rallies.

They also frequented the Alpine resort town of St Moritz and took lodgings at Suvretta House, an hotel half an hour away, hoping it would keep Margaret away from the tea dances and gala evenings at Badrutt's Palace Hotel, then a popular place to be. But Margaret was far more resourceful than Helen and George gave her credit for, and she slipped away to the Palace Hotel to enjoy sophisticated evenings with the smart set. Her defiance remained unchallenged and George decided it would be best to relocate to the Palace, so Margaret could enjoy herself under their watchful gaze. Her mornings were spent learning to ski and during her lessons she was not short of admirers who volunteered to teach her: Gene Tunney, a former heavyweight boxing champion; Viscount Carlow; the Marquis of Donegall; and Bobby Cunnigham-Reid.

However, Margaret's skiing lessons were soon abandoned in favour of the Corviglia ski club and the company of young Argentine men. She found them more sophisticated than English boys, and they taught her to tango, then a shocking dance owing to its lowly origins in Buenos Aries and its reputation as 'the mating dance'. Years later, she said, '*Everybody* danced – and fast, there was no shuffling about.'[11] Her talent as a dancer was admired by Billy Reardon, the former partner of dancing star Irene Castle, and who had taken the job of concierge and greeter at the Palace Hotel. He asked Margaret to partner with him for an exhibition waltz at the Cresta Ball, the biggest social event of the St Moritz season. For Margaret, who remained spellbound by musicals since that first glimpse of Marilyn Miller on Broadway, there could only be one answer: yes. So confident in her ability as a dancer was she that Margaret agreed without consulting Helen first, and despite her mother's natural pessimism, she was surprised when Helen agreed she could do it. There was to be one rule: Margaret had to wear bloomers with elasticated legs underneath her tulle yellow dress, to preserve her modesty while Reardon swung her around the dance floor. It was her first experience of applause and she begged Reardon to do an encore, but he refused. She was given a pair of silver birds as a memento of her brief period as a dancing star.

★

The arrival of September was bittersweet, as it removed Margaret from close proximity to Helen, which must have been a relief, and she was placed at Heathfield School. George continued his quest of turning Margaret into a well-educated young woman, but she was no longer interested in school. It would be ambitious to excuse this lack of interest as a result of her being reprimanded at the Hewitt School, for the incident did not pique her conscience at all, and unless there were prizes to be won, what was the point in applying herself academically? English schools were stricter than the liberal and artistic approaches of their American counterparts, and Margaret could not see the benefits of learning mathematics or science, or even partaking in games. Helen most certainly would not have approved of the latter, and it is difficult to imagine the young Margaret, dressed in her gym clothes, playing hockey and doing star jumps on the school lawn. Her poor performance in cricket and lacrosse meant she could never become a prefect or win the Lily Badge, the highest academic honour at Heathfield.

The gung-ho atmosphere failed to impress Margaret and she did not want to take part in the school's ethos, promoted by its founder Miss Eleanor Wyatt, of female camaraderie – the school had founded the Scouts Patrol, a decade before the Boy Scouts began – and of teaching the girls 'to see the sky'. Margaret did not view the school as encouraging but, rather, as a controlling menace in her young life. The building was shabby, a complete contrast to the luxurious setting of the Hewitt School, and the classrooms were heated by a singular tepid radiator, in front of which only the prefects were allowed to sit.[12] And the religious Miss Wyatt, to whom the girls were devoted,[13] wore a long black veil knotted on top of her head so she could visit the school chapel at any time. Hoping to enforce a similar pious outlook within the pupils, Miss Wyatt ordered them to attend prayers twice daily, for which they wore starched caps that were otherwise kept in wooden cigar boxes.[14]

The girls, many of whom were boarders, were content to follow the rules, but Margaret could not understand their conforming to a lack of privacy, scheduled baths and being told when they could wash their hair. The latter irritated her, even though it caused her no inconvenience. Her rebellion signalled her as an outsider and troublemaker, and, unlike at the Hewitt School, she had no friends at Heathfield. 'I don't like women in a mass,' she said. She was brought to and from school in a chauffeur-driven Rolls-Royce, and the lack of friendliness she felt was due to her being far more sophisticated than the others. For reasons unknown, it had been previously agreed upon that Margaret could attend lessons only until lunchtime; however, this soon upset the morale of the school and the other girls felt she was being given an unfair advantage. As the car drove away, she shouted: 'Bye-bye girls! Enjoy your hockey and your lacrosse. I'm off to a matinee in London.'[15] This continued for two months until the Whighams were delivered an ultimatum: either Margaret would remain at the school as a boarder, or she would have to leave. She left and was taught at home by an elderly governess. 'I learned more in two weeks than I had in months at Heathfield,' Margaret later wrote.

There would be no more teddy bears and no more school. Margaret turned her attention to boys, a pastime encouraged by George, who thought her friendship with the opposite sex was harmless. He often drove his Rolls-Royce to Eton to fetch a few good-looking boys for Margaret's tennis parties, despite Ascot being out of bounds to Etonians: they hid under a rug until they were out of sight. Among the small coterie of boys were Hamish St Clair Erskine, the son of the Earl of Roslyn; Desmond Parsons, brother of the Earl of Rosse; and Alistair and David Innes-Ker, the Duke of Roxburghe's nephews. The young men, with the exception of the Innes-Ker brothers, were homosexual and were keeping company with pretty girls (Diana 'Dinnie' Skeffington, and Nancy and Diana Mitford were among the favourites of Hamish and Desmond).

★

It was another boy, David 'Winkie' Brooks, the troubled nephew of Nancy Viscountess Astor, who caught Margaret's eye. Aged 17 to her 14, he was an alcoholic and had begun to attract negative attention due to his louche behaviour. Years later, in 1936, with his debts mounting and inability to hold down a job, he jumped to his death from a hotel window in New York. It was Winkie's devil-may-care outlook, though concealed from the Whighams, that attracted Margaret and she began to accept his social invitations. They went to London to see West End plays, and were chaperoned by Winkie's young aunt, Nora Phipps, whom Margaret thought 'more fun than the rest of us put together'.[16] It became clear to the youngsters that Nora was not 'fit to send anyone of Winkie's age out with',[17] and as such they were free to do as they pleased. The mischief continued when Winkie returned to Eton, for he encouraged Margaret to slip away from Queen's Hill to dine with him and his school friends. She did this without being caught, perhaps an indication of the little attention Helen paid to her, or how much freedom she was given. If the latter was true, then George and Helen must have been content with the dynamic, for Margaret was now popular and considered a catch. It was a relief to Helen, as she worried Margaret's stammer would turn her into a recluse; she would be afraid to answer the telephone, to converse with others, and would alienate herself from society because of this 'handicap'. To Margaret's surprise, the opposite sex found her speech impediment attractive, thinking her vulnerable and in need of protection. 'It was a cold comfort,'[18] she said, though she did not discourage the attention.

In the beginning, Margaret's friendship with Winkie was considered harmless, as they had much in common, namely his being half-American and her having grown up in New York, until his behaviour grew more erratic. Like Margaret, Winkie was fond of music, and his mother, Phyllis, ordered him the latest rag-time records from America, which he played on his light blue gramophone. However, a jazz record called 'Black Bottom Stomp', which had been a gift from someone other than Phyllis, provoked a violent reaction[19] and she confiscated the record. As Margaret was accustomed to Helen's moods it is possible that she did not think it strange when Winkie drank too much or became depressed, a reaction prompted by a severe mother who was also possessive and indulgent.

As Winkie had an ally in his aunt, Nancy Viscountess Astor, who treated him as a surrogate son, he invited Margaret to the Astor family seat, Cliveden House. 'I remember being overawed even at the sight of Cliveden and by the stone staircase that led up to the house and seemed to be never-ending,' Margaret wrote in her memoirs. Once inside, Lady Astor did little to put her young guest at ease. A formidable character, and the first woman MP to take her seat in the House of Commons,[20] Lady Astor's tolerance for Winkie's hijinks was running out. Girls and jazz records were one thing, but compromising her Christian Scientist views were another. Alcohol was the culprit, and, as Winkie had vomited outside the dining room before luncheon began, Lady Astor dismissed him from the table and signalled for Margaret to go with him. Margaret later called it 'a shattering experience', and George and Helen were furious with Winkie for having brought shame on to Margaret. They could not understand why Lady Astor had turned her out of Cliveden House 'in disgrace', and Margaret never found out. She had been guilty by association, but it would be one of the few times she was an innocent bystander.

*

During the years Margaret lived in New York her Easter holidays had been spent in Hot Springs, Virginia, where George took her horse-trekking in the Blue Ridge Mountains. There she met Winthrop Rockefeller, who she developed a childish crush on (albeit unrequited). Now that the Whighams lived in England,

Margaret's Easter holidays were to be spent at Bembridge, on the Isle of Wight. It was at Bembridge that she met David Niven, then a 17-year-old public schoolboy with ambitions to attend the Royal Military College, Sandhurst. During the school holidays, he and a group of friends often borrowed a car, despite none of the boys holding a licence, to drive to Shanklin and look for girls. Among the girls was Margaret, and she referred to him as 'my favourite friend' and admitted to having 'a schoolgirl crush' on him, a pointless thing, for she said Niven took no notice of her. This was not true and Margaret was being uncharacteristically modest, for during the holiday she lost her virginity to him.[21] The infatuation with Niven continued after the two weeks spent at Bembridge, and Margaret sneaked off to London with her friend Lady Georgiana Curzon, daughter of the Earl of Howe, to visit him. It was a bold and risky thing for a woman to do in the 1920s – even for a married woman, and it offered a husband grounds for divorce – let alone a 15-year-old girl, but it was typical of Margaret's rebellion and perhaps naivety. Helen had warned her about men and sex, and although it troubled Margaret at the time, her mother's views might have prompted her to see for herself.

As always, Margaret acted without a sense of consequence, but it was to have repercussions when she became pregnant.[22] Naturally, George was furious and 'all hell broke loose' in the Whigham household.[23] In the 1920s an unmarried mother was a social taboo, but being a teenaged one was out of the question for a girl from Margaret's background. Although the scandal was confined to the household (regardless, the servants were apt to talk), it was decided that she would undergo a secret termination at the London Clinic, and nobody, except for the Whighams and the doctor, would know the truth. This, Margaret confided to her biographer,* and although many would have accused her

---

* In her later years Margaret collaborated with several biographers, although during her lifetime the books never came to fruition. Charles

of lying,[24] or embellishing the truth, it was a confession most would have kept secret. In revealing this incident from her past, was Margaret boasting of how she disrespected convention or confiding a past experience that could have blighted her youth and reputation? In those days abortion was illegal and it carried a severe prison sentence, although some gynaecologists complied if the pregnancy was in its early stages. It was expensive and secretive, and the preferred method was curettage; an operation which doctors were often tricked into performing by women feigning symptoms which called for the procedure.[25] After the abortion, Margaret appeared to express neither regret nor relief, and her feelings for Niven did not diminish – she continued to adore him until his death in 1983. The problem had been fixed and the evidence swept under the proverbial carpet. George himself did not blame his precious Margaret, for as with the Winkie Brooks incident, she had surely been misled. Helen must have harboured resentment for all that had taken place, for it was decided that Margaret would leave home and spend three months at a finishing school in Paris.

★

It was hardly surprising that Margaret hated her finishing school, an establishment for English girls run by Madame Ausanne. She hated women en masse, and being with her classmates made it worse, despite charming the opposite sex in England. At Ausanne's her teachers disliked her; they refused to take her seriously until she removed her make-up and nail polish, and she was forbidden to enter through the front door until all traces of it were gone. It was a daily battle, for Margaret refused to appear without a powdered complexion and red lipstick, thus

---

Castle's biography, *The Duchess Who Dared*, released after her death, was based on his recorded conversations with Margaret.

she missed most of her daily instructions. The girls disliked her, thinking her 'fast', and she was no longer the most sophisticated girl at school, as she fancied herself to be at Heathfield; they cast scorn on her American accent and thought her stammer phoney. It did not help that a first cousin was completing a term at the school and she excelled, whereas Margaret was placed in the bottom class. The lessons instructed the girls how to dress, how to enter a room, and how to converse; things which Margaret had been doing for years, as she was never confined to nursery life like the upper-class girls from that era, many of whom were not permitted to sit in a dining room with adults until they were 16. At the end of term, she confessed to having learned nothing, as she felt nothing needed to be improved upon. Three months later Margaret left the school without a backward glance, and said: 'I emerged feeling dowdier and shabbier than I had ever done in my life.'[26]

The remark is an insight into Margaret's fragile self-esteem, as she thought to be beautiful enhanced her self-worth. It was a view which stemmed back to her childhood idiosyncrasy of having everything neat and tidy, from her toys to her appearance. And not only were aesthetic factors at play, Helen's warning that 'lovely clothes' might give the impression of a competent girl, but they could not disguise the fact that Margaret stammered and was, according to her mother, a failure. At finishing school, she was without her fashionable clothes and make-up, and had been ridiculed for her stammer. It was a blow to Margaret's confidence, for when her appearance was picture-perfect Helen was proud of her. 'I thought I was a very plain girl, but I was always vain, she later said.'[27] She was far from dowdy or shabby, as photographs from this period can attest. They show a young woman looking older than her years; her heart-shaped face painted with heavy make-up, her pencil-thin eyebrows emulating the style of Hollywood stars, and her hair cut short and waved around her face. Her posture was poor, perhaps an act of defiance against the required deportment learned at finishing school, and she often stood with her hips jutted forward and a stern expression on her face. Beautiful though she was, it was a cold, lacquered beauty which may appear strange to the modern eye. She exerted an artificial glamour that was associated with actresses, and in the 1920s it was not an occupation or an image to be proud of.

There must have been moments, during the excitement of associating with the jet-set in St Moritz and the exclusion she felt at Madame Ausanne's, when Margaret wished she were in New York, at the centre of a cosmopolitan set. However, Helen's reasoning for leaving New York turned out to be a blessing in disguise. The American economy was beginning to decline, resulting in the Wall Street Crash, a prelude to the Great Depression. George himself boasted that he saw its warning signs before its impact on 29 October 1929, as he had been in New York months before and noticed that every other apartment was for sale or to let. With his usual self-interest he managed to, in his words, 'get out' (presumably this meant out of his investments in the American stock market) in August 1929, a month before stock prices began to decline, and as a result did not lose very much money, despite America being plunged into poverty and the world's economy suffering from the fallout. The same could not be said for his contemporaries, many of whom lost everything. Margaret praised her father with having the gift of foresight, although others might have called it ruthlessness. Either way, it proved George's mettle as a businessman: he was untouchable, his millions remained intact and life continued as before, if not more lavishly.

'I wasn't aware I was rich,'[28] Margaret said when reflecting on her privileged upbringing. It was not a modest remark, but an insight into her inexperience of life and one-dimensional view of the world. While George had striven to give her an education befitting that of a young lady, his money could not broaden her mind to things outside of her social sphere. She claimed to have inherited her father's naivete, which appeared to be true, for George, with all his wealth, thought she would never need to know another life. This supposed naivete was counteracted by self-interest and the ability to rise above or exist outside of a crisis – George had, after all, avoided the First World War and the Wall Street Crash. There was also his solution to throw money at a problem, in the hope it would disappear. Thus, it instilled in Margaret the opinion that nothing was her fault and that her father could get her out of trouble. His protectiveness toward her, cushioned by his money and lack of enforcing discipline, was a misplaced love. The die had been cast, but Margaret had known no different and George could not have foreseen the damage it would later cause.

3

The Season

As with every rite of passage in Margaret's young life, she strove to be the first of her contemporaries to do it. Headstrong, wilful and with disregard for her parents' authority, she wrote in her memoirs: 'My mother must have realised there was no holding me back.' Given this stance, Helen thought it best to present Margaret at court in the summer before her eighteenth birthday,[1] rather than waiting another year. Thus toward the end of 1929, she sent an application to the Lord Chamberlain, asking for permission to do so.[2] It was a decision which pleased Margaret, and it would be one of the few occasions in which she benefited from her mother's controlling nature. Helen also gave Margaret a piece of advice, which she took to heart: 'This is the only time of your life that you will be completely carefree. Be sure to make the most of it. Once you are married you will take on many responsibilities.'[3]

Although Margaret claimed her parents were not ambitious, this statement was either a modest one on her behalf or an attempt to dismiss the effort that went into launching her as a debutante. And she did not mention in her memoirs whether or not Helen herself was presented at court, as a debutante in her youth or as a married woman. That is not to imply that Margaret was being deceitful, even if she did not specify how she came to be a debutante. As with all social classes, there were rules: only a woman who had been presented to the sovereign could act as a representative, and Helen might have received this honour after her marriage to George. It seems likely that Helen's sister-in-law, Mrs Walter Whigham (née Jacqueline de Salignac-Fenelon, the daughter of a French baron), presented her at court during the Whighams' visit to London after the First World War. Therefore Margaret's remark that Helen and George cared little about her social career was a flippant one. Helen did care, and she endured the presentation at court, not for her own advancement but to benefit her daughter when she came of age. It was far from martyrdom, however, given all George had put Helen through with his infidelities and the scandal it could have created, it was both a sacrifice and motive to ensure Margaret's reputation was not tarnished. At least not on Helen's watch.

The date for Margaret's coming-out party was 1 May 1930, the first day of the London social season. Its timing was not a coincidence but a carefully planned tactic on Helen's part. Dismissive of most things, as Helen was, she wanted Margaret to stand out from the other debutantes, whom Margaret herself assumed would be unattractive and boring. To ensure she was given the best start, and to perhaps attract attention, George gave Margaret an unlimited dress allowance, and Helen helped her to select a dozen evening gowns and day outfits for events such as the Derby and Ascot races. The couturiers chosen were, in Margaret's words, 'just down from Cambridge', and she took credit for making them famous.[4] They were Norman Hartnell and Victor Stiebel; the former had opened a dress shop in 1923, and the latter was then working as a designer for the House of Reville. It was an extraordinary thing to do, for at the age of 17 Margaret was still considered a child by most people, to be seen and not heard,[5] and not to be masquerading as a society woman. Drawing on her sharp instincts, Helen sensed that times were changing, and the

1930 season was to launch a new wave of debutantes.[6] The young women who came out that year were bright and bold,[7] a contrast to the plain-faced, retiring girls who came out in the shadow of a world war and the austerity which followed. Reporting on modern debutantes' vices, including 'making up their lips with the public watching them',[8] a newspaper wrote: 'Many of the debutantes who filed past the queen at tonight's court had brought with them a smell of cigarette smoke after the way they, their mothers, and their scarlet-tuniced fathers had smoked in closed cars during the two hours they waited in the Mall.'[9] The Whighams rented a London townhouse for the summer, and a notice was placed in *The Times*: 'Mr and Mrs George Hay Whigham and Miss Margaret Whigham have arrived at 6 Audley Square which they have rented for the season.'

Although Helen's decision to hold Margaret's dance on 1 May was an ambitious one for a girl lacking an aristocratic pedigree, it reflected how the Whighams, George in particular, did things. His entire fortune was, after all, founded on taking risks. Margaret herself said her mother was taking a gamble, for after the other girls had attended her party there was a chance she would not be invited to theirs. Were they attending out of curiosity? Helen might have wondered. And, if they were, she would not let them down. The party cost £40,000, and it brimmed with new money: Helen's jewels sparkled whereas the tiaras and diamonds worn by aristocratic mothers were dull from languishing in bank vaults;[10] the house had been decorated especially for the dance; and Ambrose, the big bandleader, was engaged to entertain the 400 guests.

The biggest gamble, however, was the presence of Helen's elderly mother, Margaret Hannay, who travelled down from Scotland for the party. Throughout the years, communication between Mrs Hannay and her daughter had been sporadic, and the tension between both women often blighted their reunions. There was no explanation as to why she accepted the Whighams' invitation, except for the obvious reason that the socially ambitious Mrs Hannay wanted to see how far her daughter had come. Mrs Hannay was also recently widowed and, no longer under her husband's influence (he refused to forgive Helen for marrying George), she was free to make her own choices. And, on the subject of ambition, could there have been an element of snobbery or competitiveness on Helen's part when it came to the cost of Margaret's party? George's niece, Sybil Whigham, the daughter of his rich brother, Jim, was given an equally lavish party in America, and that same year she was also presented at court by Lady Whigham, the wife of his brother Sir Robert. The Whigham girls might not have had blue blood coursing through their veins, but they had their fathers' millions to open doors. As Helen already knew, Margaret's party hinged on her own personal success with the old guard, whereas Sybil was living in a country where wealth was paramount. It is interesting to note that George's mother did not attend the party, even though she was also still alive and living in Scotland. There was a possibility that Mrs Whigham, a sporting woman and keen huntress,[11] regardless of her advanced age, preferred the Ayrshire countryside to that of a Mayfair ballroom.

The presence of her maternal grandmother was of little significance to Margaret, for she scarcely knew her, and her attention was absorbed by the party. However, Mrs Hannay fell deathly ill forty-eight hours before the party was due to take place, and the status of her life, or expected death, threatened to postpone it. Or worse, cancel it indefinitely. Margaret was inconsolable, not because she particularly cared about her elderly grandmother but because all of her dreams and expectations hinged on throwing the first party of the season. It had been announced in *The Sketch*, one of the first times her name and face were singled out in the press, with a pencil portrait by Olive Snell. Until then she had been mentioned in passing; there was an article[12] on jewels worth £3,500 being stolen at a house party thrown by her parents after thieves had scaled the trellis and entered through a bedroom window, accompanied by a photograph of Margaret walking alongside George, smiling for the camera. She was often grouped together with photographs of socialites at play on the Swiss slopes – 'The Saga of the Snows' ran one such headline in *The Sketch*, referring to Margaret as 'another St Moritz beauty … who is so pretty that everybody thinks she is an American'.[13] The significance of her party being announced in the smartest of magazines, and the subsequent humiliation if she had to cancel it, added to her nervous condition. She could not focus on anything; even the minutest of tasks were a challenge, and she dropped a celebratory cake that was baked especially for the servants as she carried it into the kitchen.

On the day of the party Mrs Hannay's health had deteriorated, and with her breathing growing weaker and her pulse petering out, the Whighams braced themselves for her death. There was a touch of irony, given it had been Helen who, years before, arrived at her estranged mother's home to take advantage of her hospitality and to give birth to Margaret. Now it was Helen's turn to tend to her mother, and, as with Helen's pregnancy and confinement in 1912, this medical emergency threw the household into disarray. But with the stubborn zeal that both her daughter and granddaughter possessed, Mrs Hannay made a complete (and convenient) recovery moments before the guests arrived. Margaret was triumphant; her grandmother survived and her party could go ahead.

Margaret made her entrance as Ambrose's orchestra struck the first chord, dressed in a Norman Hartnell turquoise tulle dress with a tight-fitting bodice embroidered with diamantés, translucent crystals and pearls. The dress itself should have been an indication as to how Margaret's social season would progress, for Helen insisted she wore white, the traditional colour for debutantes. However, Margaret wanted to stand out from the others, and moments before joining her parents to greet their guests she purposely stained the skirt of her white dress and had to change into the turquoise one. Given all that had happened, Helen did not quarrel with Margaret, and Margaret herself pretended the ruining of her original dress was an accident. After all, she had been terribly nervous, had she not? It concluded the dramatics that had played out over the past forty-eight hours. Mrs Hannay had lived and Margaret achieved her own way, the only thing that mattered to her. She was the unrivalled belle of the ball and society columns praised her as 'one of the most beautiful girls',[14] with another writing that '[she] shone out above everybody else, as is only fitting for the heroine of such an evening'.

★

Throughout Margaret's childhood, she thought Helen's pessimism and critical eye could tarnish even the brightest of moments. This rang true for Margaret's debutante season, as Helen began to resent the many invitations she received, as girls were always invited to attend with their mothers. 'For God's sake, do we have to go to another one of those?'[15] Helen often said. Given the money the Whighams spent on launching Margaret, and the hopes they pinned on her success as a debutante, Helen knew she could not decline. So, between herself and Margaret they devised a plan: Helen would stay for an hour before leaving, and she made Margaret promise to meet the chauffeur afterwards and return home by ten o'clock. Then Helen stopped going and she sent Miss Randall to chaperone Margaret, which was ironic given that Margaret was inside at the party and Miss Randall had to wait in the car. It meant that Margaret was left unsupervised, and was therefore given more freedom than other debutantes whose mothers sat on gold chairs all evening. She gained a reputation for being, in her own words, 'a great flirt' and she devised 'the Whigham system' to ensure her dance card was never empty. For the first half an hour she danced with any young man who asked her, and having decided who her favourites were she danced with them all evening and ignored the others. It did little to spoil Margaret's reputation with the opposite sex, but many of her female contemporaries resented her popularity and referred to her as '*that* Maggie Whigham'. This treatment of young men was not confined to Margaret, and many of her fellow debutantes acted badly toward their admirers. Cecil Beaton recalled: 'If an unfavoured young man came up to talk to them, they would sit staring at their baffled victim and then suddenly burst into derisive laughter.'[16]

With Margaret appearing to have no regard for social rules, she was taken advantage of by unscrupulous young men – a consequence of having not grown up inside the rigid English class system, so many protocols were still foreign to her. At the beginning of the season she was asked by Thomas, 'Tommy', Viscount Selby, to accompany him to a ball given by his aunt, Viscountess Cowdray, at her home on Mount Street. This seemingly harmless gesture played to Margaret's naivete and she agreed to go. However, she kept the invitation a secret from her parents, as Helen had a rule that Margaret could only attend parties given by people she knew. She sneaked away from Audley Square and met Tommy at Mount Street, where the ball was underway, and they went straight to the dance floor. To Margaret's embarrassment, Lady Cowdray approached her and asked if she had an invitation, to which she answered no and explained Tommy had invited her. Then Lady Cowdray turned her unforgiving gaze toward her nephew, and said: 'I don't remember inviting you to bring a partner, Lord Selby.' It was reminiscent of Winkie Brooks and the misunderstanding at Cliveden House, all those years ago. Margaret immediately left, followed by Tommy, and they walked around Grosvenor Square until four o'clock in the morning.

The following day Margaret confessed to her parents what had taken place the night before, and George failed to see that she had committed any wrongdoing. He telephoned Lady Cowdray and berated her for putting Margaret in an embarrassing position. Furthermore George demanded a written apology to be addressed to Margaret, and he threatened to sue if she did not comply. In those days legal cases could be brought against anyone who jeopardised a woman's reputation, and being turned out of Lady Cowdray's house was a social disgrace in itself. Listening in on a telephone extension, Margaret gloated at Lady Cowdray's loss for words and she was further vindicated when a written apology was delivered, a precautionary measure should she become the victim of gossip.

Margaret's crowning moment came three weeks later when, on 27 May, she was presented to Queen Mary at Buckingham Palace, in the third court of the season. For this, she adhered to the Lord Chamberlain's strict dress code, and wore a custom-made Norman Hartnell gown of white tulle and silver embroideries, with silver shoes, elbow-length gloves, and on her head she wore Prince of Wales feathers. Helen, who was presenting Margaret, wore a parchment-coloured gown and a diamond tiara, a gift from George. As the wait was long, owing to the cavalcade of cars along the Mall waiting to enter the palace gates, many debutantes and their mothers brought sandwiches and knitting. It was also a spectator sport and the public came to peer inside car windows, 'Come and look at this one!' some were overheard saying, as though visiting an exhibition. Of the 1930 season, one newspaper wrote:

> In the Mall tonight the crowds admired dresses and wearers with the frank and unreserved delight of villagers at a wedding. Here and there one saw the elderly woman, an old cook or old nurse, who had come to see one car or one girl, but most of them were as young as the debutantes.[17]

Once inside there was a further wait in an ante-room, filled with pale pink hydrangeas and spring flowers, while a footman called the names of the debutantes and the women who were presenting them. The guests totalled 800 – one of whom was Thelma Viscountess Furness, mistress of the Prince of Wales – and there were five courts that season to cope with the demand of girls wishing to be presented. With rules becoming relaxed (though strict rules about formal behaviour and dress code were still adhered to) as to who could be presented, it might have later inspired Princess Margaret's infamous quote: 'We had to put a stop to it. Every tart in London was getting in.' Music was provided by the Welsh Guards, and the girls could take a seat, drink coffee, or practise their curtsey which was, in Margaret's case, taught by Madame Vacani who insisted her pupils wear long curtains on their backs to mimic trains.

The presentations at court were quicker than usual, as King George V was absent due to an attack of rheumatism, and Queen Mary was accompanied by her son, the Prince of Wales.[18] The absence of the king was a disappointment to many debutantes,[19] but not to Margaret. When she was called to the throne room she curtseyed to Queen Mary, and as she rose her eyes met with a handsome stranger standing behind the queen in a white tunic and turban adorned with an enormous emerald. He was Prince Aly Salman Aga Khan, the eldest surviving son of the third Aga Khan. 'I looked at him and he looked at me,' Margaret later recalled, 'and then I passed down the line.'[20]

The following evening Margaret attended a ball at Brook House, given by Sir Ernest Cassells in honour of his granddaughter and heiress, Edwina Mountbatten. There Margaret was formally introduced to the 19-year-old Prince Aly Khan, and she thought it was love at first sight. They spent the evening dancing with one another, and at every party thereafter. He initiated Margaret into London's nightlife, and they frequented the Embassy Club (which became 'a second home' to her) and the Cafe de Paris. At 17 she was too young to drink alcohol legally, and she never touched it until the age of 30. She went to the Derby with him, a memorable day owing to the Aga Khan's horse, Blenheim, winning the first big race. George and Helen must have approved of Margaret's suitor, for they permitted Aly to stay at Queen's Hill so he could escort her to her first Ascot race week. The *Daily Express* column 'The Talk of London' mentioned her coral-coloured dress, which infuriated Margaret, as her dress was salmon-pink.

Although Margaret always maintained that Aly's behaviour was correct toward her, and he was not yet the 'cynical playboy where women were concerned', he was possessive of her and grew moody and irate if she paid attention to anyone except him. Seemingly harmless gestures irritated him, one such occasion being a party at Queen's Hill during race week, where a few female guests went to Margaret's bedroom to gossip and laugh. It prompted Aly to declare that, as he had no right to enter her bedroom, he hated the thought of others doing so. She appeared to understand his reasoning and thought it flattering that he should want her all to himself.

At the end of race week, Aly asked George for permission to marry Margaret, and he reacted furiously and thought it an opportunistic and indecent proposal. It was reminiscent of the time when George approached Douglas Hannay to ask for Helen's hand in marriage, except Aly had money, a royal title, and, above all else, he was a threat to George and his place in Margaret's life. Therefore George's answer was a simple one; he forbade Aly from marrying Margaret, and in turn, he told her she could never see him again.

Margaret could have imitated her mother and married the man she loved, regardless of her father's wishes, but she had to wait almost four years before she came of age to marry without parental consent. And she was reluctant to do anything that would hurt George, despite her parents' reasons for denying the proposal being entirely racist. Her father, in particular, did not want Margaret converting to Aly's Muslim faith,[21] as after their marriage she would become a princess of the Nizari Ismaili Muslims, a sect of Shia Islam, and their children would be in the line of succession to the Aga Khan. Aly was also mixed race, as his father was Persian (though born in Karachi, then British India) and his mother Italian, and that, too, carried a social stigma. The Whighams' views were not unpopular in those days, and the majority of Britons, especially the upper classes, disapproved of mixed marriages. Now that he had his answer Aly departed Queen's Hill and Margaret agreed with George's token excuse that she was too young to marry.

Margaret's agreeing with her father was an act, for she continued to love Aly and agreed to meet him in secret. For a time their plan worked and Margaret relied on Miss Randall, who approved of Aly, to deliver her letters to his Indian manservant, detailing the time and location of their rendezvouses. Using their mutual friends' houses as meeting places, and while her chauffeur waited at the front door, Margaret and Aly escaped through the servants' entrance and went to the Embassy Club. They considered themselves engaged, and Aly wrote to Margaret that he wanted to 'live forever if you love me and the day you stop I should like to die'.[22] Shortly after his letter, George and Helen discovered the romance was continuing behind their backs and they stopped Margaret from communicating with him, both in person and by letter. Shortly after the Whighams' realisation, Margaret saw Aly on the street and could not greet him, for she was with her parents. In his last letter, Aly wrote of their abandoned encounter: 'The moment that I passed you I felt like running back to you as fast as my body would go.'[23] Aly threatened to kill himself if he could not be with Margaret, and knowing how deep his possessiveness ran she knew he meant it and ended their relationship.

*

Since Margaret's coming-out party she had become one of the most photographed young women in London and a celebrity on the debutante scene. She was also credited with creating the 'deb ballyhoo industry'.[24] Sir John Lavery RA painted Margaret, seated on a gold chair, wearing her presentation dress and holding a fan made of Prince of Wales feathers. It was composed in preparation for his now lost work, *Their Majesties Court, Buckingham Palace*, which was exhibited at the Royal Academy in 1931.[25] Magazines called her the prettiest debutante of the season, and she contradicted the stereotypical beauty of an English rose: 'In an age of blondes came brunette Margaret Whigham'.[26] Dismissing her looks as plain, she also managed to compliment her beauty in a coquettish way: 'I don't look like either parent. Perhaps my grandmother. My mother's mother was a very beautiful woman. She had the green eyes which I have.'[27] Margaret also claimed she had star quality: 'I was my own little star in a very social world'.[28] It was an egotistical remark, though it was supported by the *Sunday Chronicle*'s observation that 'a year ago Margaret Whigham was little more than a name to me. Now I cannot go anywhere without meeting her'. As for her popularity, Margaret herself said: 'I had a knack of projecting myself, producing myself. Almost like an actress.'[29]

The reference to herself as an actress was a telling remark, for it was believed George had hired a press agent to boost Margaret's publicity and to warrant mentions of the Celanese Company, which had then become a staple of mass-produced women's lingerie and nightwear. Rumours circulated that George was spotted in deep conversation with Charles Lyttle, an important individual in the public relations industry, at the Dorchester Hotel. 'The cleverest and, they do say, not accidental publicity campaign ever hatched outside the hatcheries of Hollywood,' the *Telegraph* reported.[30] This could explain why, in the summer of 1930, Margaret's name began to appear daily in the society columns, as before that time she was overlooked in favour of upper-class girls such as Lady Dorothy Lygon, Lady Mary St Clair Erskine, Lady Joan Villiers and Miss Diana Chamberlain. Also of interest was the celebrity status of Aly's Parisian stepmother, Princess Andrée Aga Khan (née Mlle Carron), a former dress-shop owner whose rags-to-riches story captured media attention.[31] As much as George disapproved of Margaret's association with Aly, moving in his circle could only enhance her fame. A newspaper column[32] written two years after her fabled coming-out party reported that George and Helen entertained 'in royal fashion' and they wrongly credited the Prince of Wales with being present at the party. It was a harmless stretch of the imagination, and it served to demonstrate how rumours attached themselves to Margaret, and how the press did not shirk from embellishing her importance. That is not to imply the rumours of a press agent were true, but it provides an explanation as to why, from the very beginning, the media were interested in her every move.

Overnight Margaret had become an 'it girl', a media darling who did not shy away from being photographed on daily outings as well as on the dance floor. Her acquaintances were the three most prominent gossip columnists of their day: the Marquis of Donegall, known as Don; Viscount Castlerosse, writer of the 'Londoner's Log'; and Tom Driberg, the man behind the *Daily Express*'s William Hickey column. They were at the same social events as Margaret, and they quickly caught on that girls like her attracted readers to their columns. She dismissed the accusation: 'There was nothing harmful in it.'[33] Press agent or not, her looks and style ushered in a new era of the celebrity debutante. 'Miss Margaret Whigham goes everywhere, and photographs of her have appeared so often that they are as well known as those of any film star,' wrote the *News Chronicle*. 'She stood out from a row of debutantes like a thoroughbred in a field of hacks,' observed the *Sunday Graphic*. Although the odes to her beauty were many, there were a few appraisals which were written with a poison pen: 'Her stutter – stammer to you, please – which distorts the serenity of her undeniable beauty and knots up her mouth is practised by her friends and the midinettes whose claim to fame is having delivered her latest sensational garment at the tradesmen's entrance'.[34]

It helped Margaret's celebrity that she went out every night and was seen at almost every event high society had to offer. Having recovered from her heartbreak over Aly, she began to associate with different men, often seeing two in the same evening: one for dinner and another for dancing at the Embassy Club or the Cafe de Paris, which closed at two in the morning. After the earlier nightclubs closed, she 'floated on' to the Florida, the Silver Slipper, the Bat, or Uncle's, followed by a meal of bacon and eggs at dawn. Although Helen's rules about curfews and chaperones had become relaxed – the family chauffeur continued to wait outside for her – she was expected to follow her mother's rule of rising early and having breakfast with her parents at nine o'clock. Margaret was also forbidden from entering the Bag of Nails, which had a reputation for aristocratic young men picking up high-class prostitutes, or, as she referred to it, a 'rougher sort' of club.[35] Another was the Cavendish Hotel, run by its proprietor Rosa Lewis, the former mistress of Edward VII, which was said to become a brothel after dark. Rosa was a matriarch of sorts to the Bright Young Things, and they flocked to her hotel for no reason other than the scandal it courted. There was a rumour circulating, during Margaret's initiation to the social scene, that Robin Vane Tempest-Stewart had visited the hotel late one evening, intoxicated and in need of a bed, whereupon he felt something cold next to him which turned out to be a corpse, having been left there for the evening. Aly, however, was not so flippant and he stalked the Embassy Club, night after night, where he asked Jack Harris's band to play his and Margaret's favourite song, 'I've Got a Crush on You'. It was a pointless ritual, for Margaret was in Europe with her parents, who had taken her away 'to forget' him.

After coming out as a debutante and her aborted engagement to Aly, Margaret was no longer the friendless girl she had been in her youth and at school. She formed a circle of close friends which included Barbara Cartland, Cecil Beaton and his sisters Baba and Nancy, Prince George of Kent, Lady Bridget Poulett and Rose Bingham; the latter two girls were her competitors on the debutante scene. 'The girls of the 1930s not only had good looks; they knew how to dress; and they had far more self-confidence than their predecessors,'[36] Margaret said. She was invited everywhere and she met everyone; she danced with Edward, Prince of Wales and was mesmerised by his blue eyes. There were costume balls and charity performances: she dressed as the sunset for the Eclipse Ball, in turquoise for the Jewels of the Empire Ball, as Perdita for the Famous Beauties Ball, and as a china figurine for the Porcelain Ball. She set trends and was reported to be one of the first to wear pale nail polish which 'gleamed luminously in the dark',[37] and for making opened-toe shoes socially acceptable; 'I don't dare to wear my sandals,' wrote a columnist, 'Margaret Whigham sports hers every way … I'm terrified for her little toes.'[38] Her wardrobe was reported on – 'Miss Margaret Whigham in an excellent cut of tweed of strawberry persuasion'[39] – and women began to imitate her heavy make-up and tailored clothes. Another newspaper thought she should 'be awarded the prize for this year's dazzle of debutantes'. *The Sketch* claimed to have predicted her future popularity: 'I can remember Miss Margaret Whigham when she was a schoolgirl, when (if ever) she wore plaits. It was in a large house filled with people, but the remarkable child was so self-possessed that there could be no doubt of her ultimate success.'[40] She was photographed at Queen's Hill, feigning an interest in the outdoors, posing with her father by a lake with swans and walking alongside 'a favourite pony'.[41] It was rumoured that she had been screen-tested by a film studio and offered 'an entrancing contract',[42] a piece of gossip without a hint of truth, for Margaret would have leaped at the opportunity. Due to the acres of publicity she received, it was hardly surprising that Margaret was named Debutante of the Year. It was an accolade she resented, for she thought herself to be higher than a mere debutante whose main ambitions were to marry young, settle down, and give birth to an heir and a spare. 'I was the one that lasted,' she said, 'the others faded after three years.'[43]

★

Against the whirl of the social season, the streets of London were becoming a platform to oppose the National Government, led by the Labour Prime Minister Ramsay MacDonald. Hunger marches were organised, along with protests against rising unemployment – in 1930 around 2.5 million people were out of work. Naturally, it became a topic of conversation at social gatherings; even the Bright Young Things, whose fathers and brothers were killed on the battlefields of France, were championing the working classes, if only for shock value. As with the General Strike, the young people were hastily dismissed as 'ballroom communists', owing to their romantic notion of a fairer society and relationships formed across the social divide. For Margaret, there was fun to be had, and it revolved around the Embassy Club. A world within a world, its clientele of celebrities, princes and flighty debutantes were part of the tapestry of its violet, jade green and white walls; their lithe bodies slung over a pink sofa or conspiring at a private table decorated with two electric green candlesticks with pink shades and a telephone. The musicians who performed there, although well paid and earning a steady income, were onlookers to the widening gulf between rich and poor. Billy Amstell, who played with the Ambrose orchestra, recalled 'people used to come and they were well fed and they used to guzzle into their food and drink and only round the corner people were sleeping in doorways, wrapped in paper'.[44]

When Britain left the Gold Standard in October 1931, society women like Margaret became an easy target for the press. Two months after the economic crisis she attended a Buy British Ball at the Park Lane Hotel with her mother, which aimed to promote British business at home. In a way, Margaret and Helen were prime endorsements, for they shunned Parisian couturiers for the London fashion houses of Norman Hartnell and Victor Stiebel. The *Daily Express* wrote:

> As an example to the girlhood of Britain, the lovely Margaret Whigham has decided, in the interests of economy, to have her hair re-set only once a fortnight in future, and to stop wearing stockings in the evening. On the other hand, to stimulate trade, she has just bought four new evening dresses.

The *Daily Express*'s mockery of Margaret's social conscience prompted the *Daily Worker*, a left-wing publication, to respond: 'This should be a lesson to the wives of the unemployed, whose extravagant habits include setting their hair in curl-papers every day and buying no dresses at all.'

It was no use pretending Margaret had a social conscience, for she never proclaimed to be troubled by the ills of society. The charity balls she participated in, though for fun, raised money for St John's Hospital, Lewisham, the Enham Village Centre for disabled ex-servicemen, and the Highway Club for the Boys and Girls of the East End. '1930 was packed with gaiety and fun and nobody can take that away from me,' she remarked. 'I don't think anybody has had such a good time as I had. Nobody, nobody, nobody.'[45] She blamed this disregard on her extreme youth and place as a social butterfly in the abyss between the two world wars. 'Although I may have been bird-brained,' she said, 'I was never intentionally unkind.'[46]

★

A month after her eighteenth birthday Margaret fell in love with an older, married man. His name was George Pearson Glen

Kidston, a millionaire sportsman and aviator. Known as Glen to his friends, he was 32, the father of a 3-year-old son, and separated from his wife, Nancie, to whom he had been married for five years. As with Prince Aly Khan, Margaret thought it love at first sight and the attraction was mutual, though concealed by Glen. The similarities of their respective backgrounds must have struck a familiar chord with Margaret, for Glen was the great-grandson of A.G. Kidston, a metal and machinery merchant from Glasgow with interests in the Clyde Shipping Company and what became the Clydesdale Bank. With the Kidston family fortune secure for future generations, Glen was free to pursue his passion for race-car driving, which he did professionally, winning the Le Mans 24-hour race in 1930; he was also one of the original Bentley Boys, and the wealthiest of his set. Another interest was big-game hunting and safaris in remote parts of Kenya, and his excursions were filmed and remain of great interest due to their pioneering footage.[47]

In the summer of 1931, when Margaret was introduced to Glen, he was seeing her friend, Barbara Cartland,[48] and was having an affair with the actress Pola Negri, and he might have been living with the courtesan Doris Delevingne, the estranged wife of Viscount Castlerosse, for his home, Blackburne House on Culross Street, was an address which appeared on her personalised notepaper. His reputation as a philanderer should not have surprised Margaret, for she had met him through Joel Woolf 'Babe' Barnato, a millionaire and race-car driver, whose money came from his family's South African diamond and gold mines. Helen thought Babe a controversial acquaintance, and his arrangement with his wife – who lived with their two daughters at a nearby country house – inspired her feeling of mistrust. Thus Margaret was forbidden from accepting weekend invitations to Babe's home, Ardenrun Hall, in Surrey, and could only visit throughout the day. Glen, although as rich as Aly, was older, worldlier, and having served in the First World

War and survived two torpedo attacks, was determined to have a good time. 'I don't need to carry mascots,' Glen said. 'My two front teeth are widely separated. This is supposed to be lucky, and I certainly have been.'[49] He was the epitome of an F. Scott Fitzgerald character: 'They were careless people ... they smashed up things and creatures and then retreated back into their money or their vast carelessness ... and let other people clean up the mess they had made'.[50] The country mansions and townhouses were renovated, not to serve as family homes, but for entertaining on a lavish scale; his money appeared to come from an endless supply, and he played with his expensive toys of submarines, aeroplanes and racing cars. This Jay Gatsby embodiment of wealth and new money was not vulgar to Margaret, and she revelled in Glen's generosity and attention. In turn, she appeared sophisticated beyond her years[51] and her self-confessed 'dumb bunny' aura appealed to him: she did not talk back, she had no ambitions beyond her social sphere, and she was not jealous of his roving eye.

During Margaret's courtship with Glen, she could not gauge whether or not he was attracted to her, for he was undemonstrative and unromantic in person. Their evenings were spent dining with his friends, and at the Cafe de Paris and Embassy Club, where their favourite song to dance to was 'You're Driving Me Crazy'. Although Glen was known for his sexual peccadilloes, his generosity toward the woman (or women) he was seeing was not unusual, and on the mornings after his outings with Margaret, he sent her flowers and records, perhaps a clue to his feelings for her; 'With All My Heart', 'I Surrender, Dear', 'By My Side', 'Hello Beautiful', and 'When Your Lover Has Gone'.

Surprisingly, given the age gap between Margaret and Glen, and the fact that he was a married man, George and Helen approved of him. Of all her beaux it was Glen they would have liked Margaret to marry. In the short time they had known one another, Glen became a part of the Whigham family; George often played golf with him, and Helen expressed her fondness for him. Perhaps Helen was also under his spell: 'He is rich, blasé, cynical, spoiled rotten, and completely adorable; a risk-taker, a daredevil. Half the women in London are mad about him – and the only thing that saves the other half is that they haven't met him.'[52] However, as with Margaret's previous romances, this one, too, had a forbidden element, as Glen's divorce proceedings were yet to begin, and, as such, she was risking her social reputation by associating with another woman's husband. Although Margaret spent much of her time with Glen, she claimed when they were alone together he spoke of his flying ambitions and desire to break aviation records. Since piloting his first test plane, during the First World War, he had embarked on dangerous flights and each time narrowly escaped death, earning him the nickname 'the man who cannot be killed'.[53] In 1929 on a flight from Croydon to Amsterdam, his plane crashed twenty-one minutes into the flight and caught fire, killing the six crew on board, including his co-pilot Prince Eugen von Schaumberg-Lippe. Glen walked through a mile of Surrey woodland to find help, and when he flagged down a passing motorist his clothes were still smoking. Now he spoke of flying from Wiltshire to Cape Town as an experiment to see if an air-mail service was possible between Britain and South Africa, as the slowness of the British air mail 'was the laughing-stock of the world'.[54]

On their last evening together Margaret anticipated Glen declaring his love for her, but he said nothing of importance and drove her to her parents' apartment at Grosvenor House. He kissed her goodnight and she went upstairs feeling despondent. The following morning she awoke early and said a small prayer for his safe arrival in Cape Town. A moment later a letter and a parcel from Glen containing a dozen records and a Cartier watch, 'for remembrance', were delivered to Margaret's room. Helen ordered Margaret to return the watch, as it was indecent to accept jewellery from a married man, but she ignored her mother and kept it. The letter, dated 30 March 1931, detailed Glen's feelings for Margaret and the guilt he felt due to his responsibilities toward his wife and son. 'I haven't the least idea how you feel towards me,' he wrote. 'I don't think you could ever accuse me of having made love to you, even though I may have been, or tried to be, kind.'[55]

After reading Glen's letter Margaret felt stunned and helpless. She wrote him a long letter, which she knew would not reach him until his arrival in Cape Town, and so in the meantime, she cabled him and told him how she felt. All she could do was wait for his response and follow his progress in the evening newspapers. A week later a cable from Glen arrived: 'I've done it Margaret.'[56] He completed the journey in a record-breaking six and a half days, in his own specially adapted Lockheed Vega monoplane which had developed a fault in its engine on the last part of the journey, forcing him to land at Lichtenburg and stay overnight in Pretoria.[57] Given his achievement, he had become an aviation hero and his photograph was on the front page of every newspaper. 'Though his father left him the better part of a million, he is still challenging fate in the air,' one reported. It was a prophetic observation that would soon ring true. As much as he enjoyed being feted in the press, his thoughts centred on Margaret, and they cabled one another every day. 'I was living in a dream of happiness waiting for his return,'[58] she recalled. The death of her paternal grandmother, Ellen Whigham, a few days later could not diminish the optimism she felt for her future as Mrs Glen Kidston, and she attended the funeral at the Holy Trinity Church in Ayr with her thoughts focused on her beloved.

Glen responded to Margaret's original letter with an equally long one of his own, in which he confessed his past 'affairs galore … they have just come and gone and I have no lasting impression of them',[59] and he offered to settle things with his wife, as she, too, wanted her freedom. In his letter, he also spoke of wanting to marry Margaret, because 'I cannot bear the thought of your ever being married to anyone else'.[60] This, he realised, was a poor consolation given he 'was not really a tiny bit as nice as I wanted to be during our last days in London',[61] which he explained was a disguise for how he truly felt. Perhaps he refrained from showing his feelings to prevent Margaret's name from being used in a divorce petition between himself and his wife. 'I never tried to make love to you,' he wrote, 'because I knew deep down in my old heart that I did love you.'[62] Margaret arranged to meet Glen at Hanworth Aerodrome; she was to motor down in his Rolls-Royce, which he had told her to use as her own. He had also invited Margaret and her parents to stay with him at his villa at Le Touquet. The future looked bright; she would marry Glen and in doing so would become the wife of an exciting man with millions in the bank, and, more importantly, her parents approved of him.

On the afternoon of 5 May Margaret was to participate in a charity matinee entitled 'A Day in the Life of Debutantes', in the presence of the Duchess of York, at the Hippodrome theatre. She wore a shimmering blue Norman Hartnell gown and appeared alongside society girls who re-enacted their daily lives of afternoon tea, dancing, and so forth. After the performance, she stood in the foyer and watched the Duchess of York leave, when she glimpsed the front page of an evening newspaper. 'Glen Kidston Killed', the headline read. The shock was immediate, and Margaret saw the newspaper headline and the people in the room swaying before her eyes. Someone leaned forward with their arms outstretched to help, but she managed to escape the theatre and ran outside. The brief scene created a small spectacle and the next morning newspapers falsely reported that Margaret had slipped on the stairs and experienced a fall. She went to the nearest kiosk and bought a newspaper, scarcely believing the headline she had seen. Glen and his mechanic, Captain Gladstone, had been killed at 11.20 that morning when the aeroplane he was piloting crashed into the Drakensberg Mountains, its engine landing on Glen and decapitating Gladstone.[63] A shopkeeper in Mauba witnessed the crash and rushed to the scene, where he found two bodies and an identification card, which confirmed one was Glen.[64] There were several factors at play that might have caused the crash: Glen had undertaken that particular flight path to see Table Mountain, and his plane had fallen victim to heavy crosswinds, thick dust and poor visibility. In a letter to Margaret, sent before take-off, he wrote: 'I'll try hard to get back by June. Don't be annoyed with me if I try a record flight back from Kenya.'[65]

Margaret's grief had to be kept private as nobody, with the exception of her parents, knew the true nature of her relationship with Glen. Later that day Nancie Kidston spoke to the press from her home on Cavendish Street: 'I cannot believe the report of the accident is accurate. I have had absolutely no news, and I should have heard if anything had happened.'[66] Her statement was a telling one, for it was Margaret, and not his wife, who knew of Glen's news. Nancie received a marriage settlement after his death, and she remarried six months later, to Edmund Sheffield, a man she had been in love with while Glen was still alive. The following day and owing to the delay in overseas post, a letter from Glen arrived, confirming to Margaret his itinerary for the return flight ('I hope the return flight succeeds. It will be hard work')[67] and he signed off with: 'Sweetheart I'm terribly in love with you.'[68] For several weeks his letters continued to arrive in the post, detailing his plans for their marriage and future together. A letter from Glen must have also reached Nancie, for word began to circulate that Margaret was having an affair with her husband, and Nancie herself did not mention their separation or the fact that she was in love with another man. 'It seems like some terrible dream,'[69] Nancie said, and she banned Margaret from attending Glen's memorial service at St Mark's church. However, Dale Bourn, the golfer and a friend of Glen's, escorted Margaret to the church and they slipped into a pew at the back, she kept her head down and her presence was undetected. Margaret knew then, as she did all her life, that Glen was the man she should have married. 'Had I become his wife, my life would have been happy, protected, and with never a dull moment.'[70]

★

The London season began a month after Glen's death, and although it was a solemn one for Margaret, she threw herself into socialising. She continued her debutante existence, and at 18 she was now the same age as the girls who came out that year. Little had changed; she had received two marriage proposals in the past year, both had foundered and she was once again single. Helen and George must have been eager for Margaret to move on, and in July they gave two lavish parties at Queen's Hill. The first was to coincide with Ascot race week; and the second was a dinner for sixty-four guests and a further 600 were invited to a dance held in a marquee assembled in the garden, which was lit by 3,000 lanterns. Now, in her second season, Margaret knew more people and the party was a grander affair than her coming-out dance at Audley Square. Newspaper gossip columnists were also in attendance, with Lord Donegall sitting on Helen's right. As before, her grandmother Margaret Hannay came down from Scotland, this time in robust health, though she wore an electrical hearing aid around her neck, its cord concealed by a fur-trimmed opera coat.

For the remainder of the summer, Margaret motored around the Continent with her parents. They stopped at Baden Baden and took lodgings at the Stephanie, so Helen could take the cure at Dr Dengler's sanatorium, a health retreat with a clientele of aristocrats, film stars and millionaires. Some went to rest, to cure their neurosis in the solitude of the Black Forest, and others went to lose weight by eating a prescribed diet of red meat, and to undergo anti-ageing treatments. At the end of August Margaret went to Eze, to stay at the Chateau de

Madrid with Lady Phyllis Allen, daughter of the 3rd Earl of Lovelace, an eccentric individual who had a pet bear named Susan and gave cocktail parties in its honour. Then it was back to London in September for the re-opening of the Embassy Club, where Margaret was one of the few unmarried women to be given honorary membership. For those who were affluent enough to gain membership, the fee was £21, the average cost of nine months' rent in London.

Once again Margaret's life appeared to be happy and carefree, and although her mind often strayed to Glen, she focused on the present. The future did not enter her thoughts, for she was too preoccupied with having fun – her circle of friends became known as the 'Ritz Set'. Her new and steady boyfriend at the time was Murrough O'Brien, grandson of the 14th Baron of Inchiquin, but it was nothing serious and she was also friendly with Max Aitken, who had fallen in love with her. She also began to socialise with Charles 'Charlie' Sweeny, who, unlike the various men she had known, claimed to dislike her. 'I could not stand her,' Charlie wrote. 'To me, she was a conceited, garrulous show-off, whose company I avoided as much as I could.'[71]

As Charlie was friends with both Max and Murrough, avoiding Margaret was almost impossible as they were often at the same parties and in one another's company. They were to encounter each other at the wedding of Peter Horlick and Rosemary Nichols, for which Charlie was an usher and Margaret a bridesmaid. The wedding party went to a luncheon at the Ritz, and afterwards, Max suggested they go to the Embassy Club. Charlie was without a partner, as was Margaret, and he asked her to accompany him only because he was certain she would say no. She said yes, and cancelled her evening date with Murrough to go out with Charlie, and he did not learn of this gesture until years later. 'Bit by bit I fell under the spell of Margaret Whigham's charm,' Charlie wrote in his memoirs. 'That evening she became fascinating.'[72] Margaret, too, must have felt the same way, for after a few more dates she agreed to marry Charlie and they 'swore to love one another forever'.[73] Proposals meant nothing to Margaret; the promise of marrying someone had become an impulsive gesture, which she discarded at a moment's notice. However it meant everything to Charlie and he began to think of himself and Margaret as an engaged couple, and for several months he existed in 'a euphoric haze'.[74]

With Margaret appearing to recover from Glen's death and her romantic life experiencing a renaissance, Helen announced the family was going to Egypt for the month of December. For some time Helen had been suffering from debilitating aches and pains, which were eventually diagnosed as arthritis. And, although there was little by way of treatment in 1931 except for the spa treatments she sought at Dr Dengler's sanatorium, she was advised by her doctor to escape the British winter for the good of her health. As much as Margaret did not want to go, she knew she could not argue with her mother and did as she was told. In an attempt to make light of her impending trip, she disguised it as another one of her jolly japes. For the *Daily Sketch* she wrote:

'Margaret has gone mad!' My friends really did not conceal their thoughts when I announced, last autumn, that I was going to Egypt. I mean they have always seen me around Bond Street, in and out of the Ritz, or at Ascot, and they considered the Embassy Club my spiritual home. Now Egypt really does come up to expectations – but not from a Ritz Carlton point of view. I found I had to abandon all that and appreciate it in the light of stepping back into the Bible. The natives are just heavenly in their colourful robes, and especially at Assouan. Cairo, you see, is only a pretty poor imitation of London, Paris and Cannes, and although I love that kind of life I only love it at its best. Actually, the best thing about

Cairo is the Gezira Club where they have polo, racing, tennis, golf, and everyone who is anyone goes for tea.[75]

On 17 December Margaret left with her parents on a boat-train from Victoria station. Her friends came to see her off,[76] and soon her compartment was filled with flowers and had become an impromptu *bon voyage* party. To give an indication of Margaret's popularity with the press, or if the rumours of George hiring a press agent were true, Lord Reading was on board the same train; however, the *Daily Express* dismissed him as 'after all, he is only an ex-Viceroy'. Her absence from London society that winter was aptly described by *The Bystander*: 'Her departure shows that the Little Season is quite finished.'[77]

4

Fate

In late December 1931, Margaret arrived in Cairo harbouring a secret. Before leaving London she had become unofficially engaged to Max Aitken and wore his garnet ring, despite telling him she needed more time to get to know him better. Presumably neither Max nor Charlie Sweeny knew of this double betrayal from Margaret, as she had asked both men to keep their relationships with her a secret. She had known Max since her coming out the summer before, and after Glen Kidston's death she began to see more of him, and although she did not love him, he meant a great deal to her. At the age of 21, Max was over a decade younger than Glen, and despite his youth, there were similarities between both men; like Glen, he was a talented golfer and an enthusiastic flyer, and as the 1930s progressed he piloted his own aeroplanes around Europe and America. However, unlike Margaret's romance with Glen, which played out in their letters before his fateful flight from Cape Town, Max was demonstrative toward her and she was certain of his feelings. As the eldest son of Lord Beaverbrook, one of the richest men in the world, he lived in his father's shadow and father and son shared a strained relationship. Max feared and admired his father in equal measures, and Beaverbrook demonstrated his love through intense jealousy, especially if Max's attentions were spent elsewhere. Much of Max's unhappiness stemmed from his father's expectations; he was being pressured by Beaverbrook to take control of the Manchester *Daily Express* newspaper, and was tasked with making it 'the greatest in all the world'.[1] 'Little Max', as his father called him, could not muster any enthusiasm for politics or journalism, and was, therefore, a disappointment.

Margaret was a sympathetic listener, as both she and Max were the children of self-made men and a possessive parent. As George had been jealous of Aly and the risk that Margaret might transfer her devotion to him, Beaverbrook was threatened by Margaret's power over Max and told him he 'would be God's biggest fool to get married'.[2] The warning was a senseless one, for Margaret was not attracted to Max's money; she had her own unlimited supply from George. Beaverbrook, however, wielded his financial power over his family and friends, and unlike George, he was not demonstrative without a motive and was prone to berating and humiliating his son in public. 'He is the loneliest man I know,' Max wrote to Margaret. 'I seem to be the only person he will confide in and who he enjoys having around.' This Margaret could sympathise with, for her own mother's mood swings, now intensified by chronic pain, were a storm she often weathered alone and over the years she became accustomed to, even tolerant of, similar traits in others. As Margaret had been brought up to respect nobody except her parents, she was unafraid of Beaverbrook and was never awed by his fortune. It must have intrigued Beaverbrook, as everyone else was 'frightened of him because he has such unlimited power',[3] for he responded to her request to meet with him. Margaret went to Beaverbrook's London residence, Stornoway House, where they dined alone, and her plea was simple and direct: she told him to stop being 'so unkind to his son'.[4] Could this courage have been inspired by her longing to confront Helen? The outcome of her meddling was unknown, as Margaret departed for Egypt shortly after, and Max was to become a distant memory.

★

In 1931 Egypt was under British rule, and although it was a period of political and economical unrest for the country in their quest for independence, the rich were not discouraged by the poverty and rioting, and they frequented Cairo and Aswan during the winter season. Margaret's arrival in Cairo was noted by the press and with the usual amount of jest, a newspaper paid tribute to her importance: 'I hear Sheiks are clipping their camels.'[5] As of late, English society girls were making an impression in Egypt, with Peggy Salaman, a 19-year-old pilot and former debutante, landing in Cairo aerodrome on her successful attempt to beat Glen Kidston's flying record from England to Cape Town. There was also a visit from David Lloyd George, who was in Cairo at the same time as the Whighams, and who went on a much-publicised moonlight visit to the Sphinx and pyramids before joining his boat at Port Said. With the press taking note of such visitors to Egypt, it was only natural that George would want Margaret mentioned too, and he reputedly cabled his press agent, Charles Lyttle, in London. As a consequence Margaret's photograph was printed in Egyptian newspapers and it was widely circulated that this glamorous Debutante of the Year and heiress to the Celanese empire was in Cairo for the festive season. Significant events had previously sparked a similar excitement for expatriates, especially those who were of the male sex – the 'Mummy Rush' of the 1920s; the presence of Enid Cavendish, an Australian wine heiress who resided in Cairo and as a dare had slept with her husband's entire regiment; and the arrival of Miss Margaret Whigham.

It had the desired effect and Margaret was invited to parties that were held every night in sandstone villas and hotels, frequented by the British Guards who were stationed there. A young man serving in the 1st Battalion of the Grenadier Guards learned of Margaret's arrival and invited her to a dance on Christmas Eve. His name was Charles Guy Fulke Greville, a 20-year-old aristocrat known as 'Fulke', who, four years earlier, had succeeded his father as the Earl of Warwick. Years later Fulke went to Hollywood and became one of the most famous Englishmen in the film industry, with his louche behaviour attracting press attention rather than a film career, which, aside from a role opposite David Niven in 1938, failed to launch. After Fulke's first meeting with Margaret he fell in love with her, and learning she had reservations on a train headed for Aswan, he jumped aboard and followed her there. Having found the Whighams' carriage, he pretended it was a chance encounter and he told Margaret he would be spending the weekend at Aswan.

Margaret and her parents stayed at the Old Cataract Hotel, overlooking the Aswan Dam, which George had helped to build. Although Helen loved Egypt she worried Margaret would be bored, as the resort was popular with people who had come to take the cure, and they spent their days buried up to their necks in sand, which was said to help their rheumatism. In her memoirs, Margaret described her time there as though it were an Angela Brazil novel; she rode a camel into the desert every day accompanied by an Egyptian bodyguard, stopping to chat with English tourists along the way. It was also likely that Helen was in a pleasant mood, her aches and pains relieved by the dry, desert heat. Margaret remained coy about her involvement with Fulke, which had developed into a love affair. They spent every weekend together, taking camel rides into the desert for moonlight picnics and daytime cruises on the Nile to visit the Temple of Philae and Coptic churches nearby. She did not tell Fulke of the daily letters she received from Max Aitken, detailing his daily routine: his car had caught fire outside Stornoway House and it took three fire engines to extinguish the blaze; he was miserable at his newspaper job in Manchester, where he became stranded for three days due to heavy fog; and he mentioned a rumour he had read in the *Sunday Dispatch*, that she was being romanced by a well-known peer and he wrongly guessed it was Lord Tennyson. The content was true, even if Max's estimation was incorrect, for Fulke had proposed to Margaret and she accepted. Of her deception, she said: 'I thought, well, Max and Fulke are a long, long way from each other, so they won't meet.'[6]

Although Margaret had not considered that she would soon leave Egypt, and perhaps Fulke would amount to nothing more than a holiday romance, her mind often wandered to Max, whom she knew was in love with her. Her diary, dated 15–23 February, detailed her inner turmoil and she wrote of her plan to break off her engagement to Max, which had been thwarted by a letter from him; then she wrote to Fulke and broke off her engagement to him, and changed her mind after she received a 'sweet letter' from him 'that upsets me terribly'. She also thought of Charlie Sweeny, whom she had also promised to marry, and wrote him a short letter saying 'although it had been lovely'[7] she was going to marry Fulke. Further complicating matters was the unsettling discovery that Fulke's best friend and fellow officer, Napoleon 'Naps' Brinckman, had also fallen in love with her and began to send her letters. Fulke was accepting of this and he urged Margaret to respond to Naps's letters 'since his love was the most sincere tribute he could pay' to her.[8] The fact that Naps was married might have inspired Fulke's lack of jealousy, and Margaret herself thought him 'a wonderful person' and was surprised by the coincidence that his father, Sir Theodore Brinckman, had been in love with Helen, years before when she lived in Egypt.

From the beginning, Margaret's engagement to Fulke was fraught with problems. His mother, Marjorie Greville, Countess of Warwick, travelled to Egypt to meet Margaret and her parents, and she announced that her son was too immature to marry and she doubted he could make any woman happy. Lady Warwick's opinion was perhaps inspired by the men in her family, many of whom played a prominent role in British politics – her brother was Anthony Eden, Prime Minister of the United Kingdom from 1955 to 1957, and her mother was descended from the Earls of Grey. By contrast, Fulke's paternal grandmother was Daisy Warwick, a Victorian society hostess noted for her extramarital affair with Sir Joseph Laycock, an Olympic sailor, which produced two children, and for being the mistress of King Edward VII. This poor impression of Fulke was enforced not only by his mother, as George, too, expressed his concerns; namely Fulke's lack of ambition, his modest annual income of £2,500, and the fact he had no job lined up for when he left the army.

Against the advice of their naysayers, Margaret decided she would marry Fulke, removing Max's garnet ring and replaced it with a sapphire from Fulke. On 4 March 1932, which also happened to be Fulke's twenty-first birthday, Margaret, her father, and her new fiancé sailed home, leaving Helen behind in Aswan to continue the cure. The press was informed of the engagement and of her arrival, and while at sea she responded to cables from the press: 'Why, there is nothing simpler; we've just fallen in love, and are both looking forward to our wedding day.'[9] The ship was met by the press who, quite rightly, called Margaret 'the most-discussed young woman of the hour',[10] with the *Daily Express* reporting that she 'was handed a great basket of dahlias six months out of season … Miss Whigham discarded the dahlias with the absent-minded touch of a film star, and rotated before the cameras'. The story of the debutante and the earl was the silver lining that many young women in her position dreamed of. Or, from a cynical point of view, the millionaire's daughter and an impoverished peer.

★

Margaret's time in Egypt had filled her with a false sense of security, particularly in accepting Fulke's proposal and avoiding

Max and Charlie. She went along to a party given by Max at the Embassy Club, and seeing him in person made her doubt whether or not she should marry Fulke. Charlie was also there, and in her memoirs, Margaret dismissed him as someone she often danced with, despite their having been secretly engaged. 'I preserved a dignified silence but it didn't make me feel any better,' Charlie wrote in his memoirs. 'I was still in love.' Margaret was also in love with both Max and Charlie, and she said: 'I seemed to be suffering an emotional schizophrenia and was unable to decide what and who I really wanted.'[11] In the end, she chose Fulke, as their wedding plans were underway.

Although George did not begrudge Margaret becoming a countess, he thought the financial burden of maintaining Fulke's family seat, Warwick Castle – which outweighed the money the estate earned from tenants' rent and other endeavours – outweighed the incentive of a title for her. He also relied on Helen's instincts, and she proclaimed that she disliked Fulke, a decision that was influenced by Lady Warwick, who had telephoned her with the advice: 'If you love your daughter, don't let her marry my son. He's a liar, he's ill-mannered, and he picks his nose.'[12] It enforced George's initial feelings about Fulke, whose personality traits he thought unworthy of Margaret. Such feelings were validated when George and Margaret accepted an invitation from Lady Warwick to stay at Warwick Castle. They arrived too late to attend a luncheon given to mark Fulke's coming of age, and after a toast to his health, Fulke said: 'I very much look forward to the day, and I hope it will be as soon as possible, when my wife and I shall be able to come and live at Warwick and take as active a part as possible in everything associated with the town.'[13] The words were meaningless, for Fulke ignored Margaret and left her to explore the castle with the head guide, and during her stay he seldom bothered with her. She thought it a premonition of the lonely life she would lead at Warwick Castle, as the youngest countess in England, alone with only her disapproving mother-in-law for company. After returning to London, Fulke went a step too far, when he failed to greet George as he entered the drawing room. What was worse, Fulke did not stand up when Helen came into the room. 'You've got to break your engagement off to that young man,' George said. 'He's so rude *now*. What's he going to be like when you're married to him?'[14]

For weeks Margaret had reservations about marrying Fulke, which she kept private as she felt trapped. There had been an engagement party, given by the Whighams, at the Embassy Club and several dishes on the menu were renamed to mark the occasion; Salmon Welcome Back, Caviare Supreme de Notre Happiness, and Petit Pois Prosperity. A notice was placed in *The Times* and a wedding date had been set for June, and they were to marry at Westminster Abbey. Furthermore, Norman Hartnell had begun making Margaret's wedding dress, along with eight bridesmaids' dresses, and Fulke had bought her a large solitaire diamond engagement ring to replace the cabochon sapphire he had given her in Egypt. It was George who helped Margaret to change her mind after he asked if she was in love with Fulke. She admitted she was not, and George told her to call off the wedding. Although Margaret knew her father was right, she was reluctant to disappoint Fulke. 'What does it matter,' George said, 'compared to your whole life and happiness?'[15]

Fulke's ill-treatment of Margaret might have been inspired by his love for Rose Bingham. When he returned from Egypt he realised he wanted to marry Rose, and rather than breaking the news to Margaret he hoped his behaviour would drive her away. Thus it was Margaret who took the initiative and broke the news to Fulke that she no longer wanted to marry him. It was said by their mutual friends that he was relieved by Margaret's decision; however, she claimed he tried to win her back, and owing to Fulke's promiscuity both statements could be true. She returned the ring and an official announcement was printed in *The Times*: 'The Marriage arranged between the Earl of Warwick and Miss Margaret Whigham will not take place.' Helen spoke to an Ascot newspaper, telling them: 'She just changed her mind.' Lady Warwick, despite encouraging Helen's disapproval for her son, merely said: 'I have nothing to say. Any statement must come from Miss Whigham or her family. Lord Warwick is not at the castle.'[16] It was also reported that Margaret 'objected to sitting in state as a countess'.[17] As for society, it had a 'violent surprise',[18] and many wondered how 'any girl could be so foolish'.[19]

Despite Margaret and Fulke no longer being romantically involved, they continued to see one another socially and remained 'awfully good friends'. Their reunion, albeit a platonic one, served to encourage his erratic behaviour and he accumulated bills he could not pay, and the Metropolitan Police requested he surrender his driving licence after being accused of dangerous driving. It did not take long for rumours to circulate that Margaret and Fulke had become re-engaged, which complicated matters for his romance with Rose Bingham, and he announced he was leaving for a five-month tour of Egypt. 'Miss Whigham staunchly denies the engagement, but there is something in the manner that of her doing it that still leaves room for doubt,'[20] a newspaper wrote. They were, however, quick to add that Margaret and Fulke dined at separate tables; she with another suitor, and he with Miss Bingham. Eventually, Fulke went to Cairo, and Margaret began to cast her attention elsewhere. In her later years, she spoke of her regret in not marrying Fulke and thought her father had given her bad advice, 'which was sad in a way because I think I did love him'.[21]

*

In the weeks before Margaret ended her engagement to Fulke, she had rekindled her friendship with Charlie Sweeny. They encountered one another at the Ritz; Charlie was dining with Max Aitken, and Margaret was with her friend Lady

Bridget Poulett. Both made their apologies and departed, leaving Margaret and Charlie alone, and they proceeded to sit in silence before she said: 'Why don't you take me to a film?' The request infuriated Charlie, and he replied: 'The way I feel now, I wouldn't take you to a dogfight.'[22] Moments later they were sitting in the Empire Cinema and she confessed that she loved him, not Fulke. Of the two men, Margaret said: 'Fulke was not a bad person. I think he was as good as Charlie who, I must say, was always waiting in the background.'[23] She also found Charlie more attractive than Fulke: 'I have always found American men attractive and he was the epitome of male glamour.'[24]

Charlie was born in Pennsylvania on 3 October 1909 and was raised in San Francisco, Los Angeles and New York. He was a fifth-generation American and his Roman Catholic family's roots were established in Counties Donegal and Armagh, in the Irish province of Ulster. Although he was not aristocratic his parents, Robert and Theresa (née Hanaway), came from rich families whose fortunes were founded during the Gilded Age; his maternal family were involved in the Pennsylvanian coal-mining industry, and his paternal family had interests in oil and smelting. His grandfather and namesake, Charles Sweeny, described as 'a rough diamond', followed the wagon trail to Nevada in search of gold, and moved on to Washington where he found it in the Spokane Mountains (renamed the 'Morning Glory' mine), the headquarters of what became the Federal Mining and Smelting Company, which he co-founded with the Guggenheim brothers. Charlie's father, Robert, also took an interest in mining, and he, too, was a canny businessman. 'If you ever get your hands on a good mine,' Robert Sweeny told his son, 'there's no price at which it's worth selling.'[25] Charlie's uncle, also named Charles Sweeny, did not go into the family business but he established his own identity as one of America's most celebrated soldiers whose bravery and reputation inspired Ernest Hemingway,[26] then working as a foreign correspondent for the *Toronto Star*.

In her memoirs, Margaret wrote that the Sweeny fortune diminished over the years, and she referred to the family as 'terrific gamblers'.[27] The latter statement was partly true, as Charlie's paternal grandfather spent his retirement gambling on the stock market against the advice of his friend, John D. Rockefeller Jr, and he gifted vast sums of money to the Roman Catholic church and built several cathedrals in the American Midwest. However Charlie's father did not believe in gambling and he moved his wife and two sons to San Francisco, where he founded a successful law practice and became a leading figure in the Republican Party. After several years in San Francisco and having also lived in Los Angeles, Robert and Theresa settled on the East Coast; she thought it a far more sophisticated place to raise children, as Los Angeles was then a small desert town. Thus Charlie spent a large part of his childhood in New York, attending Loyola School, and going to the Ziegfeld Follies with his godmother, Millicent Hearst, wife of the newspaper magnate William Randolph Hearst. Then, after graduating from Loyola, Charlie went to Canterbury School in New Milford, Connecticut, where he excelled at sport and was offered two scholarships to Yale, one for basketball and one for baseball. Charlie laughed at the offer and said he would be attending Yale with or without the scholarship, as his father could afford the tuition fees. This display of arrogance provoked Robert to react furiously, and he accused Charlie of showing 'a disgraceful lack of respect for money'.[28] Although Robert was a millionaire he treated money as a precious commodity which he held in trust, with the view that it could earn him more money. Unlike Margaret's upbringing and her father's generosity with his money, Charlie was raised with the understanding that, despite having a rich father, money was not to be squandered.

Margaret spoke of a rumour regarding the Sweeny family, and how they had to leave America in a hurry. She did not elaborate on the reasons for their leaving, nor did she speculate as to how Charlie came to live in England. During his adolescence, his summers were spent at his parents' villa in Le Touquet, and on the golf course with his brother, Bobby, determined to become a champion golfer. The location had been a compromise for both Robert and Theresa, for she loved the Continent and he had business interests in London, trading under the name of the Federated Trust. It was Charlie's decision to attend Oxford that had inspired his mother to move to London, and she took a flat at Grosvenor House, and Robert eventually joined her and adopted the city as his business headquarters, which, by the 1930s, also included mines in South Africa. Following Charlie's graduation from Oxford, where he failed to complete his law course and instead studied 'groups' (humanities), he moved to London and took an apprenticeship at an investment banking firm, Charterhouse Investment Trust, for which he earned £100 a year. Margaret wrote that Charlie's modest salary, although less than Fulke's income, did not trouble George. She assumed it was because he did not have an estate to manage, and her father could always supplement their living expenses. 'Charlie always worked,' she said. 'He was at the office every day. He was never idle.'[29]

However the idea of Margaret marrying a Catholic troubled George and Helen, for they knew any future children would be raised in the faith. The subject of Charlie's money and religion might have seemed presumptuous on the Whighams' part, but they knew that Margaret, when in love, acted on impulse. At the age of 19 she had been engaged four times, and each time an obstacle presented itself; Prince Aly Khan's religion, Glen Kidston's marital status, her reservations to commit to Max Aitken, and Fulke's lack of money and manners. Now, it appeared, Charlie's confession that he loved Margaret and wanted to marry her as soon as possible troubled George. He thought Margaret was being pressured by Charlie to convert to Catholicism, and that it was an unnecessary gesture on her part. As she had been prepared to convert to Islam in order to marry Aly, she treated Charlie's religion as no exception to her original plan.

On 17 November 1932, an announcement of Margaret and Charlie's engagement appeared in *The Times*, and George was relieved, for the time being, that she remained a Presbyterian. Their first experience as an engaged couple began badly, as Charlie had arrived at the Whighams' suite at the Ritz Hotel and presented Margaret with a four-carat diamond ring from Cartier. She was furious that he had done it in front of George and Helen, rather than waiting until they were alone, as 'romance and sentiment were very important to her'.[30] Having agreed to postpone their official engagement for six months, perhaps Charlie did not think the circumstances and setting were important, as he had already proposed and she had accepted. Robert and Theresa Sweeny gave the couple an engagement party at the Embassy Club, the setting for many of Margaret's love affairs, and they hired Larry Adler,[31] then a fledgling harmonicist, to entertain the guests. There was also a cocktail party hosted by the Whighams to introduce Charlie to their extended family, and he recalled an elderly woman remarking: 'He's not bad looking – for a Catholic!'[32]

For a period of two months, Margaret went several times a week to a church on Farm Street to receive religious instruction from Father Colin Woodlock, an Irish Jesuit priest. By then George had come round to the idea of her conversion, though he never entirely approved. 'Anyway, thank goodness you'll still be a Christian,'[33] he said. Although serious in wanting to convert, Margaret fought many of the church's teachings and she questioned everything she was taught. 'When I pray it's going to be to the Head Man, and to nobody else,' she said. She agreed to become a Catholic on two conditions: she would not accept the infallibility of the pope, as he had only been infallible since 1886, nor would she pray to any saint. According to Margaret, the Catholic Church accepted her terms, as they were pleased with the publicity her conversion would attract. Despite this view, Margaret received letters from both Catholics and non-Catholics, the former accusing her of making a mockery of the religion. And her close friend, Jeanne Stourton, a Catholic, called it a 'Conversion of Convenience to Catholicism'.[34]

On 11 February 1933 Margaret was received into the Catholic faith at Farm Street Church, during the Feast of Our Lady of Lourdes. She telephoned Charlie and ordered him to report to the church at six o'clock, and there he found her with Father Woodruff, who delivered the news. 'And from now on,' Margaret said, 'you'll be coming to church with me on Sundays instead of playing golf!'[35] Helen and George, who had little interest in or knowledge of the religion, sat against the confessional without realising they were an obstruction to Margaret going to the booth to give her first confession. Charlie approached the Whighams and, after some whispering, they moved away. Despite George telling a reporter that 'the reception into the church will be a quiet affair,'[36] it was an overwhelming experience for Margaret and after returning home she fainted. A day later she received her First Communion and was confirmed as a Catholic at the Sacred Heart Church, Westminster.

The wedding date was set for 21 February, and Margaret's time as 'the Whigham', as the press had begun to refer to her, was coming to an end. 'So no longer will the gossip paragraphs contain references to the Whigham's hats, dresses, lunch-companions, and poodles. It is goodbye to all that,' wrote *The Sketch*. George and Helen sent out 2,000 wedding invitations, printed in silver, and rented a house at 55 Prince's Gate, as it was close to Brompton Oratory, from where Margaret would be married. Over 3,000 wedding gifts filled three of the large rooms at her parents' house, and among the things she was given were decanters, silverware, a coffee set, an electric kettle, and a gong. She did not want champagne or brandy glasses, nor did she ask for furniture, and Fulke, who claimed to have no ill feelings toward her, sent a cocktail cabinet in green shagreen. Her favourite gift was a caricature drawn by

Cecil Beaton and decorated with tinsel and embroidery, and it remained one of her prized possessions. George and Helen bought her coats of mink and ermine, two silver foxes, and a six-skin sable stole; and they gave Charlie a pair of Boss single-trigger guns. There was one present in particular which caused excitement in the press, a pair of gold cufflinks, sent by Charlie's golfing friend Edward, Prince of Wales, engraved with three feathers and the inscriptions: *Ich dien* ('I serve') and *Honi soit qui mal y pense* ('May he be shamed who thinks badly of it'). However, after the wedding when the gifts were delivered to Margaret and Charlie they discovered the cufflinks had been stolen from Prince's Gate, a secret they kept from the press as they did not want to offend the prince.

The wedding dress, designed by Norman Hartnell and stitched by thirty women, took six weeks to complete. It was to be ivory satin with orange blossoms cut out of lace outlines to give the appearance of a star pattern, and embroidered with seed pearls and silver glass bugles. The sleeves were angel-cut and white tulle, and the train, measuring 28ft long and 3ft wide, also had a border of white tulle. The dress cost £52 and Margaret asked for the headdress to be included in the price. Before her wedding, she broke from tradition and 'acted as a mannequin in her own lovely bridal gown for a small party of intimate friends', during which cocktails were served and Turkish cigarettes were smoked.[37] There was a trousseau-and-present party, and instead of a customary rehearsal party, Margaret gave a lunch for her parents, her future in-laws, and the wedding party, before going to a rehearsal at Brompton Oratory. The press followed Margaret's every move, and she was happy to oblige their enquiring questions and pose for photographs as they captured her daily life from dining with friends, to leaving a dress fitting at Norman Hartnell's studio on Bruton Street. There was also a rumour that Margaret was retiring from society and, after her marriage, she planned to settle in the 'quietude'[38] of the countryside. A newspaper wrote: 'For the last couple of years there has hardly been a society function of importance which she has not attended'.[39]

Before leaving her parents' home for the last time as Miss Margaret Whigham, George took her to one side and said: 'Margaret, you are leaving us now to be married and start a new life. Just remember one thing: if you are ever in trouble or need any help I will always be there.'[40] In years to come, she would learn that her father was the only man on whom she could depend.

5

Mrs Sweeny

The preparation that had gone into the Whigham–Sweeny wedding was on par with a grand production, evident in the order of service which resembled a theatre programme; alongside the hymns and prayers was a list of acknowledgements, thanking florists, milliners, choristers, and confectioners. Margaret chose nine of her friends as her bridesmaids; Bridget Poulett, Jeanne Stourton, Molly Vaughan, Dawn Gold, Sheila Berry, Pamela Nicholl, Angela Brett, Margaret Livingstone-Learmonth and Baba Beaton. Of the nine, three were celebrity debutantes, with Jeanne Stourton often pinned by *The Sketch* and *Tatler* as being Margaret's lookalike. However, as with Margaret's coming-out party, three years before, Helen's influence over the proceedings was apparent, and she forbade the presence of children in the bridal party. Children, Helen said, were apt to walk on the train of the dress, or be sick, or loudly interrupt the most solemn moments. She also feared that Margaret's friends, who were beautiful, would outshine the bride.

Helen's latter sentiment proved to be a pessimistic barb, for the publicity surrounding the wedding was reminiscent of royalty. On the day of the wedding, 21 February 1933, traffic in Knightsbridge came to a halt for three hours, and news-cameras filmed Margaret's arrival with George, and departure with Charlie, inspiring a news-paper to report: 'No film star has had a more enthusiastic welcome from her fans than this debutante of a season or two ago.'[1] In addition to the 2,000 invited guests, another 2,000 gatecrashers arrived and surrounded the church, many of whom managed to get inside despite the best efforts of the ushers, Lord Birkenhead, Randolph Churchill, and Margaret's ex-fiancé, Max Aitken. Referred to as 'The Great Whigham Scramble',[2] the uninvited guests stood on pews and climbed on top of pillars for a better view, and the noise distracted from the Nuptial Mass and sound of the choir. It prompted reporters to write that the service was 'more reminiscent of a circus than a wedding'.[3] *The Bystander* noted:

> There seems to have been a certain number of people at the Brompton Oratory for Miss Margaret Whigham's wedding who had never been to a fully choral Roman Catholic wedding, and to judge from the behaviour of at least half the congregation, they had never even been inside a church before.

Although Margaret was a darling of the society columns, many found the publicity surrounding the wedding to be vulgar. The *Daily Mail* wrote:

> While reaching the peak of 'showy' society marriages will probably be responsible for a swing in the pendulum of fashion. Certainly church dignitaries hope that brides will not emphasise too much the social side of church ceremonies, and one or two informal conversations have taken place to see if any official steps are necessary.

The Telegraph agreed: 'The only thing that could have improved upon that show was to install a Lido in the church, with guests in bathing suits and beach what-nots.' *Tatler*, who had been instrumental in Margaret's rise to fame, echoed a similar sentiment:

'A lovely bride, of course, but the whole thing seemed just mildly shocking. Somehow just all those hundreds of fashionables spoilt what should have been a lovely happening.' Continuing with their negative appraisal of the wedding, they added: 'It seems odd that we actually live in an age when a celebrity has to be married in order to induce people inside a church.'

Margaret did not begrudge the public their behaviour, and 'smiling and confident [she] sensed the desire of the crowd and gratified it'.[4] As she went to her car, a young man[5] approached her and placed a single red rose into her hand and muttered a few words that she could not hear before disappearing into the crowd. She later discovered that he was an unemployed clerk from Battersea, who had been following her around for three years, waiting outside restaurants and nightclubs to catch a glimpse of her. 'You've chosen a very good moment to get married,' George said to Margaret. It was the height of an economic depression, which began in 1929 and reached its peak in Britain in 1933. However, it was not only the poor who suffered; the royal family were claiming a decline in their wealth, demonstrated when King George V ordered the Prince of Wales to donate £10,000 from the Duchy of Cornwall to the Treasury. In Britain, Sir Oswald Mosley and his British Union of Fascists were gaining popularity, and in Germany, the Nazi Party had risen to power. It marked a period of political and economic uncertainty; whereas before when Margaret came out as a debutante the public swooned at such displays of wealth, now they resented it. 'It was the darkest moment of the Depression, with millions of unemployed,' Margaret later wrote, 'but I think they felt our wedding had brought a flash of colour into a grey world. I hope it did.'[6]

*

The honeymoon lasted for six weeks, during which time Margaret learned of the various facets of Charlie's character, and he hers. They spent the first two days in Paris, and Charlie told a reporter: 'After twenty-four hours of married life we both find that it agrees with us vastly.'[7] Then they boarded the *Colombie* for a six-week cruise of the West Indies. As they sailed through the Bay of Biscay Margaret was overcome with seasickness, but she pretended it was a headache so as to not trouble Charlie. By then his moods caused her concern, and when alone with him she discovered he had 'an almost pathological streak of jealousy in his make-up'.[8] She claimed he knew everything about her life, including her past love affairs, but it did not stop him from making 'ridiculous scenes'[9] if she happened to mention any man she had been out with.

This form of jealousy, described by Margaret as pathological, is also known as Othello Syndrome. It causes the sufferer to become preoccupied with thoughts that the other person is being unfaithful without having any solid proof. As Margaret and Charlie had met during her brief engagements to both Max Aitken and Fulke Warwick, could his outbursts of jealousy have been inspired by his own insecurities or her prior conduct? Margaret felt, at the age of 20, that she was too young to cope with those early marital rows; and his reaction, in her own words, 'puzzled' her. All of the men who had been in love with her, with the exception of Max who had treated her as a confidante, had been possessive in their own ways. Prince Aly Khan's jealousy, Margaret said, had flattered her at the time; Glen Kidston treated her aloofly and then showered her with gifts, and so she never knew where she stood; and Fulke was happy for his best friend to bombard her with love letters but reacted badly if she danced with anyone else. Now the man she had married, whose looks and talent as a dancer she had prized above all else, surprised her with his behaviour. She had known then, a mere week into her honeymoon, that marriage was not going to be easy.

It should be noted the description of Charlie's personality traits was told from Margaret's point of view. In a way, she must have been attracted to men who sought to control her, or who, in a way, were not entirely welcomed by Helen and George. Her mother, in particular, Margaret hoped to displease, as she had made her childhood so unhappy. George, however, remained her hero and the only man who never said no to her, thus it must come as a surprise when she married a man who did. 'I was never so happy … knowing I was to be with my husband and have his attention, and knowing nothing could take him away from me,'[10] she said when describing her ideals of marriage, which proved that she, too, was possessive. Regardless, Margaret described Charlie as having 'a quick Irish temper' and criticised him for being 'excessively possessive'.[11] The freedom she sought from marriage and leaving home was naive on her part, for she was now a Catholic and was expected to behave as such. 'While we were engaged we talked and talked of our honeymoon and looked forward to it, so it was up to both of us to make it come up to scratch, wasn't it?' she later said.[12]

Charlie's remembrances of their honeymoon were different, and he recalled having a 'wonderful' time with the 'most beautiful girl'.[13] During their stop in Colón, a small port in Panama, he mentioned to Margaret how thrilling it must be to sail through the Panama Canal. 'That can be easily arranged,' remarked a gentleman, who had overheard their conversation. As they were only there for the day, Charlie thanked him and explained the logistics were impossible. They were shown to the gentleman's small aeroplane, and his pilot flew them over the canal and landed at the other side so they could take lunch in an hotel overlooking the Pacific Ocean. As they made their way through Venezuela a purser drew their attention to a prison, where he said the prisoners were kept in dungeons and tortured as their punishment for disobeying the commanding general of the army, General Gomez. As the ship sailed out of the port, word reached the passengers that a revolution had taken place, and Gomez was now president. While all Margaret recalled from their honeymoon was her seasickness and

Charlie's moods, he remembered their adventure. Incidentally, a book, *The Technique of Marriage*,[14] written by Mary Borden, was published around that time and it declared the honeymoon should be abolished, as it 'is very often a painful, difficult, disappointing and nervous experience for the man and woman'. Margaret herself commented on Borden's book, stating:

> Abolish honeymoons! What an idea! Why I adored mine! I frankly confess I needed the rest of a honeymoon. There's such a rush before – wedding presents, thanks, people, and the ceremony. I was a wreck – I won't tell you my husband's funny little ways or anything about it, except that the full moon shone from Panama to the West Indies, and we had honey for breakfast.[15]

When the ship docked in Plymouth Margaret was detained by the immigration authorities as an alien. This was the consequence of her having married an American, as after her marriage she had automatically lost her British nationality without being allowed to acquire her husband's. She was now a stateless person. Difficulties had apparently arisen when they were both questioned by the authorities and Charlie answered that he intended to work in England.[16] They were ordered to remain on the ship after the passengers had disembarked, and Margaret could not enter the country until she produced an affidavit. 'I still feel English, and never thought I was an American until now,' Margaret said.[17] Charlie added, 'I have lived in England so long that I almost believe I am English.'[18] Not only had she forfeited her Presbyterian religion to adopt her husband's Catholicism, she had also taken on his nationality and, it seemed, a new identity: 'London will scarcely seem the same now that Miss Margaret Whigham has changed her name!'[19]

★

After returning home from their six-week honeymoon Margaret and Charlie rented a furnished house at 39 Hans Place, Belgravia, until they decided where to live permanently. As Charlie's earnings of £2,500 a year were scarcely enough to afford Margaret the lifestyle she had grown accustomed to, their expenses were supplemented by each of their parents. They had six servants, including a parlour maid, a butler, a cook, and Miss Randall, who had become Margaret's lady's maid. 'There were no money problems,' Margaret recalled, 'of course both families were behind us.'[20] Unlike when Helen had married George, Margaret's allowance was not stopped nor did her father think it important for her to make her own way in the world. 'But Charlie always worked,' she said, years later. This must have impressed George for, although he was not happy about Margaret's religious conversion, he respected hard work.

Although Margaret felt Charlie's moods had blighted the first few weeks of their married life, she was, in her own words, 'thrilled' to discover she was expecting a baby and looked forward to its arrival in December. She was in good health and things were progressing as they should, until seven weeks into the pregnancy, while out walking her dogs in Hyde Park, she was startled by nearby gunfire to honour Queen Mary's sixty-sixth birthday. The dogs bolted and she chased after them, searching for an hour before going home. They were returned later that afternoon, as the address was on their collars. By then Margaret was ill in bed, but she did not think her symptoms were serious. Four days later, Margaret continued to feel unwell, and despite this she went with Charlie to the Capitol Cinema for the opening night of *A Kiss Before the Mirror*. She recalled she wore a white satin evening dress and white shoes, and that the previous symptoms persisted but she ignored them. When it was time to stand for the National Anthem she realised she had begun to miscarry, and Charlie draped his overcoat around her and they swiftly left the cinema without any fuss. She blamed her dogs for 'causing me to lose my first child'.[21]

A few months later Margaret was pregnant again. It was the end of summer and the London season, and newspapers reported that she was looking forward to 'a happy event'. Her social life continued as before, now dominated by Charlie's golfing tournaments and there were many golfing weekends spent in Le Touquet. Despite several of her Whigham relatives being keen golfers, with her cousin Sybil Whigham gaining a reputation as a competent sportswoman on the golf courses of Scotland and America, she never showed any enthusiasm for the sport. Her disinterest suited Charlie, for he believed wives should be spectators.

In the New Year of 1934 Margaret, who was in her eighth month of pregnancy, caught a cold and began to complain of a pain in her chest, only for it to be dismissed by doctors as nothing serious. It was diagnosed as indigestion, a common complaint during pregnancy. The diagnosis was an odd one, Margaret thought, for she had not eaten anything in twenty-four hours and she compared the feeling to having a stone resting on her chest, and as the days passed she complained to Charlie that she could not breathe. Thinking her doctor had been correct, and dismissing her ailments as harmless, she attended the theatrical producer C.B. Cochran's party at the Dorchester Hotel. However, over the weekend Margaret's health began to decline and Miss Randall noticed that she was turning blue; a specialist was called to the house and he diagnosed her with double pneumonia and ordered an ambulance to take her to hospital.

After arriving at a nursing home on Welbeck Street, Margaret's temperature was recorded at 104 degrees and, along with double pneumonia, she also had a kidney infection. Before falling into a coma, she recalled various tubes being put up her nose, 'that's all they had … there was no such thing as penicillin and they didn't have the antibiotics or the oxygen tents'.[22] For the next five days, she remained unconscious and dangerously ill. Newspapers wrote that her condition was 'critical' and daily reports of her health, or lack of it, were announced on purple placards – the colour reserved for royalty. To save her life, the doctors induced labour and a baby girl was stillborn, a consequence of the pneumonia that had been originally dismissed as indigestion. There was a funeral and the child was buried according to the rites of the Catholic Church, with Charlie in attendance while Helen and George remained at Margaret's bedside. When Margaret awoke from the coma, she asked for her baby and a nurse suggested placing another woman's child in her arms, as she, too, was not expected to live. The suggestion was dismissed. George sent for the best doctors to tend to her, one being the king's physician, Lord Dawson of Penn, only to be told nothing could be done. As a last resort, she was given a blood transfusion, written about in cinematic detail by newspapers as far away as Australia:

> A young London business man hung up his office telephone receiver recently, hastily cleared his desk of papers, explained to his principal that he required a few hours leave 'on urgent private affairs' and within a few minutes was speeding westward in a taxicab. This unknown young man was No. 1 on the stand-by list of London's anonymous blood-donors – men who give their blood for transfusions. The telephone bell had summoned him from his prosaic ledgers to a higher work.
>
> He knew that his mission was to give his blood to try to save a human life – but whether it was that of man, woman, or child he neither knew nor cared. It was not until many hours later that the young man realised he had given a blood transfusion to Mrs. Charles Sweeny, who, before her marriage, was Miss Margaret Whigham.[23]

The blood transfusion made little difference to Margaret's health, as her temperature had begun to fall below what is deemed

normal for survival, and her loved ones were told she had hours
to live. Charlie asked a priest to perform the last rites, during
which he sprinkled holy water from the Grotto at Lourdes on to
Margaret's head, which had been sent by an anonymous admirer.
All Margaret recalled was a shadowy figure standing at the foot
of her bed, murmuring prayers. Three hours later she began to
make a slight improvement and her temperature gradually rose,
and two days later she was declared out of danger. Charlie issued
a statement to the press: 'I especially thank the people who sent
the Holy Water from the Grotto at Lourdes. This water, as you
know, has made wonderful cures, and it can be sprinkled on the
bed or the patient can be blessed with it.'[24] Margaret, although
not religious, believed the Catholic Church and the holy water
had saved her life when all medical practices had failed.

Now that Margaret was beginning to recover, Charlie, who
had seldom left her bedside, went to celebrate at the Embassy
Club. Helen thought it cruel and she never forgave him, for on
that day Margaret was given the news that her baby had died.
'There I was lying in hospital on the critical list, my child gone
and feeling very weak and ill,' Margaret recalled. 'I'd only been
married a year and I was miserable. I was crying half the night
through and that wasn't helping much.' Each night Charlie visited for half an hour, dressed in a white tie and on his way to a
nightclub, and after a brief conversation, he looked at his watch,
kissed her goodnight, and said: 'Well, darling, it's nice to see you
looking better. I'll be in tomorrow.'[25]

After a month spent in the nursing home Margaret fell into a
deep depression, prompted by the loss of her baby and Charlie's
absence. The doctors, thinking she had recovered enough to be
discharged, suggested she go abroad to convalesce in the sun.
She refused to go, knowing that Charlie could not leave the
office, and decided on the Princes Hotel in Brighton, thinking
he would accompany her and commute into London each day.
He refused to do so, and confined his visits to the weekends. She

was furious, and dismissed him as 'very selfish'. Miss Randall, along with a trained nurse, kept Margaret company, but aside from their companionship, she was restless. Brighton in March was a resort out of season, and with nothing to do, she passed her days watching an elderly Princess Beatrice, the youngest child of Queen Victoria, being wheeled in a bath-chair along the seafront.

There was a time when Margaret would have taken comfort from press attention and letters from her admirers, and despite the newspapers reporting on her health and describing her as having 'a sort of film star reputation',[26] it left her cold. She had also been referenced in P.G. Wodehouse's Anglicised version of Cole Porter's song, 'You're The Top', from the musical *Anything Goes*. A topical look at what was popular in the 1930s, the lyrics in Wodehouse's version were: 'You're Mussolini/ You're Mrs Sweeny/ You're Camembert.' Flattered[27] as she was at being included alongside Mickey Mouse, the Louvre Museum, a Shakespeare sonnet, and Greta Garbo, years later she said: 'I did not care for being sandwiched between Mussolini and Camembert.' She also disliked Porter's music and preferred the Broadway hits of Jerome Kern and Oscar Hammerstein, particularly the songs from *Show Boat*. Her mind centred on Charlie, and she read *Tatler* and *The Sketch* for clues of his social life, as he was photographed on the golf course and on nightly jaunts around London restaurants with his bachelor friends, and she wondered who he danced with after dinner. She also feared he was at risk of being tempted by other women, and for some time wondered if he had been unfaithful. 'Charlie was very attractive,' Margaret said, 'and the danger of having a good-looking young husband loose on the town minus a wife is only too obvious.'[28]

★

After an uneasy six weeks spent in Brighton, staring at the seafront and worrying about Charlie's social life, Margaret returned to London. Her homecoming was timely; it was the beginning of the social season and, although she felt both emotionally and physically weakened, she looked forward to being presented at court as a married woman. It was a mixed blessing for Margaret, as she was married to an American and now considered as such – a letter from the Lord Chamberlain informed her that she could only be presented by a fellow American. The honour was performed by Mrs Robert Bingham, the wife of the United States Ambassador to the United Kingdom. For her presentation, at the third court of the season Margaret wore a satin dress of pale coral with crystal shoulder straps and a velvet train of dark coral and crystal embroideries; in her hair, she wore diamonds, and carried a shaded feather fan. 'She is as beautiful as ever, if a little frail-looking after her comparatively recent serious illness,'[29] a newspaper reported. The tiara had caused Margaret considerable worry, for Charlie had asked Moss Bros, from whom he had rented his court-wear, to supply one. Instead, she went to Cartier and asked to loan a tiara. 'Now if the Queen asks where I got my marvellous tiara I can truthfully say "from Cartiers." Would you really expect me to have to say "I rented it from Moss Bros, Ma'am – if you ever need one, let me know and I'll pick it up for you?"'[30]

Before Margaret left for Buckingham Palace *The Sketch* photographed her kissing Charlie outside their home; her feelings for him had not diminished despite how he had treated her during her illness.[31] Among the 200 debutantes who were presented at court during the season of 1934 Margaret stood out, despite having three seasons behind her. The acres of publicity she warranted, as a debutante and now as a married woman, set the bar for the emerging girls who were expected to follow in her wake but somehow failed to do so. 'She understands publicity better than anyone else. Without benefit of profession or title she has made herself a front-page story, whether she is engaged, disengaged, married, ill, well, or convalescent,' wrote *The Bystander*. It was reported that the secret of Margaret's success was her ability to treat journalists and photographers as if they were 'charming hosts who can give her a good party'.[32]

Although Margaret went to parties she was not free to enjoy herself as she had done before marriage. Charlie forbade her to go out alone, and their social lives revolved around his interests. A few years before, it was fashionable for society women to dine with men who were not their husbands; however, the Roaring Twenties and its louche morals were a distant memory and people were content to revert to tradition. The hours Charlie spent at the office would have restricted Margaret's activities throughout the day, and the luncheons at the Ritz, which she had enjoyed before marriage, were few and far between. A few years before she thought of herself as a star; a golden girl inhabiting her own universe in which everything revolved around her. Now she was a respectable married woman, and, from her own perspective, a model wife. 'A new side to Margaret has come out, one that few people ever knew existed – a completely devoted wife anxious for family life,' wrote Lord Donegall.

Margaret's complaint that her social life was relatively quiet compared to the past might have been an exaggeration, for the society columns were abuzz with mentions of herself and Charlie, and they were frequently photographed out on the town. Although Margaret described married life as pleasant but narrow, during the season she continued to receive and accept invitations that were reminiscent of her debutante years. There was Ascot race week and the customary house parties that went along with it. And she attended the wedding of her old friend (and, as some believed, former love interest) Prince George of Kent to Princess Marina of Greece and Denmark, at Westminster Abbey. Margaret and Charlie gave the royal couple a silver cruet stand as a wedding present, and on the night before the wedding they attended a ball given by King George V and Queen Mary at Buckingham Palace. Around that time Margaret gave a dinner dance at the

Embassy Club for 150 of her friends, and Charlie's golfing friend, the Prince of Wales, was the guest of honour. She also did a 'confessional album' with *The Sketch*, answering their trivial questions of her likes and dislikes; June was her favourite month, going to the cinema was listed as her hobby, green was her preferred colour, and ordering food was her pet aversion. Reflecting on that period, however, Margaret dismissed her social circle as a gathering of young married couples of 'exactly the same age group, traipsing into dinner just like the animals boarding Noah's Ark'.[33] To mark Margaret's twenty-first birthday Charlie gave a party at the Embassy Club for 100 of their friends; every woman was given a spray of cattleya orchids and the men a bright red buttonhole. The interests from her youth prevailed and she was naturally drawn to showbusiness, but Charlie was not and he preferred golf and to associate with his friends from the business world. Perhaps Margaret felt her social life was dominated by pleasing Charlie and his friends, and it had become an endless task of talking shop, which she thought 'a useless waste of time … if I want to talk business I will go to an office and talk across a desk'.[34] Though, by her own admission, she was often sick or convalescing, and so she gave Charlie her blessing to go out alone.

★

After Margaret's return from Brighton, and when she was declared sufficiently healthy, she spent her time 'trying to catch up' and was soon pregnant again. It was to end in a miscarriage, as did the others, and she was to suffer eight in total. 'I don't think it distressed Charlie as much as it distressed me,' she said. 'I was obsessed with it. I felt a complete failure as a woman.'[35] Her desire to have a child was the opposite of how Helen had felt, who thought the ritual of sex and childbirth was 'terrible' and, perhaps, a messy business. The physical implications of pregnancy and the pain of childbirth, followed by a confinement period before and after the birth, did not appeal to Helen. It is therefore interesting to speculate whether Margaret's determination, or 'obsession' as she referred to it, to have a successful pregnancy stemmed from a childhood of being told, by her mother, that she was not good enough. The stammer, the lack of a sense of humour, the improvement on her looks beginning at the age of 5, and now her inability to bear a child. Of course the aforementioned could have been purely psychological, and it does not mean to suggest that Helen was not sympathetic towards Margaret. It was Helen, along with Miss Randall, who had remained at Margaret's bedside when she was delivered of a stillborn baby, ill with pneumonia, and on the critical list.

During this period George sold Queen's Hill and bought Margaret and Charlie a twenty-one-year lease on a house at 6 Sussex Place, in Regent's Park, overlooking the lake. It was a six-storey Georgian house, designed by John Nash, with a large garden, which Margaret thought would be perfect for children and dogs. George also bought Margaret a Rolls-Royce and paid the wages of a chauffeur, which amounted to £3 a week. Having left the countryside, the Whighams bought a lease on an eighteenth-century townhouse at Upper Grosvenor Street. Both homes were decorated by Syrie Maugham, the interior designer and former wife of W. Somerset Maugham, renowned for her extortionate prices and white-on-white decor. The rooms of Upper Grosvenor Street were entirely white; antique furniture was 'pickled' in the colour, regardless of how valuable it was, and a bathroom was designed especially for Helen with mirrored walls and a sunken bath.

George balked at the cost of Helen's vision of a modern and feminine home, and he was furious that the Chippendale and Queen Anne furniture had been stripped of its originality and painted white. Margaret envisaged a similar style for her own home, but Charlie, who lacked George's funds, put his foot down when he rightly sensed the cost of Syrie's decorating bill. His father, thinking he had the better deal as George had taken care of the lease, agreed to pay for it, and knowing of Robert's dislike of squandering money on unnecessary things, Charlie discouraged Margaret's vision. However, she achieved her way and a gossip columnist reported that in Margaret's bathroom she had white walls with light shining through Lalique, and white rugs on the floor;[36] and a telephone room was installed next door to her drawing room, decorated with green and white wallpaper in a bamboo print, 'so telephone conversations may be conducted without interruption and in a charming setting'.[37]

Margaret, having created a home that was decorated to her taste, longed to establish an identity as a society hostess. She asked Charlie if they could introduce new people to their circle of friends; she wanted to invite writers, actors, politicians, and diplomats to dinner. 'What on earth do you want them for? They won't fit in,' Charlie said.[38] His reaction was an ironic one, given that his friends and acquaintances were from different backgrounds owing to his hobbies and business interests. Was it their youth that inspired his remark, as they were each in their early twenties, and the men Margaret had known, with the exception of their mutual friend Max Aitken, had wastrel tendencies. Margaret's mother-in-law, Theresa, was an intellectual woman; she studied piano and voice at the Boston Conservatory of Music, and was well-read and widely travelled. Unlike many women, after they married, Theresa retained a level of independence and would often travel alone to the Continent, to Paris and Le Touquet. Throughout Charlie's childhood and until he left for Oxford, his mother remained a strong figure, often making decisions[39] on behalf of the family and her husband was content to let her do this. Perhaps this was a reason why Charlie wanted, from Margaret's point of view, a wife who obeyed him in all aspects of their marriage. Margaret knew her knowledge was limited and that her interests were narrow, and she tried to educate herself on world affairs and to read literature beyond *The*

Sketch. Having broached a conversation on world affairs, Charlie dismissed her with: 'What's all this? You're getting to be quite a little intellectual, aren't you?'[40]

Margaret knew, as she had done during the first week of their honeymoon, that Charlie was the boss in their marriage and 'all [he] wanted for a wife was a pretty, brainless doll'.[41] During this time, when Margaret had been moulded into a passive wife, had she paused to think of Helen's plight, and how George had treated her the same way? The heartache her mother suffered due to George's infidelities and long absences would also become a common theme in Margaret's marriage. Therefore it was hardly surprising that her interests remained largely superficial, as it filled a void in an otherwise empty existence. 'I began to feel like a bird in a not-so-gilded cage.'[42]

6

Idols of Consumption

When Margaret reflected on her marriage, after the first few years and during a period when Charlie had risen in the world of finance and was earning substantial money, she did not acknowledge how they had grown as a couple or as individuals. Instead, she recalled the repression she felt, and despite this private opinion she gave an impression of a happily married life:

Unquestionably the leader of the young marrieds in London Society to-day, Mrs Charles Sweeny, who will always be remembered as Miss Margaret Whigham, most beautiful and glamorous of debutantes, is taking her place as a hostess among the younger set. Comfortably settled in one of those modernised Sussex Place period houses in Regent's Park, she and her good-looking American husband take large parties to Claridge's, have always entertained for the season's round of charity balls, done much to enrich many a hospital's cheque from a charity film premiere. On one occasion, they hired a private plane to fly their friends out of London to a week-end party. Like her husband, Mr Charles Sweeny, who is a brilliant amateur golfer, Mrs. Sweeny plays a good game of golf, and is a lover of the outdoors.[1]

Just as Margaret had cloaked her private feelings about Charlie, she never acknowledged the social prominence of the Sweeny family, or their connections to the showbusiness, horse-racing, and sporting worlds (two of Charlie's uncles competed in the Olympics). Nor did Margaret refer to the popularity of her mother-in-law as a hostess in New York, London, and Le Touquet, and of her talent as an opera singer and the requests[2] she often received to sing around the world, all of which she refused. And writing of Charlie's nightly outings, during her recuperation, Margaret was surprised he had a social life as active as hers. 'When I married Charlie I married, in a way, a commoner who was a very glamorous man but he had no great wealth, or title, or anything,' she said. 'I made *him*. I put *him* on the map.'[3] It might have been a coincidence, or not, that he was friends with Charles Lyttle, Margaret's rumoured press agent.

Charlie's popularity should not have surprised her, as he had grown up among the elite circles of the 1920s and 1930s; his father was a close friend of Joe Kennedy, the American Ambassador to the United Kingdom, and in his youth he played golf with the Princes Edward and George on the course at Le Touquet. Given Charlie and Bobby's popularity as young men about town, they were introduced to Louis B. Mayer, head of MGM, who offered to take the brothers to Hollywood and give them a salary of $30,000 for appearing in three films. Charlie thanked him and refused, stating he was to be married soon, and Bobby was discouraged by their father, who thought an Oxford degree was a better investment. Therefore, when Charlie did marry, he gave up the pleasure-seeking ways of his youth to focus on his career. It was a natural progression for him – 'I suppose I could have won the British Amateur if I had changed my priorities'[4] – and he expected Margaret to do the same.

An indication of Charlie's expectations for a wife can be found in his relationship with Miss Dotty Smith, an American debutante and a Smith Brothers Cough Drops heiress. The romance developed during the summer before he went to Oxford, and he spent Christmas in New York with Dotty, and promised to return at Easter. Dotty and her family spent the summer at the Sweenys' villa at Le Touquet, and one evening she asked Charlie: 'Are we going to marry when you graduate from Oxford?' He was startled by Dotty's direct question, and by her strength of character, something which he admitted he did not possess. Instead of responding, he went to his mother and asked for advice. Theresa thought Charlie, at not quite 19, was too young to marry, and she told him to tell Dotty they would 'have to wait and see'.[5] It was an answer he came to regret, for a few months later he received an invitation to Dotty's wedding to Chester Bayliss of New York, a gesture that left him broken-hearted, despite being repelled by her forceful nature. Perhaps they would have been ill-suited in marriage, but Charlie never had the chance to find out. So, although he married another celebrated debutante in a similar mould as Dotty, he did not want a headstrong wife.

What Margaret failed to mention during her retrospective of marriage was a new friendship that began in 1934 and continued sporadically until the summer of 1937. Through her mother-in-law, Margaret was introduced to Wallis Simpson, whom Theresa had known from New York and for whom she gave a luncheon party upon her arrival in London with her second husband, Ernest. Far from thinking Wallis outstanding or fashionable in any way, Margaret wrote: 'My impression was of quite a plain woman with a noticeably square jaw, and not particularly amusing.'[6] She also thought Wallis's hairstyle, parted in the middle and wrapped in a coil-like way at each side, resembled earphones. This unfavourable appraisal was noted in hindsight, and as much as Margaret dismissed Wallis's shortcomings, she said: 'We were to remain friends.' Their friendship, however, developed as a result of Charlie's connection to Edward, Prince of Wales, by then King Edward VIII, and his American mistress, Thelma Morgan Furness, the former wife of Marmaduke 'Duke', the 1st Viscount Furness, a shipping magnate and one of the richest men in the world. It was a circle formed of American ex-pats who had married into the British aristocracy, and Margaret, having grown up in New York, considered herself as such. The Sweenys had known Thelma and her parents since their days of living in New York, and Charlie's father had thrown a coming-out party for Thelma and her twin sister, Gloria (later Vanderbilt) in 1922. Adding to this tangled web of mutual friends, who were also royal concubines, both Margaret and Charlie were on friendly terms with Edward's former mistress, Freda Dudley Ward, whom Margaret favoured over Thelma and Wallis.

It was Thelma Furness who had drawn Margaret and Charlie further into the king's affair with Wallis, of which the present mistress remained oblivious. Thinking Wallis would be lonely, as her husband was often away on business, she asked Charlie to partner with her at social events and he agreed. It seemed a surprising gesture, given Charlie's reaction if Margaret were to suggest dining with a male friend or going out alone without him. Charlie wrote in his memoirs of his few dates with Wallis, as platonic as they were, and thought of her as an 'odd-man-out'.[7] After Thelma left London to visit America, the king was free to pursue Wallis, and Margaret became part of the foursome. After this change of status, Margaret began to think of Wallis as 'a witty, brilliant hostess, one of the best-dressed women in the world, and a femme fatale'.[8] Now an intimate of the king's inner circle, Margaret observed his behaviour and thought he had become 'a pathetic, desperately unhappy man'.[9] She must have felt out of her depth, or perhaps Charlie sensed the scandal that was simmering behind the king's obsession with Wallis, for Margaret began to distance herself from the set.

After it became known that King Edward was to abdicate to marry Wallis, Margaret and Charlie no longer accepted their invitations, nor did they boast of such a friendship. This was due to Wallis and Edward's visit to Nazi Germany, undertaken after his abdication and subsequent exile from his country. Charlie claimed it was 'a much misunderstood'[10] trip, but he and Margaret were not taking any risks with their social reputation. Her last association with Wallis was to be in print, as she had ranked ninth in the 'Ten Best-Dressed Women in the World' list. 'Her hats inspire millions,' the list declared. 'She is a businesswoman in the sphere of clothes. She allows nothing to distract her attention, knows exactly what suits her and exactly what she wants.'[11] First place was given to Wallis whom, Margaret noted, 'had since discarded the ear-plaits she wore at my mother-in-law's luncheon party'.[12]

★

To relieve Margaret's boredom and give herself a purpose, she turned her attention to charity work. 'No premiere would be complete without her,' wrote the *Tatler*, as she had been participating in fundraising events since her teens. Often the mainstay of society women, this new vocation as chairwoman of the London Society for Teaching and Training of the Blind Fund must have given Margaret a new sense of confidence in her abilities to form an identity outside of the gossip columns and her role as a wife. However she was under no illusion that her celebrity[13] was the reason she was offered the post, and she wholeheartedly threw herself into committee meetings.

The timing conflicted with her private life, for after accepting the charitable post Margaret became pregnant and was ordered by her doctor to rest as much as possible. Before her pregnancy she went to Freiburg, Germany, to be operated on by Dr Siegert, a famous surgeon, to reduce the risk of miscarriage. She obeyed her doctor, and held the committee meetings at her home, and was forbidden to travel to the funeral of her grandmother, Margaret Hannay, who died on 23 December 1936. She did, however, spend Christmas and New Year's Eve at Leeds Castle in Kent, a medieval castle surrounded by a moat filled with swans that had been the home of

Eleanor of Castile and Catherine of Aragon. Through centuries of changing hands and architectural styles, in 1926 it was bought and restored by Olive Baillie, an Anglo-American heiress said to be worth £100 million, and her third husband, Sir Adrian Baillie. Enshrined with new money it had a cinema, tennis court, squash court, and a swimming pool with a wave machine. The landscaped park was home to Olive's menagerie of exotic birds, and on the grounds, her pet llamas and zebras ran free.

Prior to accepting the invitation, Margaret had been warned by friends that Olive was eccentric; she dined on her favourite staple of pheasant, drinks were served at eleven o'clock in the morning, and lavatories were decorated to resemble thrones. Aside from her idiosyncrasies in entertaining, Margaret was also told that Olive might not greet a new house guest until a few days into their visit, and sometimes she did not appear at all. Olive took to Margaret at once and invited her to take tea in her Louis XIV-style bedroom, although such meetings were largely secretive because she disliked publicity and did not take kindly to other guests knowing her business. She also liked Charlie, and on occasions would summon him from London to the castle to play poker with her guests, where losses of £10,000 in one night were not unusual, nor was the sight of Olive with a cigar in her mouth and a mountain of poker chips in front of her. Sometimes Charlie refused, but Margaret would urge him to go; 'Look, Olive is such a nutcase if you don't accept we won't get invited again and we love her weekends!'[14]

Returning to London in the New Year of 1937 Margaret resumed her charity work and held a committee meeting for the London Society for Teaching and Training the Blind. She had promised to sell out the premiere of *Beloved Enemy*, which was being screened to raise funds. On the afternoon of the meeting, word reached her that Charlie had been diagnosed with a perforated stomach ulcer, and emergency surgery was performed to save his life. 'Worried as I was about him, and very pregnant, I went on with the job,'[15] she said, emphasising both her commitment and her condition, which, given her previous medical history, caused her doctor concern. She left Loelia, Duchess of Westminster to chair the meeting, and rushed to the hospital and waited outside the operating theatre. The operation was a success, though Charlie had to remain in the hospital for a month. With little else she could do, Margaret returned to arranging the charity premiere, which was to be held at the Leicester Square Theatre, and Bobby Sweeny accompanied her. 'She was disappointed that there were no arc-lights illuminating Leicester Square to herald the film premiere of *Beloved Enemy*, but on reaching the theatre we realised how unnecessary they would have been,' wrote *The Bystander*. Merle Oberon, the star of the film and 'heroine of the evening', was in attendance, and afterwards, she and Margaret went to the Cafe de Paris. Margaret raised £1,800 for the charity, and despite being well connected and using it to her advantage to sell tickets, it was a worthy achievement as until that period she was often lamented for her choice of dress or colour of lipstick, rather than noble endeavours.

Throughout their marriage, Charlie had suffered from an incipient duodenal ulcer, brought on from overwork and a poor diet. He had previously travelled to Baden Baden with his father to take the cure at Dr Dengler's sanatorium, which he found boring and pointless. His father went every year, as did Helen, even though Charlie himself thought there was nothing wrong with his health; and on that particular visit he went in place of his mother, who had grown tired of the Bavarian scenery. He believed Dr Dengler's patients were hypochondriacs; the cure was nothing more than mind over matter. Instead he went to Dr Martin in Freiberg, as he had been recommended by some friends he met at a casino, and he thought the treatment had better results. For three weeks he received daily injections of larostidine from an enormous syringe, and when his London doctor learned of the treatment he worried about the strain on Charlie's kidneys.

In her memoirs, Margaret made no mention of Charlie's visit to Dr Martin, and instead wrote of a visit, in 1935, to a Swiss clinic to help cure him. Now, two years later, he went with Margaret to the Princes Hotel in Brighton, to recuperate from his operation. The irony was not lost on her, and she said: 'When I was ill, which happened all too often in those years, Charlie would go out to various dinner parties with my blessing. But if he was ill, or away, he forbade me to dine even with close friends of ours.'[16] Margaret recalled they returned to London in May, in time for the coronation of King George VI, and she took a box on Oxford Street to see the royal carriage on its way to Westminster Abbey.

A month later and despite being ordered to rest, Margaret went to Swerlings, the milliners on Bond Street, where she lost her footing and fell down a flight of stairs. She was unhurt, and her maternity nurse, whom she recently engaged, took her home and put her to bed. Charlie did not seem worried, and he spent the afternoon at the Ascot races. Two days later, at three o'clock in the morning, Margaret awoke with labour pains and was taken to Beaumont House, a nursing home in Marylebone. She gave birth to a baby girl at half past nine on the morning of 19 June. Charlie had wanted a son, and Margaret thought he would be disappointed with the news of a daughter, but he wrote: 'When she looked up at me with her slightly bleary, beautiful blue eyes, I felt I had been blessed with the most wonderful daughter anyone could ever have.'[17] During Margaret's stay at the nursing home, an employee cut the bell wires in the other mothers' rooms, so they would not ring and disturb her. It was to have dire consequences when another woman went into labour at the same time as Margaret and rang for a nurse and her call went unanswered. It was a reminder of Margaret's celebrity, and how she was given preferential treatment, though at the time she knew nothing about the wires being cut.

The baby was christened Frances Helen Sweeny, by Father Woodlock, at Brompton Oratory; her godparents were Bobby Sweeny, the Marquis of Queensberry, Count John Bendern (a golfer, better known as John de Forest), the Countess of Dumfries, Lady Bridget Poulett and Jeanne Stourton. *The Sketch* reported that Theresa Sweeny gave Frances a diamond bracelet with a rose formed in the centre. And Margaret, they wrote, 'looked lovely as ever in black chiffon and lace, with a large black picture hat, two diamond clips, and two silver foxes'.[18] The birth of Frances caused significant fanfare in the press, and Margaret, 'facing the camera with wide-eyed surprise',[19] was photographed with the child in her arms. An article, accompanying the pictorial study, wrote:

> There was a pilgrimage of well-dressed young women to a house just off Regent's Park during the mornings. They are friends of Mrs Charles Sweeny, and they visit to become better acquainted with tiny Frances Helen Sweeny, who was born just three weeks ago. Mother and daughter are now back at Sussex Place, where a delightful nursery suite of three rooms awaited little Miss Sweeny. It comprises a bathroom in pink and blue (with a soap container in the shape of a big pink duck); a day nursery, spacious and airy, with primrose walls; and a night nursery in similar tones to the bathroom.[20]

In August Margaret and Charlie left Frances in the care of her nurse and departed for a tour of Europe in their Rolls-Royce, driven by their chauffeur, who also doubled as a gun loader for Charlie. They stayed at Schloss Mittersill, a medieval castle near Salzburg, run by Baron Hubert Panz and Count Hans Czernin, which had been renovated into an exclusive resort and, later, a sporting and shooting club. Margaret's afternoons were spent socialising with the guests; among them were Charlie's god-mother, Millicent Hearst, and Lady Mendl, better known in other echelons as a former actress and interior designer Elsie de Wolfe. As Margaret had witnessed in her teens and driving through Nuremberg during Hitler's first rally, Charlie, too, sensed the tension between Germany and Austria. 'Those of us who travelled the Continent should have been better informed than we were,' he wrote. 'Only occasionally did we get a glimpse behind the curtain and see the danger signals.'[21]

The danger signals were observed and largely ignored by pleasure seekers. This was particularly true when Margaret and Charlie motored from Austria to Venice to join their friends on the Lido, where Joseph Goebbels, Nazi Germany's Minister of Propaganda, was also holidaying. Although, years later, Margaret described him as sinister, at the time it was the latter part of her holiday and not the company that troubled her. She persuaded Charlie to visit Budapest, and he agreed even though he did not want to go. They drove through Yugoslavia, the rough roads causing discomfort and threatening to damage the car, and upon reaching the Hotel Duna Palota in Budapest he was bad-tempered, ill with sunstroke, and went straight to bed. Determined to see something of the city, Margaret took a taxi to Lake Balaton, but her enthusiasm had been spoiled by Charlie's moodiness. His pessimism was not out of place; that same year, in 1937, a conspiracy theory had come to light regarding the mass suicides in Budapest,[22] believed to have been inspired by the 1933 song 'Gloomy Sunday', also known as the 'Hungarian Suicide Song'. To counteract the problem, which had peaked in the late 1930s, a professor and hypnotist invented a 'smile club', and patrol boats were stationed along the Danube to rescue anyone who attempted suicide by throwing themselves in the river. During Margaret's visit, it would not have been unusual to see individuals out in public wearing a piece of paper taped to their mouths, with a smile illustrated on it. It can be assumed Charlie overlooked the odd display, given his reluctance to leave the hotel, which made headlines four years earlier after a young

British journalist checked in, and although in high spirits when she arrived, succumbed to the epidemic and slit her wrists with a safety razor.[23] Margaret and Charlie's trip ended with him refusing to ever again visit any of those 'God-damned places'.

Forms of eccentricity were better suited to England, or so Charlie thought, and Margaret was undoubtedly drawn to unconventionality. This was particularly true of their first Christmas with Frances, which was spent at Wentworth-Woodhouse, the family seat of the Earl and Countess of Fitzwilliam. With 240 rooms, 1,000 windows and a frontage of 200 yards, it was the largest house in England and its size exceeded Buckingham Palace. The Fitzwilliam fortune was predominantly founded in the coal-mining industry and the Wentworth-Woodhouse lawn was permanently blackened from coal dust from the nearby mines. Given that Margaret was 'intrigued by the idea of being a duchess',[24] this display of pre-war grandeur appealed to her; liveried footmen stood behind each chair, and a miniature railway track brought food from the kitchen to the dining room. It was a lost world, even by the standards of the late 1930s, and as the mining industries declined the Fitzwilliams' finances suffered and the house became impossible to run. However, during this period when several industries were collapsing and once-powerful families were becoming bankrupt, Charlie was beginning to build his fortune; he had bought Serocalcin, a cold cure developed in Switzerland, and a year later he sold it for a profit of £45,000. Although his and Margaret's lifestyle became more affluent during a period of economic depression, she measured his wealth against that of their respective fathers, and continued to think of themselves as poor.

After Christmas Margaret was given the news that Miss Randall was leaving to marry their chauffeur, Bertram Parker, and to have a family of her own. It was a painful loss, as for the past nineteen years she thought of Miss Randall as her most loyal companion and mother figure. Now that Margaret was married and had become a mother herself, perhaps Miss Randall, at the age of 43, thought it time to move on. During Margaret's childhood Miss Randall tolerated the Whigham household because of the child, and, then, drawing on the scenes Margaret accused Charlie of making, it can be assumed she was privy to them too. In Margaret's later years she recalled, '[Helen] was extremely good at running the house and the servants adored her. But she was tough with them, much tougher than I've ever been.'[25] It conjures up a dual life; the kindness of strangers and Margaret's readiness to accept love and adoration from those who were not family. It was a dynamic learned in the nursery; the foundation of what others referred to as a false facade of vulnerability. The relationship between Margaret and her staff often breached the professional boundaries between employer and employee; years later this was true of the maids she hired, and of a butler who drank too much and, one on occasion, Margaret dragged him under the table before her guests arrived and they ate their dinner, oblivious he was there.

*

In the New Year of 1938, Margaret was once again pregnant. The operation she had in Freiburg and the subsequent birth of Frances had perhaps given her a false sense of security and she ignored the doctor's orders to rest. She went to Vichy, so Charlie could take the cure, though this contradicts his memories of the summer of 1938,[26] for he bypassed Vichy completely. Margaret recalled the setting as a significant one; for it was during luncheon at a golf club, which was situated on an island, that she began to miscarry. 'It was no fun getting me home after that fiasco,'[27] she later said. Sitting in a chair and covered with blankets to hide the blood, she was carried to a ferry for the mainland. For several weeks she stayed at the Clinique La Pergola, a nursing home run by nuns, and a doctor there warned her not to attempt to have any more children as it would risk her life. She decided to ignore the medical advice; 'I loved having children. They're a great joy to have and whatever heartache they are, they're worth it.'[28]

By then Margaret and Charlie's marriage was in trouble; they each wanted different things and neither was prepared to compromise. Perhaps serving as an omen, or an indication, as to what was on the horizon, she lost her engagement ring after she accidentally threw it away with some paper wrappings. It had cost £1,000, and her carelessness warranted mentions in newspaper columns; 'Mrs Sweeny's Loss' was one such gloomy headline.[29] 'I would rather have lost anything than my engagement ring. It was never off my finger,' she told a reporter.[30] Then, keen to know what the future held, Margaret had her palm read at the Derby Ball. Charlie, who did not believe in such things, agreed on the condition he could enter the gypsy's bower and listen to any predictions told to his wife.[31] Presumably, nothing of interest was predicted, for Margaret did not take anything to heart. She would have been accustomed to being told what she wished to hear; 'beautiful', 'charming', and 'stylish' were the adjectives often used to describe her. It was not terribly imaginative, but for Margaret, it was enough.

During the time between Frances's birth and the declaration of the Second World War Margaret and Charlie travelled frequently. It was a period spent wandering the Continent, observing first hand the tension provoked by Mussolini and Hitler, and the dismissive views of British politicians, who sunbathed on the Riviera and did not, or would not, heed the warning until it was too late. 'My memories are not of fears of impending disaster so much as keeping up the old friendships and traditions we treasured, precisely because we sensed that things would never be the same again,' Charlie wrote, with the benefit of hindsight.[32] He could have been describing his marriage, rather than the threat of war.

Margaret and Charlie kept up appearances and broadened their horizons, and in February 1939 they sailed to New York on the *Ile de France*, as she longed to visit the place of her childhood. However, Charlie, whom Margaret accused of being 'completely Anglicised', did not share her enthusiasm. An invitation from his friend, Stephen 'Laddie' Sanford, convinced him to go, and they were to spend the latter part of the trip with the Sanfords in Palm Beach. As the boat sailed into the harbour, and the Manhattan skyline came into view, though much had changed by the addition of the Empire State building, Margaret felt at home. The American accent, too, evoked in her a feeling of familiarity, although hers was now replaced with an upper-class English drawl, an outcome of adhering to Helen's enforced elocution lessons. 'Obviously, one's childhood environment is very important,' she wrote of her thirteen and a half years spent on Park Avenue; the setting of her infant nightmares of boats sinking, the raised voices of her parents, and the unconditional love from Miss Randall.

During the trip, Margaret and Charlie were received by Byron and Thelma Foy, the Chrysler heiress, the Winston Guests, and the William Paleys. Trips to Broadway always ended with supper at the Colony Club, the Stork Club, El Morroco, or the 21 Club. There was an invitation to the opening of the Monte Carlo, a nightclub run by Fete Fefe Ferry, who led a troupe of dancers called Les Girls. After their stay in New York they took a night train, nicknamed the 'Florida Special', to join Laddie and Mary Sanford in Palm Beach. Las Incas, the Sanford ocean-front mansion, was a lost world hearkening back to the Gilded Age; there was a room entirely decorated with shells, and Mary caused a sensation on the tennis court by playing it as a rigorous sport rather than a gentle form of exercise, as was the style of Edwardian women. Although Laddie was a celebrated polo player and heir to the Bigelow-Sanford carpet fortune, it was Mary, a former actress, hailed as 'Queen Mary' by Palm Beach society, who was the leader of their social world. At night there were dances under the stars at the Everglades Club, and by day Charlie and Laddie played golf at the famous Seminole Club. Mrs Jessie Woolworth Donahue invited Margaret and Charlie to attend the Hialeah races, and she sent her private railway coach to fetch them. She was a collector of royal railroad carriages, and this one was air-conditioned, with solid gold taps and fittings in its bathroom. The races were watched from Joseph E. Widener's box, with a view of the pink flamingos in the centre of the track, and of the visiting Seminole Indians in their tribal dress. After their jaunt to Palm Beach, Margaret and Charlie returned to New York for two weeks, and she recalled watching the St Patrick's Day parade, which, incidentally, occurred on the day she heard that Hitler's troops had occupied Czechoslovakia. The following day Margaret and Charlie boarded the *Queen Mary* to sail home.

They continued their travels during the summer, 'that last summer of peace', as Margaret wistfully remembered – a foreboding remark, as it would turn out. She went with Charlie to Monte Carlo, to meet their friends Douglas Fairbanks and his wife Sylvia Ashley, and while there she discovered she was pregnant. Although each pregnancy signalled a worrying time for Margaret, who longed for another baby after the birth of Frances, her thoughts were preoccupied with war and it cast a dark shadow over their fun. Their original plan was to holiday with the Fairbanks in Venice, but it was thwarted after Charlie asked his friends in the Air Ministry if it was a good idea, given the political situation, as Mussolini's fascist troops had invaded Abyssinia and furthermore he endorsed Nazi Germany's annexation of Austria.

During their stay in Monte Carlo, the German–Polish crisis began, and in an attempt to forget the news Margaret and Charlie attended a gala as the guests of Hollywood stars Norma Shearer and George Raft. It was a poor attempt at gaiety, for each day they sat around the pool discussing the impending war. And when Margaret was not listening to talk of war she was observing Douglas Fairbanks, whom she thought 'dapper, vital and handsome, with very white teeth and immense charm'. The physical attributes of Fairbanks were overshadowed by her views of him being 'pathologically jealous' of his wife, as he would insist on Sylvia sitting next to him at dinner parties and never allowing her out of his sight. This she felt was on par with Charlie, and she placed the two men together in the category of jealous husbands. Sylvia, a former chorus girl and the ex-wife of the Earl of Shaftesbury's son and heir, was renowned for her promiscuity and extramarital affairs. Margaret never elaborated on such, except to accuse Fairbanks of unreasonable behaviour. What she did not know at the time was that Fairbanks was gravely ill (he died four months later) and had become dependent on Sylvia more than ever, and this might have explained his behaviour.

Another guest at the hotel, Leslie Hore-Belisha, was Britain's Secretary of State for War, who had asked Charlie when he and Margaret intended to go home. In his memoirs, Charlie wrote of an exchange he shared with Hore-Belisha while sitting next to him and his French actress girlfriend at the pool; 'I understand the international situation is getting dangerous and we were thinking of leaving tomorrow. What do you think?' he asked.[33] Hore-Belisha agreed it was a wise decision, so, acting on his advice, Margaret and Charlie left for London with their fellow guests Simon and Miriam Marks. Simon suggested they stop in Paris, as he and Miriam had to collect three Renoir paintings, costing £10,000, with a view of saving them from the Nazis should war come. As they were Jewish, Miriam did not want to stay in Europe longer than she had to, and the paintings were not collected.[34] Margaret and Charlie proceeded with their Parisian plans, as she hated Monte Carlo and the resorts he liked, and she wished to lunch with Elise Mendl at her home at Versailles.

They arrived in London at the beginning of September, and went to Margaret's uncle Walter Whigham's country house,

Highlands, near Canterbury. It was there, on the third, that they listened to Neville Chamberlain's declaration of war. The news left both Margaret and Charlie anxious, and they feared the worst. Having followed the political situation developing in Europe, although with a degree of denial that another world war would happen in their lifetime, Charlie's approach was far more pragmatic than Margaret's. The German torpedoing of a British passenger ship, the SS *Athenia*, on 4 September, confirmed Charlie's fears and he began to make plans for his own future, as part of an impending war effort, and for his family. For Margaret, it disrupted her lifestyle and travelling;[35] she loathed the countryside and wished to remain living in London, and after her previous trip to New York she wanted to return. She pinned her hopes on, and then resented, Chamberlain's promise of 'peace in our time', which she understood as a solution to the conflict. Reverting to the familiar pattern of her youth she turned to her father for reassurance and thought his opinion was of far greater value than Charlie's. It would, in many ways, create an irrevocable dynamic in their marriage, which became magnified by the war.

War

In the early days of the Second World War, the general consensus was to leave London, with children being evacuated to the countryside, and many of Margaret and Charlie's friends leaving for America. Margaret's fate was to be decided by Charlie, and along with Frances she went to his parents' house at Cooden Beach, a small seaside resort near Bexhill-on-Sea, in Sussex. She was restless; it was the period known as the phoney war and she longed to return to London, where George and Helen were. When France was invaded by the Germans, followed by the Dunkirk evacuation, Charlie persuaded his parents to close up the house and return to America.

In March 1940, after a long winter in Sussex, Margaret returned to London. The phoney war was coming to an end, and an eerie stillness prevailed over the city. Air-raid sirens were tested day and night, their wailing signalling to her nothing more than an unbearable sound. As a precaution, and perhaps a practicality owing to the lack of domestic staff during wartime, George and Helen closed up their Upper Grosvenor Street house and moved into the Dorchester Hotel; its concrete and steel infrastructure earned it the reputation of being the safest building in London. Margaret proposed to Charlie they do the same, and they, too, took a suite at the hotel. It was there, in April, that her son, Brian Charles Sweeny, was born, his birth occurring on the day Germany invaded Norway. 'It was a divine way to have a baby, in a hotel,' she said. Owing to the decline of the gossip columns to make way for news of war, the birth was not extensively covered, like the birth of Frances, but it still garnered a small mention: 'News of the arrival of a son to Mrs Charles Sweeny is a reminder of the quite wonderful popularity of this young Mayfair hostess.'[1] She was also the subject of an article, which asked 'where are all those society lovelies whose pictures used to adorn the glossy pages of the illustrated weeklies?', and she was grouped between Anna Neagle and Vivien Leigh, who were in Hollywood, while Margaret, they falsely reported, 'whiles away the train journey [to Sussex] by knitting socks and scarves for the troops'.[2]

The question of Margaret and the children's safety continued to trouble Charlie, and as he had done with his parents, he made plans for them to sail to America. It was a decision prompted by the United States Ambassador to the United Kingdom, Joe Kennedy, who said: 'Get out of England, Margaret. This country's finished.'[3] Elaborating on his view, Kennedy predicted England would be invaded by Germans, and that war refugees would descend on the country, 'all the roads will be blocked … just as they are now in France'.[4] The warning troubled Margaret, as did the onus of making a decision on behalf of not only herself but her children too. 'They kept sending ships over for us and every time the ship came I was upset because I didn't know what to do with the children who were half American … I wished to God they wouldn't send any more ships.'[5] Incidentally, her parents-in-law had left in May 1940, on the SS *Washington*, the last passenger ship to leave the British Isles for America.

It was her father who had the final say on whether or not Margaret and her children would go to America: 'Margaret, if you leave Britain, or if you send your children away, I shall never speak to you again.'[6] It seemed a hypocritical stance, given

George's own predicament during the First World War and how he remained in New York, a safe distance from battle. And, far from patriotic in his view that Margaret and her children ought to remain in Britain and display great courage, it appeared to be a selfish one. There was a risk, should she go to America to live during the war years, that she might settle there indefinitely; she had, after all, felt homesick for New York during those first few years in England, and after her holiday in 1939 she was planning to return.

Although George had the final word over Margaret and the children's departure for America, it was Charlie who decided that if Margaret wished to jeopardise her safety by remaining in London, the children could, at least, be spared. Accompanied by their nursery maid and nanny, a 2-year-old Frances and a 1-month-old Brian were sent as paying guests to Bodnant, Lord and Lady Aberconway's estate at Tal-y-Cafn, in Denbighshire, North Wales. In her memoirs Margaret wrote: 'Christabel Aberconway had decided to take the children of her friends as paying guests at £10 a head, in preference to having the Liverpool evacuees forced upon her.' The snippet which Margaret shared in her memoirs was inspired by having known Christabel, 'a lady of great wealth but of diminutive intellect',[7] for years and had been accustomed to her eccentricity. Christabel's father, Sir Melville Macnaghten, had been Assistant Commissioner of the London Metropolitan Police and heavily involved in the Jack the Ripper case,[8] thus prolific criminal cases fascinated her.[9] Christabel was also fixated with the imprisonment of her friend and neighbour, Oscar Wilde,[10] whom she had known briefly at the age of 2. Another childhood friend of Christabel's was Josephine Kipling, daughter of Rudyard, and she inspired his poem 'The Way Through the Woods' as she did Sir William Walton's Violin Concerto.

The billeting of Frances and Brian to the countryside gave Margaret the freedom to resume her social life. It was summer, but the season was bleak; her contemporaries, who had not deserted their country for America, were consumed by the war effort, and all the men whom she had known had enlisted in the armed forces. In May the Germans marched into Belgium, the Netherlands and Luxembourg, and in June, Italy entered the war; this marked the end of the phoney war and the threat of a German invasion had become a reality for many Britons. By September the first bombs were dropped on London, and Charlie became frustrated all over again by Margaret's refusal to obey his orders to go to the countryside, to join their children at Bodnant. On the night of a significant attack, Margaret and Charlie were coming out of a cinema at Marble Arch and saw the flare from an explosion, and heard the distant sound of bombs and anti-aircraft guns. They ran down Park Lane, to the Dorchester, and Margaret sat down and lit a cigarette, and Charlie went up on to the roof to watch the explosions. Selfridges on Oxford Street was ablaze and dozens of neighbouring buildings were burning, and looking in the direction of the East End he could see a bright glow across the landscape.

There would be many near-misses as Margaret and Charlie conducted their social life around the half-mile square of the West End, its pavements pitted by bombs. 'London looks like a tired woman, people said,' reported the *Sunday Express* in a mocking tone, for they dismissed the notion that the city had succumbed to the Luftwaffe. Instead, the newspaper wrote encouragingly of the upper classes and exiled royalty who had moved into hotels, namely the Dorchester, Claridges, and the Ritz, thus providing a new focal point for the diminishing gossip columns. It spurred Margaret's nightly jaunts, even if Charlie was reluctant to ignore the air-raid sirens and unpredictability of the bombing raids. His fears were not unfounded. The Cafe de Paris, considered to be the safest club in London due to several of its floors being located underground, was blown to pieces, killing its bandleader Ken 'Snakehips' Johnson and thirty-four others; the power of the blast sucked the air out of their lungs, leaving them frozen in the pose they had been in when the bomb exploded. And Princess Catherine Galitzine, an acquaintance of Margaret's, was killed in a daytime air raid as she travelled on a bus to her job at the Postal Censorship Department. The 400, a frequent haunt, was a reminder they were playing cat and mouse with death, as Charlie suspected it would collapse like a deck of cards if it was hit. On another occasion, they were passing the Lansdowne Club in Berkley Square when Charlie impulsively pulled Margaret into the entrance of the club to find shelter behind a pillar. It was a timely gesture, for a bomb fell across the street and filled the space where they stood with glass and debris.

With the Luftwaffe attacking London every night, and with British anti-aircraft gunners failing to shoot down enemy planes, Margaret and Charlie followed the advice of Mr Ronus, manager of the Dorchester, to sleep in the Sauna Room which was 12ft below street level. For a few nights they did this, along with Diana and Duff Cooper, with whom they likened the atmosphere to sleeping in an underground station. Cecil Beaton wrote of his wartime digs at the hotel: 'What a mixed crew we are! Cabinet ministers and their self-consciously respectable wives; hatchet-jawed, iron-grey brigadiers; calf-like airmen off duty; declasse society people; cheap musicians, and motor-car agents.' It was a seemingly pleasant and safe arrangement until Charlie heard a clang above his head and the next morning he went outside to investigate, to discover there was nothing but a couple of feet of earth and a few inches of concrete protecting them. They soon moved back upstairs to their suite. A short while later a bomb fell on Dean Street, shattering the windows of their suite and filling the room with plumes of black smoke. Although it startled Margaret, she did not care about the near-miss; she had survived, had she not? Charlie disagreed with her philosophy and ordered her to leave at once.

A few days later Charlie took Margaret to Euston Station to catch a train to north Wales. A bomb exploded while she waited on the platform, paralysing her with fear as glass from the windows fell around her, and she saw a woman dive under a stationary train to emerge with her hat covered in soot. It struck Margaret as funny; the surreal Anna Karenina-esque scene that had played out before her eyes, evoking her childhood dreams of ships sinking. 'Look, you're getting me killed. You've brought me to this station to get killed!' she shouted at Charlie.[11] The scenario could have served as a clue to her lack of a sense of humour, for it was not conventional scenarios which struck her as humorous, but that of the macabre. The frustration which she felt toward Charlie and at being forced to go to north Wales overwhelmed her, and sitting in the train carriage, filled with evacuees going to Liverpool, she began to cry. A well-meaning businessman patted Margaret on the knee and attempted to raise her spirits by telling her they would soon be out of London. 'That's what I'm crying about,' she snapped. She gave up her seat to a woman with a baby and moved into the guard's van, which she shared with a goat.

Margaret's arrival at Bodnant was as equally uninspiring, and she thought the Georgian house, rebuilt in an Old English style, was large and uninteresting. Then she saw Christabel Aberconway descending the stairway, with a candle in her hand, and decided she looked like Lady Macbeth 'and that really did it, the *gloom*!'[12] However, prior to reaching the house, her mind was made up, and she stopped at a post office and sent herself a telegram, citing Charlie's ill-health and saying that she was needed urgently. It arrived the following morning, and Margaret kissed her children goodbye and left for London. The train journey took six hours, and for the duration there were air-raid warnings every few minutes and passengers lay on the floor of the carriage. Margaret admitted she was 'beaming', which attracted curious looks from those fearful of London and the bombs: 'They must have thought I was mad.'[13] Charlie, too, thought she was mad but admitted defeat. 'I give up,' he said.

It was one thing to remain in London, it was another to neglect her children entirely. Margaret visited them every other weekend when the trains were running, as they were often delayed or cancelled due to air raids. She accused Charlie of showing little interest in Frances and Brian, and said he seldom accompanied her and visited only briefly before making his excuses to leave for London. In his memoirs he recalled spending Christmas with Margaret and the Whighams at a local pub a few miles from Bodnant, with the intention of seeing Frances and Brian, but the chief attraction for the men was the shooting on the Aberconway estate and they had brought their guns with them. They were invited to Bodnant for Christmas dinner, and although they heard the guns on Boxing Day, Charlie and George were not asked to join the shoot. Charlie thought his hosts' generosity had its limits; their housing the Sweeny children was a formal arrangement and not an invitation for familiarity, confirmed by James Lees-Milne's remark that Lord Aberconway had 'an old-fashioned keep-your-distance manner'.[14] After Christmas Frances and Brian moved with their nanny to Stony Stratford, near Bletchley, close to Helen and George's rented country house, Calverton Place.

Charlie's absence from family life was due to his war work and, as Margaret accused him of, infidelities, although, in the present time, having closed up the Federated Trust, it was the former which occupied his attention. With Charlie's decision to remain in England and with his bouts of ill-health[15] making it impossible to enlist in active service, he wanted 'to do his bit'. He was certain that other American expatriates in England would feel as he did, and although America had not yet joined the war, he was approached by an individual named Buchor, who spoke of forming an American volunteer unit. This inspired Charlie to seek out General Sir Sergison Brook, the commanding general of London Air Headquarters, and he suggested those Americans who were interested should set up a mobile volunteer unit prepared to help with any emergency. Aside from strengthening the war effort, Charlie sensed it would boost the government's propaganda machine.

In theory it was an attractive proposal; however, when it came to executing their plan both Charlie and Buchor failed to impress General Brook, as he rightly sensed their voluntary unit infringed on America's neutral status. Despite the rejection, Charlie recruited his friend Charles Lyttle and they founded the First American Motorised Squadron, made up of 100 volunteers. His father sent 100 Tommy guns and 100,000 rounds of ammunition, donated by the Thompson Company. Sir Malcolm Campbell, the racing motorist, offered to equip their cars with armour and to supply a few personnel armoured carriers, of his own design, for around £2,000 per car. The personnel carriers failed to materialise, and although it was a setback the squadron attracted support from the Scots Guards at Pirbright, who trained the volunteers in night marches and range work. They were now a respectable unit and those American volunteers who were not fit for active service joined the Home Guard.

Having learned that many of the American men had flying experience, Charlie asked his uncle Charles Sweeny, the decorated war hero, who, in 1939, was responsible for recruiting American pilots to join the Finnish Air Force in their war against Russia, to become an honorary commander. A new name was decided upon, the American Eagle Squadron, and those men who were trained pilots eventually fought alongside the RAF in the Battle of Britain. When the unit was presented to Winston Churchill, Margaret and Clementine Churchill were the only two women present on Horse Guards Parade to watch what would become a moment of Anglo-American history.

Although Margaret was proud of Charlie's achievements, she also wanted to help the war effort. She volunteered at the Beaver Club, close to Admiralty Arch, founded for Commonwealth troops, predominantly Canadians, who came for the reduced rate of dining and drinking. According to Margaret she was happy to do the washing up, but it was waitresses the club was short of, and so she stepped into the role alongside Winston Churchill's daughter-in-law, Pamela. The work was hard and the hours were long, and she began to suffer from exhaustion and various health complaints. It would be a brief stint, for she was ordered by her doctor to give it up, as he thought it too soon after the birth of Brian to undertake such strenuous work. Her next post was the RAF Benevolent Fund, where she worked at a gentler pace under the management of Lady Portal of Hungerford. It must have been too sedate for Margaret's tastes, as she claimed she was praying for America to join the war, if only to liven things up.

On 7 December 1941, the Japanese bombed the United States naval base at Pearl Harbor, and Margaret was 'thankful' when news came that America had joined the war. There and then she rushed to Mayfair to see Harvey Gibson, head of the American Red Cross, and asked for a job. It was an exciting time for Margaret; she described the period as 'tremendously gay' and 'dangerous', and she became the second woman in England to wear an American Red Cross uniform, 'a frightfully pretty' ensemble of Air Force blue trimmed in red, with a white shirt or white jersey. She had hers made at Molyneux and modelled it for the society photographer Dorothy Wilding.

The first woman to wear the uniform was Margaret Biddle, wife of Anthony 'Tony' Biddle Jr, who had served as a United States ambassador to eight countries and minister to five. Mrs Biddle was Margaret's superior, and aside from having a certain amount of clout in political circles, she was a wealthy mining heiress in her own right, and like Margaret, she possessed enough arrogance to do as she pleased. Uniform restrictions or not, Mrs Biddle wore pearls with her white jersey, and Margaret was inspired to do the same. She was photographed in this fashion, and the portrait was placed in the window of Dorothy Wilding's Bond Street studio. It caught the attention of Henry Gibson, who demanded to know 'who the hell is that dame wearing the pearls with her uniform?' The pearls were forbidden, for both Margaret and Mrs Biddle, which undoubtedly irritated the latter as she had been wearing her pearls unnoticed until her charge drew attention to them. Said to have a man's brain, believed to have been influenced by her billionaire father, Mrs Biddle rarely took no for an answer, and therefore her Red Cross club, run for women officers, was the finest in London, and if she could not source luxuries such as strawberries or asparagus from the Catering Corps, she bought them at her own expense. Despite the Ministry of Food enforcing rationing in 1940 their menu was exceptionally good and it attracted patronages from the Women's Army Corps, the United States Naval Reserve (for women), and various regiments of male officers.

Margaret was given the position of entertainments officer, a role that drew on her connections and celebrity status. Among her responsibilities she had to book a dance band or cabaret to perform one or two nights a week, and she also attracted stars such as Bob Hope, Jack Benny and Marlene Dietrich to appear. She managed to persuade Bing Crosby to sing for two hours, as well as engaging Vera Lynn to give several concerts. At her suggestion David Rose, head of Paramount Studios in Hollywood, held a screening of *Road to Morocco* for General Eisenhower, General Bradley and other top military personnel. Some thought the film to be a secret message, as it was shown on the eve of Operation Torch, the British–United States invasion of French North Africa, and it caused an undercurrent of panic and paranoia among the generals. 'It was Dorothy Lamour, Bing Crosby, and Bob Hope in a film. No more, no less,' Margaret said, unmoved by the conspiracy theory.

Lady Charles Cavendish, the former dancer Adele Astaire, looked after the Red Cross Rainbow Corner, which was run for American GIs, and she said, 'You're such a snob, Margaret, working for all those officers.' There were moments of controversy, too, especially surrounding the racial prejudices. One evening Margaret was told to expect a number of black officers and nurses, who were to be given a dinner to welcome them to England, and word came from the American First Lady, Eleanor Roosevelt, that there should be no discrimination. During the evening Margaret entertained a black doctor and two nurses; however, when the dancing began the southern officers stood up and walked out, to show their disapproval of white women dancing with black men. Margaret was embarrassed, both for herself and on behalf of the guests, though there were to be no consequences for those who breached Mrs Roosevelt's protocol.

However Margaret was not restricted to looking after women officers, and soon began to socialise with the men, much to Charlie's jealousy. 'Charlie's possessive jealousy, which had always been a problem, now became a nightmare,' she wrote in her memoirs. If he spied Margaret in the company of a male officer, or if one happened to speak to her while they were out together, he would be 'embarrassingly rude'.[16] He recalled the version of events quite differently, and in his own memoirs wrote that Margaret's new role was a favourable one and that she enjoyed meeting new people. On one occasion she invited two American generals to dine with her and Charlie at the Dorchester; he appeared to like the men and found them charming and everyone had been on first name terms from the beginning. They were General Eisenhower and General Beadle-Smith. For Margaret to dine with her husband in the company of men was deemed acceptable by Charlie, but to dine alone with her male friends was another thing entirely. He thought not all her friends were 'so nice', and he suspected a few were far from platonic.

Margaret disputed his claims, thinking his imagination had run wild with jealousy and speculation. 'I didn't ever go out with anybody but Charlie,' she said. 'Never, never, never. I mean, I was being a model wife all the time, *which is quite ironic, isn't it?*'[17] He accused her of seeing a chief of staff of the 8th Air Force, known simply as Colonel T, whom he thought 'fat, bald, and a bit deaf', and decided it was not her betrayal which had upset him but the fact her paramour was not a handsome fighter pilot or a charming navy man. Furthermore, Charlie approached the man in question and decided that, as he was far from a gentleman, he should like to handle it man to man. Had Charlie carried through with his threat, he would have been court-martialled for assaulting an officer.

The man in question was Savannah-born Major General Frank O'Driscoll Hunter, known as the 'swashbuckling ace', owing to his dark looks and distinguished war effort dating back to the First World War. Contradicting Charlie's appraisal of his rival, Hunter, ironically known as 'Monk', was a dedicated bachelor and ladies' man. The accusation of an affair between Margaret and Hunter remains unvalidated, as neither mentioned a wartime fling, and Margaret was candid about the men in her life. Charlie himself had only seen her in his company, possibly at the Red Cross club, and had reached the conclusion they were romantically involved. It could also validate Margaret's claims that such associations were indeed platonic. As for Charlie's alias for Hunter, it risked directing the speculation toward General Carl Andrew Spaatz, known as 'Tooey', and therefore the name Colonel T would have applied to him and his rank. However, Charlie and Spaatz were on friendly terms, and he often hosted parties for him and their mutual friend, General Ira Eaker of the 8th Air Force.

Charlie approached Hunter's superior and was told little could be done to stop the affair, and that he should accept that his marriage, like many marriages during wartime, was over. As a Catholic he would not entertain the idea of a divorce, nor did he want to give Margaret up so easily. The Matrimonial Causes Act of 1937 reformed the reasons for which women could divorce their husbands: one significant ground was adultery, and this meant Margaret could now divorce Charlie on the grounds of his adultery, if she could prove it. For many marriages it would have signalled a shift in dynamics, though at the time Margaret did not wield this power over him, nor did she want to pursue a solution as final as divorce. Her suspicion of Charlie's infidelities was enforced by her friends, who approached George and Helen with the news that he was seeing several women, and in doing so they felt he was making a fool out of Margaret. She now realised that during the weekends she spent with the children at Calverton Place and he remained in London, offering excuses from business meetings to exercises with the Home Guard, that he was being unfaithful to her. At the time Margaret had made no assumptions, nor did she want to accept the truth.

It was her mother and father who broke the news to Margaret, an action provoked by the unhappiness Charlie had been causing her. Marital rows had become all too familiar, and what was once carried out behind closed doors was now blatantly obvious to her friends and parents. Margaret's reaction was not of anger or jealousy, but that of relief, and it surprised her parents as much as it did her. 'Charlie was now proven to be certainly no paragon of virtue, and I did not have to put up with those nerve-racking scenes anymore,' she recalled.[18] With a clear view of what she wanted from her marriage she confronted Charlie about the rumours and he did not deny them. She claimed he confessed to his infidelities and begged for her forgiveness, and he asked her to attend Mass with him, so they could pray together and begin anew.

The following weekend Margaret went to Calverton Place and she asked Charlie to join her, but he refused and said he had to dine with an American general. This general, Margaret was soon to discover, was an attractive blonde-haired woman. Could it have been her friend, Sylvia Ashley, the much-married former showgirl who, at the time, was widowed from Douglas Fairbanks and married to Edward Stanley, the successor to three baronies? 'Gossip ... Edward Stanley [found] Charles Sweeny in bed with his own wife,' wrote Charlie's friend, Eric Siepmann, in a letter.[19] Margaret knew she was being taken advantage of, and for a long time she accepted his shortcomings; 'I put up with this – everything has its price, and in many ways Charlie was a devoted, faithful, almost model husband.' Or, as things stood, it was wishful thinking on her part.

The turn of events, as related by Charlie, differed to Margaret's version of the truth. In his memoirs, he wrote that he sought counsel from George Whigham, and in so doing acknowledged he was putting his father-in-law in a difficult position, as George loved Margaret more than anything and would likely defend her behaviour. George's advice was to begin divorce proceedings as soon as possible. Perhaps the answer, although not what Charlie had wanted to hear, confirmed Margaret's side of the story. It was also hypocritical of George to think ill of his son-in-law's philandering when he, too, was known for his infidelities. Margaret's conversion to Catholicism never sat well with her Presbyterian parents, and this could explain George's reaction, for he never proclaimed to be a religious man, nor did he want his daughter to change her faith, and in doing so she had given up so much. There was a brief mention of Calverton Place, which Charlie stated that he and Margaret took a lease on with a view to live there and commute to London for her war work. In reality, this would have been impossible, as daily trips to London by train were often delayed or cancelled due to air-raid warnings. Aside from that, it was her parents who had leased the house, and she would never be happy in the countryside. In a final attempt to remedy the discord between himself and Margaret, he asked his brother for advice. The answer was simple: to move out of the suite he shared with her at the Dorchester and to rent his own flat. Charlie eventually moved around the corner, to 20 Charles Street, the former home of the British Prime Minister Archibald Primrose.

After returning from Calverton Place, Margaret learned that Charlie was being posted to a supply depot near Lytham St Anne's, in Warton. He insisted she come with him, but she refused as it was a three-month post and by then her mind was made up: their marriage was over. The posting, as he wrote in his memoirs, came as a surprise and he claimed it was done out of spite following his altercation with Frank O'Driscoll Hunter, who had arranged the transfer. When Charlie returned he asked Margaret to reconcile; he explained that after Hunter's meddling came to light he was dismissed from his post and sent to a desk job in Arizona. While it was true that Hunter played a role in having Charlie transferred, his dismissal was due to disobeying an order from his superior, General Ira Eaker, mandating the use of wing tanks on P-47 fighters. Margaret appeared indifferent to the news which, instead of giving Charlie hope, made him see the situation could not be salvaged, as he could not satisfy her ego.[20] 'Although she sought it, I don't think she ever found true happiness,' he later wrote.[21] Shortly after this realisation Margaret moved out of their suite at the Dorchester and into another one, on a different floor. It was a ridiculous scenario, she knew, but with the war and lack of safe accommodation in London, she was left with no other choice but to remain at the hotel. In her memoirs, she made no mention of Charlie's flat on Charles Street, a lively meeting place for politicians and American generals. From Charlie's own perspective he was happy, a feeling that was marred by a cable from his father, in July 1941, informing him of the unexpected death of his mother.

Throughout her life, it was no secret that Margaret lived in the comfort of her own reality and when reflecting on her life she rarely, if ever, cast herself in an unfavourable light. It was the consequence of her upbringing, and rather than viewing it as a blind spot she merely thought herself naive and easy prey for others. However, when considering the reasons why both Margaret and Charlie committed adultery neither were willing to accept responsibility for the part they played in ending their marriage. She blamed him for making the first move to break his vows, and he reciprocated her accusation. Their relationship, as she admitted, was entirely physical, and so when he strayed she followed suit and blamed it on the constriction of a Catholic marriage. It was the opposite of what her parents' marriage was, for as unhappy as Helen was at times, there were many things about George that had made her happy and outweighed his personal faults. This was particularly true during the war when the Whighams were living at Calverton Place, and Helen's health began to decline, leaving George to tend to her. It began with a pain in the soles of her feet, which moved up her legs and gradually gripped her body, and within weeks she was confined to a wheelchair, unable to stand or walk, and needing constant care. Although Helen had been suffering from arthritis since the 1930s and had travelled to warm climates all over the world to seek a cure or respite from the pain, she was belatedly diagnosed with osteoarthritis and rheumatoid arthritis. The woman who had criticised Margaret's flaws was now facing her own shortcomings, and instead of adopting a heavy-handed approach with her mother, as that was how she was treated by Helen, she sympathised with her helplessness and thought her brave. Helen, however, wished she were dead.

Not yet 30, Margaret had her entire life ahead of her, and there were no shortage of admirers willing to take her out. Before, at the Red Cross club, she thought the work fun and dangerous; the two ingredients driving the risky behaviour of many during the war. It was a period of uncertainty and given the shadow of death which hung over her, relevant with the near-misses she had experienced during the Blitz, she chose to live as she pleased. Friends told her to arrange a quick divorce, but she seemed reluctant to do so, and Charlie was against the idea of a divorce or an annulment. It begs the question as to why, if she was as unhappy as she claimed to be and knew that he was guilty of adultery, Margaret did not begin divorce proceedings. She admitted that she 'loved' being married; she enjoyed the idea of companionship and permanency. It stemmed from her childhood with Miss Randall and always having a person to turn to, a person in whom she had a natural ally, but like Miss Randall's position as a servant, Margaret preferred to have financial ascendancy over those she attached herself to. Charlie had ceased to be those things, or, rather, he failed to become those things. Her money, she believed, gave her power over people, including the men she entered into relationships with, but it also cast her as an anomaly and she never felt on equal footing with any man. By her own admission, she liked to encourage the men in her life, to see them reach the heights of George Whigham, though it was an accomplishment that few, if any, could achieve. There was also the probability that both she and Charlie were waiting for the hedonistic period to end; that she knew this behaviour was only temporary and when peace came everything, and everyone, would fall into their pre-war routines of married life and raising children. Reflecting on the era, she said: 'We were young and pretty, and the men were all terribly good looking and male. But we weren't bitchy or unkind. And we tried to be good wives and mothers.'[22] It was an element of domesticity, regardless of having servants, that she could never recapture.

A change in Margaret's behaviour came about as the result of a head injury gained in 1943, when she fell 40ft down a lift shaft after an appointment with her chiropodist, Mr Wiberg, at his office on Bond Street. She landed on her knees, as a lift cable had broken her fall, the impact cracking her head off the wall. The caretaker heard Margaret's whimpers, and thinking it was a cat, he called 'puss, puss', and halted the lift from descending. It saved her life, as she would have been crushed to death. When she was eventually rescued she was found to be covered in blood and clutching the lift cable, her fingernails torn off from doing so. Margaret was rushed to St George's Hospital and without anaesthetic was given thirty stitches in her head, and it was discovered she had broken vertebrae in her back. Three days later she was moved to University Hospital, and her parents were given the news that one side of her body was paralysed and that she might never walk again. George and Helen agreed to keep the news from Margaret, during which time she was growing restless in the hospital, where she was to remain for three months. After spending several days in bed, she convinced a nurse to let her get up, and she almost fainted from the pain and effort it took to walk. Regardless, she did not give up and three weeks later she left the hospital, the paralysis cured and her mobility restored. Given the blow to her head and damage to the olfactory nerve, she lost all sense of taste and smell for the next four years. Some believed it also altered her personality, awakening what might be described as nymphomaniac tendencies. 'It changed her totally,'[23] Charlie later wrote, and not for the better.

★

As the war drew to an end Margaret began to take stock of her life. In 1945 she was presented with an American Red Cross Theatre Ribbon on behalf of the military authorities of the US Army. It had been a hectic period; her work at the Red Cross continued throughout the breakdown of her marriage and her dangerous fall. An element of stability came from George, and he offered Margaret his house on Upper Grosvenor Street, which had thirty years remaining on its lease, as Helen could no longer manage the stairs. As George and Helen were to remain living at the Dorchester, Margaret also inherited the household staff – Mr and Mrs Duckworth, the butler and cook, and Gertrude Giltrap, the housemaid – and she brought with her a personal maid and the children's governess. Owing to Margaret's dislike of boarding schools, she sent Frances to a nearby day school and paid for her to have private lessons in French, Italian, painting, music, riding and tennis.

There was also the question of divorce and whether or not Margaret would begin proceedings. The best thing to do, she thought, was a trial separation, so in February 1946 she kissed George goodbye at Tilbury Docks and sailed to New York. It was an extreme step, for wartime travel restrictions still applied to international travel and one had to be an important individual or conducting business of national importance to go abroad. Since Margaret was neither, obtaining a passage would have been impossible had she not connections at government level. She approached the Ministry of War Transport and was given two options: as she was still married to an American she could travel as a GI bride, which meant sharing a cabin with three women, or she could sail on a banana boat, the SS *Rippingham Grange*. The latter appealed to her; she would be the only woman among twenty-five men and would, therefore, have her own cabin. It was a small price to pay, or so Margaret thought, but she regretted her decision when she realised the sailing would take longer than usual (it had taken three days to reach Brighton from Essex). 'Captain, dear, surely we can do better than this?' she said at lunch, emphasising she had a date in New York on 10 March. Her request was not only impossible but dangerous – the ship was neither insured nor seaworthy and the March weather was against them. They ran into gale-force winds and the decks were flooded for the next ten days, forcing the passengers to remain indoors and without fresh air. Margaret spent her endless days in the lounge, and she lived off tinned food, as all the passengers did, and after a week her skin looked dull and blotchy, and she was diagnosed with onset scurvy.

Arriving in New York on 9 March, despite the captain's gloomy prediction, Margaret was met by Admiral Luis de Flores, a wartime friend who often promised to meet her in the city. She was given Freedom of the Port, her luggage was whisked through customs and she was escorted by wailing police sirens to the Plaza Hotel, where she stayed for a few days. The remainder of her three-month stay was spent at her uncle Jim Whigham's apartment on Park Avenue; an ironic turn of events, as it was where Helen began her life in New York, and it was where Margaret hoped to relaunch hers. There were plenty of men willing to take Margaret to dinner and dancing; old friends from the Beaver Club and eligible bachelors, with whom she was photographed on the dance floor of El Morocco. When the photographs appeared in the press the rumour mill began and there was talk that Margaret would soon be divorced. Such images, if Charlie were inclined to initiate divorce proceedings himself, could have served as evidence for not only a divorce case but a custody one, too.

Aside from liking the attention, Margaret claimed her confidence was knocked by 'how fresh and healthy' the American women looked, as they were not the products of German bombing or strict rationing. There was no mention of her cousin Sybil, so like Margaret with her lithe frame and dark looks, and who one can assume fitted her description of American womanhood – she had since married Robert Young, a millionaire steeplechaser and racehorse breeder. Regardless of this view a change of scenery and male attention improved Margaret's outlook and restored her health.

★

In London Margaret's social life began again, only without Charlie, but it did not hinder her. She went to Leeds Castle, as the guest of Olive Baillie, who had recently divorced her husband. During the war, the castle was used to treat the expeditionary forces repatriated after the retreat from Dunkirk and to rehabilitate burned pilots who were operated on by Sir Archibald Mcindoe, a renowned plastic surgeon. The first big social event, hosted by Olive, was the wedding of her youngest daughter, Susan Winn, to Captain Geoffrey Russell, elder son of Lord Ampthill.

Although Margaret was yet to fall in love and forget Charlie, she began to accept they had each moved in different directions. During the war he had fallen in love with Lady Isabel Milles-Lade,[24] whom he thought of as 'one of the most popular and beautiful girls around … she always sparkled and charmed everyone'.[25] In her early twenties when they met, Isabel had been a popular debutante, and, like Margaret, she was renowned for her striking looks and nicknamed 'a Mayfair beauty'. Margaret, however, dismissed her as 'the sister of a peer' and, at the time, viewed her as the woman who had compromised the Sweeny marriage. As with their differing views on their behaviour and what contributed to the collapse of their marriage, Charlie hinted that Margaret's treatment of him might have influenced his affair with Isabel, and his wartime encounters with other women. In 1944 he was posted as an officer in the SHAEF (Supreme Headquarters Allied Expeditionary Force) mission to Paris, and later transferred to Chambery, thus enforcing a separation from Margaret, even though she herself stated she had left him the year before. One night, on a sleeper train from Chambery to Paris, he invited a pretty young woman to share his compartment, and she accepted. 'All I can say about that night is that it could have only happened in France in wartime, and that it was wonderful.'[26] He never saw her again, though he did not forget her.

During his sporadic trips to England, Charlie tried to contact Margaret, but she refused his requests to reconcile and would not talk to him when he enquired about the state of their marriage. When he returned to London a year later she did not acknowledge his absence, and she did not wish to heal the rift between them. 'As far as she was concerned, I might as well have been in Outer Mongolia,' he said.[27] By coincidence, or not, around the time of the D-Day landings, Charlie encountered Glen Miller at his base known as Tent City, in Portsmouth. He mentioned that he was needed in Paris, as his commanding officer ordered him to go as soon as possible, and Miller offered him a seat on his Norseman. Charlie politely declined, thinking he would arrive in Paris at an unsociable hour and decided to go to London for the night and fly to Paris the following day. The Norseman took off and vanished without a trace, and Charlie was the last person to see Miller alive.

When it seemed certain Margaret would begin divorce proceedings, Charlie began to take an interest in her, and she responded to his attentiveness. 'What about Isabel?' she asked, and he said the affair meant nothing to him. She wanted to take the children to St Moritz, and Charlie arranged a chartered flight and, to her surprise, he was waiting for them in Zurich. It was a gesture she would have welcomed during their marriage, but in light of the divorce case, it unnerved her. He asked her to dine with him on the terrace of the Baur-au-lac Hotel, and although she did not want to she thought it would be ungrateful to say no, so she agreed. There was caviar and champagne, and an orchestra played Strauss in the background, and despite the setting, she thought it a difficult and emotional evening. Charlie begged her to reconsider the divorce, and, succumbing to his charm, she relented. She was taking Frances and Brian to St Moritz the next day and invited him to join them, as they would have ten days together to decide if their marriage was worth saving. Despite Charlie wanting Margaret to abandon her idea of a divorce, he was hesitant to go to St Moritz and said he could join her two days into the trip. He offered the usual excuse of business meetings in London, and she believed him and telephoned her solicitor to postpone the divorce proceedings. A day later Charlie rang and explained that his plane had run out of fuel and was forced to land in Cannes, which delayed him further. The following day Margaret telephoned his office, to ask when he might be joining her in St Moritz, to be told by his secretary that Charlie was on holiday in Cannes. She then realised he had never intended to join her and that it had been a ploy to make her call off the divorce.

Ten days later Margaret arrived in London and was surprised to see Charlie at the airport. He embraced the children and told Margaret how wonderful it was to see her, and he suggested they all go back to her house at Upper Grosvenor Street. She rejected the idea and they went their separate ways. Later that evening Margaret went to Ciro's with a male friend and was placed at a table next to Bridget Poulett, who had just returned from Cannes, where she had stayed in a neighbouring hotel room to Charlie and Isabel. The news, as jarring as it was, allayed Margaret's guilt of divorcing him against his wishes. Finally, she made the decision to file for a divorce. He had fooled her for the last time.

From the early days of their marriage to the brief reconciliation during their separation, Margaret was willing to overlook Charlie's shortcomings and to give him another chance. In their assessments of what went wrong in their marriage, they each blamed the other for its failure. He thought her egotistical and claimed she was the first to commit adultery. She said the same of him and added that it was his temper, jealousy, and thoughtlessness that ruined their life together. Regardless of his moodiness and the abandonment she felt following the birth of their stillborn daughter, she was willing to put her trust in him entirely. In a way, although Margaret fell into the traditional role of being a wife and mother, she could never be satisfied in a marriage that asked her to morph her identity into that of her husband's. For despite having no ambitions or aspirations outside of socialising, holidaying and taking care of her appearance, her daily existence consumed so much of her time.

By leaving Charlie and filing for a divorce Margaret was taking charge of her own destiny; a courageous stance which has often been overlooked, though many would have thought her foolish and, to a degree, reckless. From a stammering little girl so afraid of her mother's moods to a self-absorbed young woman interested in only having a good time, she had decided to take a step that could ruin her socially – the very thing her life had revolved around. It was far from taking a stand to protect her self-worth, but rather a means of freeing herself from conventionality; she wanted to throw parties, to be in charge of the guest list, and to go out with whom she pleased. 'Charlie was always so orthodox and boring,' Margaret said.[28] Everything had come full circle; she had come out as a debutante in the shadow of the First World War, and now she was free to revive her social life in the aftermath of the second.

Clockwise from above:

Helen Whigham (née Hannay).

George Hay Whigham.

The Hewitt School. (Jim Henderson)

Margaret and Charles Sweeny, after their wedding at Brompton Oratory, 1933. (Author's collection)

Crowds outside Brompton Oratory, 1933. (Author's collection)

Clockwise from above:

Margaret's wedding dress, designed
by Norman Hartnell, as exhibited
at the Victoria and Albert Museum.
(Elisa Rolle)

48 Upper Grosvenor Street.
(Reproduced by kind permission of
Dr Roger Bowdler)

Margaret and her children (and Marcel
the dog) at Brian's twenty-first birthday
party. (Author's collection)

On this page:

Top: Margaret and Ian with members of the Tiree Association, circa 1950. Photograph by George Outram & Co. (By kind permission of Tiree Historical Centre)

Middle: Margaret and Ian with Mrs Nancy MacLean, at the Tiree Association's annual concert, circa 1950. Photograph by George Outram & Co. (By kind permission of Tiree Historical Centre)

Bottom: Inveraray Castle. (Phil Sangwell)

Clockwise from above:

Day one of Argyll versus Argyll, 1963. (Author's collection)

Margaret campaigning to save the Argyll and Sutherland Highlanders regiment from disbandment. (Author's collection)

Margaret and Lieutenant Colonel Colin Campbell Mitchell, 'Mad Mitch', at Euston Station with crates containing 1 million signatures to 'Save the Argylls'.

Clockwise from left:

Margaret, Michael Thornton and Brodrick Haldane at Bleakholt Animal Sanctuary, 1968. (Reproduced by kind permission of Michael Thornton)

Arriving at Lord Dudley's memorial service, 1970. (Author's collection)

Leaving Lord Dudley's memorial service, 1970. (Author's collection)

Margaret and her friend Virginia Martini at Coral Casino Beach Club. (Reproduced by kind permission of Beverley Jackson)

The Grosvenor House Hotel, as it looked upon opening in 1929.

Margaret, circa 1986. (Reproduced by kind permission of *Scottish Field*)

Margaret, photographed at the Grosvenor House Hotel, 1992. (Reproduced by kind permission of Allan Warren)

8

The Golden Age

When Margaret and Charlie divorced in February 1947 they did so quietly and on the grounds of his constructive desertion. Although he agreed to the conditions of the divorce, it was against his will and perhaps something he came to regret, as a year later his love interest Lady Isabel Milles-Lade married Edward Stanley, the 18th Earl of Derby. Since their separation in 1943, this final step was a natural progression for Margaret, as she claimed she gave Charlie many opportunities to be a loyal husband. Her reputation remained unscathed; she had been married for fourteen years, was the mother of two young children, and, from an outsider's perspective, she had tried her best.

Margaret's status as a divorcee in the late 1940s offers a unique insight into social mores after the war, as the divorce rate increased between 1939 and 1945 and many post-war divorces were the consequence of hasty marriages, infidelity (58 per cent of divorce cases were filed by husbands) and incompatibility when men returned home. Margaret did not list Charlie's adultery or unreasonable behaviour – the two things she accused him of and the vital reasons, from her point of view, why her marriage failed. Desertion was a respectable cause for divorce, making it look as though Margaret had been another casualty of wartime circumstances and a victim of her husband's behaviour. The *Daily Mirror* embraced the changing social attitudes and reported that a divorce between two unhappy individuals should be granted: 'Even the most conservative figures of the legal profession today would not deny that our divorce law contains much that is stupid, vexatious and unfair.' It was a subject that divided opinions, and Mr Justice Denning claimed that a divorced couple with children 'have no absolute right to decide the future of their children … they have disabled themselves'.[1] The Church of England criticised the decline in moral standards and the collapse of family life, and in America the former president, Herbert Hoover, suggested that couples should understand that 'war relaxes moral standards on the home front and that this imperils the whole front of human decency'.[2]

None of the aforementioned were apparent in Margaret's household, and the children, she said, never suffered as a result. Nor did she exclude Charlie from family events; he was invited to tea in the nursery,[3] to accompany Margaret and the children to pantomimes, and to help decorate the Christmas tree. It was, after all, an era when upper-class children were accustomed to absent parents and their nanny taking responsibility for their upbringing, and so, as Margaret attested, Charlie's absence from their home life did not trouble Frances and Brian. The children would have also been used to not seeing either parent during the war years, when they were billeted to the countryside, and Brian, a mere baby at the time, knew no different.

This was particularly true when Margaret, dressed in Molyneux's post-war fashions of a long skirt and peplum jacket, left Frances and Brian at home and sailed to New York on the *Queen Mary*. She had been a divorcee for all of five days, and planned to make the most of it. Perhaps she wanted to have an affair with an American man, as they were, to her mind, the most attractive. Life on board the ocean liners, in an age before commercial air travel, was a social stratosphere within itself, and

Margaret often met friends who were also travelling alone, and in turn, there was always someone to dine with. On one occasion, she encountered Cecil Beaton, who was avoiding her friend – and his nemesis – Maureen, Marchioness of Dufferin and Ava, whom he called 'the biggest bitch in London'. One evening they were dining in the ship's Verandah Grill, when Margaret spied Lady Dufferin approaching in a black cape with a chartreuse-green lining, and Beaton quipped: 'And a chartreuse-green lining to her mouth, no doubt?' And sailing home aboard the *Queen Elizabeth*, Margaret was in the company of famous entertainers Florence Desmond and Arthur Askey, and Hollywood film star Ray Milland. The latter passenger was an interesting coincidence, for in her memoirs, Margaret wrote that, from New York, she flew to Los Angeles to stay with Ray Milland and his wife, Muriel. On that particular crossing a gossip columnist, reporting from the ship, wrote:

[It] is loaded with money, full of fat-faced cigar smoking men and mink-clad women. Over Martinis, champagne, and later brandy they talk heatedly of the workers, insist they are bone-idle, and that the prohibitive tax on tobacco and cigarettes is a damn good thing. I don't like them, and prefer to watch beauteous Margaret Sweeny, pencil-slim, stroll through the lounge.[4]

During this period of Margaret's transatlantic crossings, she met Theodore 'Ted' Rousseau Jr, the son of a rich American banker and German mother, who had spent his childhood in Paris and was educated at the Sorbonne, Eton, and Harvard. With Ted's connections to Europe's upper classes and as the stepson of Princess Nicole Xantho de Broglie, he considered himself aristocratic, and furthermore his sister, Marta, was a concert pianist who in 1940 had married Giovanni Jean Bagarotti, a famous violinist. It was through such high-ranking connections that Ted became curator of paintings at the Metropolitan Museum of Art in New York, where his colleagues called him 'the golden boy ... because he lived such a favoured life'.[5] During the war, Ted had served as a United States Naval attaché to the American embassies in Lisbon and Madrid, and after the war, he worked for the Office of Strategic Services (OSS) and was assigned to the Art Looting Investigation Unit (ALIU), and along with the 'Monument Men', he was responsible for uncovering art stolen by the Nazis from occupied countries. For this Ted was awarded with the Legion of Merit, named a Chevalier of the French Legion of Honour, Chevalier de l'Ordre des Arts et des Lettres (France), Officer of the Order of Orange-Nassau (the Netherlands), Order of Alfonso X el Sabio (Spain), and Knight Officer of the Order of Merit of the Republic of Italy.

After Margaret's first meeting with Ted, she thought it love at first sight, and was dazzled by his charm and striking looks – it was rumoured that Douglas Fairbanks Jr had undergone a facelift to look like him. However, Ted was a notorious womaniser and often fell for actresses and dancers (a future love interest was prima ballerina Alicia Markova), but he was always discreet, and, presumably, Margaret was unaware that she was not the only woman in his life. 'He seduced women not because of some Casanova complex, but because he delighted in pleasing them,' a colleague wrote.[6] Margaret accompanied him on his investigative trips to Rome, Milan, and Florence, to look for paintings stolen by Adolf Hitler's right-hand man, Hermann Goering. And later, while in Spain, Ted met Goering's banker and during the questioning he plied him with brandy and successfully learned of the art's whereabouts. It revived the sense of adventure Margaret had felt during the war; Ted's secret missions, the intensity of code-breaking and interrogation, and her role as confidante, waiting in hotel rooms for his return, learning of his games of cat and mouse.

When Ted asked Margaret to marry him she said no. She sensed the experience was a temporary one, and that he would return to

New York and devote his life to the Metropolitan Museum of Art, and fall in love with other women. Although Margaret loved Ted, she thought him arrogant and self-involved,[7] and these, she felt, were unsuitable qualities in a stepfather. Despite her rejection, they continued to see one another, even if it would never end in marriage. It was a dynamic that appealed to Margaret; she liked being attached to a man without the restraints of marriage, and despite many thinking her promiscuous (when such relationships came to light) her expectations were ahead of their time. She had her own money, her own home, and aside from her father, she was not forced to depend on a man. 'I think I'm something rather strange that men can't understand,' Margaret said. 'I want to be protected very much, but one can't wait forever for that glorious man to come round.'[8]

The distance of an ocean between Margaret and Ted cooled their romance, and having returned to London she accepted an offer from Mr R.J. O'Connell, the editor of *Woman's Illustrated*, to work as a reporter. Her first commission for the magazine was to go to Berlin and write an article on the conditions under which the wives of British soldiers were living. Flying in on the Berlin Airlift, Margaret arrived at Tempelhof Airport and was met by Anthony Marreco, chief staff officer to Sir Christopher Steel, the political adviser to the British Military Government in Allied-Occupied Germany. The first stop in her week-long post was to lunch in Potsdam, in what would become East Berlin, the Soviet sector, and she discreetly took photographs, which put herself and the magazine at risk, as it breached censorship rules. She also met with several Russian, French, American and British officials. Of her stay in Berlin, between the abyss of the Second World War and the beginning of the Cold War, Margaret wrote: 'The sight of a devastated Berlin shocked me, and walking home at night in the light of a full moon is a memory that will always haunt me.' Margaret received 30 guineas for her article, and her post as a reporter lasted for another eighteen months until she lost interest.

Love continued to dominate Margaret's attention and, although she continued to hold Ted in the highest regard, she had fallen for another man. Joe Thomas, whom she called 'a Texan charmer', fitted the bill of her former lovers: handsome, athletic, and a self-made millionaire said to have a healthy disdain for money, he did not shirk from enjoying the spoils of his dealings at Lehman Brothers, where he was a senior partner. Throughout the years Margaret and Joe had vaguely known one another, as he was married to her old schoolfriend Eleanor Bangs, and following his divorce in 1940 and Margaret's post-war visit to New York, they had become acquainted. 'You are the loveliest thing ever brought back by the Berlin Airlift,' Joe wrote in a telegram to Margaret, shortly after her return from Germany. It was an instant attraction, and as she had done before, she said goodbye to the children and crossed the Atlantic in pursuit of love. She went with Joe to Vermont, to stay with Josephine Hartford, heiress to the Great Atlantic and Pacific Tea Company, who had divorced her third husband and would soon marry her fourth. Josephine invited Margaret and Joe to the Saratoga Race Course, where several of her horses raced, and there they encountered Elizabeth Arden, who asked Margaret how she kept her complexion so cool in the 100-degree temperatures. 'By using Elizabeth Arden make-up,' was Margaret's clever reply. It resulted in an invitation to dine with Arden at her 5th Avenue apartment and, confiding that she found Arden's lipsticks too greasy, the following day a box of drier lipsticks, which had been specially formulated, arrived for Margaret. It did little to inspire loyalty for Arden's brand, for Margaret also lunched with Helena Rubinstein, who also had an apartment on 5th Avenue, and it was there that she met a young and aspiring photographer named Antony Armstrong-Jones. The highpoint of this American visit was not the social invitations she received but her brush with death, for while she was swimming at Easthampton, Long Island, a wave swept her out to sea and Joe swam out and saved her life.

Given the company that Margaret kept in America, it was clear to see why she preferred to spend long periods there, as nobody thought her conduct socially unacceptable and being a divorcee did not spell exile. Her hostess was proof of that, as Josephine had enough money to disobey social mores and to live as she pleased, as did her mother who had recently married Prince Guido Pignatelli of Belmonte, a man two years older than Josephine. The idea that money could trump any social wrongdoing, or what was perceived as unacceptable, appealed to Margaret. In America, with her own money and status as an heiress, she could do things that would have classed her as a pariah among her set in London. In public, that is, for the private lives of the British aristocracy have always been tinged with scandal, but it was often kept from the gaze of the chattering classes. However as Margaret settled into life as an unmarried woman she came to the conclusion that the English 'although they may pretend, are very impressed by money',[9] and so they would continue to look the other way if she misbehaved. Above all else, she could be with a man without the expectation of marriage.

Margaret's point of view regarding marriage changed after Joe saved her life, and it could explain why she fostered ideas of marrying him. She knew of his arrangement with another woman, Poppi de Salis (née Martha Paula Ruppaner), and although he had also loved her, he promised Margaret that his former relationship was over. After he proposed, and Margaret accepted, they went to London for a dinner party she was hosting in his honour, and to spend the weekend at Leeds Castle with Olive Baillie, who approved of Joe despite being fond of Charlie. Helen and George thought Joe a suitable husband for Margaret, perhaps thinking him a steadying influence in her life after her divorce from Charlie. George had also begun a new romance, with a 35-year-old Scotswoman and former actress named Jane Corby, whom he had met at the captain's table on the *Queen Elizabeth*. Naturally, George's affair was kept a secret from Helen, though

Margaret knew of Jane and claimed to like her, an opinion that would change throughout the years.

Life for Margaret, to quote her Whigham grandmother, appeared a little too *couleur de rose*. Although Joe was American, and Margaret had previously declined Ted's proposal due to his living and working in New York and her having to uproot the children, she and Joe agreed to keep her house in London and spend half of the year in America. It was then, after they had reached a compromise on their living arrangements, that he said he had to go to Switzerland to break the news to Poppi, as he did not want her to read about it in the newspapers. 'Could you not write to her, or telephone?' Margaret suggested, but Joe refused. She instinctively knew something was amiss, despite his promising to telephone her when he arrived in Switzerland and asking her to meet him at the airport in a few days time. As Joe had promised, he did telephone Margaret, but with the news that he was going to marry Poppi instead. The news devastated Margaret and she 'cried for a long time'. Aside from wounding her ego and betraying her trust, it might have offered her an insight into how she had treated men prior to her marriage to Charlie, accepting their proposals and discarding them at her leisure. Self-reflection was never Margaret's strong point, and she merely said: 'Perhaps it was for the best, for Poppi has certainly made him a wonderful wife.'[10]

However, there were other factors influencing Margaret's relationship with Joe and the ambiguous love triangle with Poppi. In the New Year of 1948, several months before Joe had telegrammed Margaret after her return from Berlin, he went to St Moritz, where he met Poppi, who was estranged from her husband, Max de Salis. During the two weeks that Joe was there, he and Poppi began an affair and agreed to meet a year later to see whether or not they were still in love, and if they were she agreed to divorce her husband. During the interim of Joe going to St Moritz and his return to New York, Margaret had entered his life and they, too, fell in love. He did not forget his promise to Poppi, nor did he estimate how ambitious she was; she was a popular figure in St Moritz, her father was a prominent doctor, and through him, she knew his patients – foreign royalty, Greek shipping magnates, old money. And Joe, coming from humble beginnings in Texas, was drawn to Poppi's circle of friends and knew he could benefit from her social connections, he also knew that she had the power to destroy his reputation.[11] It was not blackmail, exactly, but Poppi was determined he would see his promise through, despite knowing of Margaret, and her friends imploring her to forget about Joe, who 'was making an absolute fool of himself with Margaret Sweeny'.[12] A few months after Joe ended his engagement to Margaret, he and Poppi were married in Portofino.

★

Not even Margaret's naysayers could deny her ability to move on and reinvent herself. With two failed romances behind her, she turned her attention to entertaining. It signalled a new beginning for her, and she would refer to this period of her life as 'the golden age'. The statement was partly inspired by her independence, and because she was free to entertain in a way she had always dreamed of. She gave dinners for eighteen people, often with another ten joining the party afterwards, and her guests were 'not just the boring aristocracy' (as she called them) but were made up of politicians, American ambassadors, Hollywood film stars, theatrical producers, gossip columnists, and new money. Her role as a hostess was a new one and she considered it an experiment: 'The word entertaining is such a large one. It compromises dinner parties, of course, luncheons which I think are ridiculous events because everyone is watching the clock and no one can relax.'[13] Having never ordered wine or cigars before, as that had been Charlie's responsibility, Margaret gauged whether or not her parties were successful by how late the guests stayed, which was often past midnight.

Margaret made up the rules of entertaining as she went along, and when she settled on a style that worked not only for herself but her guests, she rarely changed it. Above all else, she thought the measure of a good hostess was one who did not enjoy their own parties, for they were to control the evening like a stage manager. Women guests preoccupied not only Margaret's guest list, but her thoughts; she wanted only beautiful women to come to her parties, for she thought it gave men something to gaze at and lightened the mood, and if a woman's physical appearance was lacking she then settled for intelligence, but rarely. There was no room for what Margaret called 'dead wood', her explanation for a woman whom she thought a crashing bore – years later she held a party and afterwards a young female guest picked up a satin cushion and sat on the floor, 'What a fun party, Margaret. Let's swap gossip,' she said. Margaret coldly responded, 'It's not that sort of party. And it's not that sort of cushion.'[14] She also liked to mix professions and placing witty raconteurs and political-minded guests together, or, as she said, 'brain meets brain'. As with having attractive women at her parties, Margaret was preoccupied with inviting foreign guests, as she thought they brought glamour and excitement; 'I'd be happy to have Arabs here anytime. Particularly the Lebanese. I'd be happy, that is, if only I could get a hold of them. And naturally, if they came to dinner with you, I'd hope they'd take off their masks.'[15] As for her male guests, there were few rules, except they were not to linger in the dining room for more than twenty minutes after dinner, as she thought it unfair to the staff who had to clear the table. Margaret's rules and her memories of grand parties were later compiled into a 1986 book, appropriately entitled *My Dinner Party Book*.

Although Margaret's parties were popular there were those who considered them second or third rate in comparison to the great hostesses who came before her. She had maids serving in the dining room, rather than a butler, as he was an alcoholic and often drunk. 'I'm frightfully sorry but the butler passed out five minutes before dinner. I'm afraid I had nowhere else to put him but he has been under the table all this time,' she told her guests after one such indiscretion. Elements of her parties could be amusing, and many found her 'endlessly chatty' and candid in her criticism towards those she disliked. Her male guests found her attractive and many of her parties were constructed to appeal to men and their egos. In a lot of ways she had a masculine trait to her personality; she instinctively knew what men wanted, especially those at the top of the hierarchy, and although a modern woman in many senses, she was not sympathetic to her own sex. Women, particularly those who knew her well, found her 'so austere, so cold ... she always had this don't touch me, don't disarrange me aura about her'.[16] Or, as one guest put it, 'You liked her, but you could never really take her seriously, despite her unshakeable poise.'[17] As much as Margaret's guests were considered great raconteurs of the twentieth century she failed to match their wit, and it has been said that she possessed no wit at all. 'No aspect of life, to her, was comical ... it made her strangely inhuman. Almost spooky.'[18]

Margaret's life continued with its familiar pattern of entertaining in London, foreign travel and men. She went on a shopping trip to Paris; the post-war city was in ruins after the Nazi occupation and had set upon reviving itself through fashion. The Théâtre de la Mode, an exhibition of miniature porcelain dolls wearing haute couture, was created to raise funds for war survivors and the fashion industry. It also toured Europe and America, and in doing so had inspired rich and affluent women to commission their wardrobes from French couturiers, namely Christian Dior, a young designer credited with creating the New Look. However, Margaret, who was often ahead of certain trends, said she wore a similar design by Molyneux a year before it became popular.

On this particular shopping trip, Margaret took a suite at the Ritz Hotel and at the end of her stay she asked the concierge to book her a seat on the Golden Arrow. In many ways, it was an uneventful trip and an unremarkable request. However, this was in 1947, before she met and fell for Ted Rousseau and Joe Thomas, and it would have been insignificant had it not been for the consequences it sired. 'Momentous encounters in life often pass by without our realising their importance,' she later wrote.[19]

Taking her seat aboard the luxury train Margaret was greeted by a fellow passenger who had travelled to Paris from his wife's home in Biarritz. He was tall and thin, with narrow eyes, a crooked nose, and wry grin; in physical looks, he was not unlike George Whigham, perhaps this inspired the familiarity Margaret felt for him despite their not knowing one another. His name was Ian Douglas Campbell and he had been born in Paris in 1903, to a French-American mother with connections to an old New York stockbroking family, and a father of Scots origin. Although Ian was penniless he had aristocratic blood running through his veins; he was the great-grandson of George Campbell, the 8th Duke of Argyll, and Lady Elizabeth (née Leveson-Gower), daughter of the Duke of Sutherland; his great-uncle, John Campbell, the 9th Duke of Argyll, had married Princess Louise, a daughter of Queen Victoria. For two generations there were no sons born to the 9th and 10th dukes, and thus Ian became the heir to his second cousin Niall, the 11th Duke of Argyll. Niall was an academic prone to madness, and for this reason, he chose to remain unmarried and childless; he also claimed he could see fairies, greeted tourists with recitals from Italian operas, and his neglect toward Inveraray Castle, the Argyll family seat, saw it fall into rack and ruin. It would therefore become Ian's responsibility when he inherited the dukedom, which he anticipated being sooner rather than later, to either restore the castle or to lose it entirely. His rich wife's generosity had petered out, and he was beginning to cast his sights on another millionairess to help him with his quest. Margaret, he sensed from their first meeting, was only too willing to help.

Those who knew Ian Campbell, both personally and from his reputation, thought him idle and an opportunist; he had no job to speak of and by coincidence, or not, his first two wives were heiresses in their own rights. His first wife, Janet Aitken, whom he married in 1927 when she was 18, was the only daughter of Lord Beaverbrook. And his second wife, Louise Clews-Vanneck (known as Oui-Oui), was the former wife of the Hon. Andrew Vanneck, and the daughter of Henry Clews Jr, a famous painter and a scion of a wealthy New York family which was related to James Madison, fourth President of the United States. It was during Ian's marriage to Janet that he had met Louise, as they were neighbours in Biarritz, and each woman, during their respective time as his wife, would accuse him of cruelty and of squandering their money. 'Both she and her father's fortune were in for a bit of a battering,'[20] Janet observed when Ian announced he was to marry Louise, though she did not warn her. Janet, in particular, came to realise that Ian was drawn to vulnerable women; they had met when she was 17 and he 25, and they married ten days after her mother had died. 'That's why he was in such a rush to marry me,' Janet wrote. 'He was in debt up to his eyebrows and I was to bail him out.'[21] Like many seasoned fortune hunters, he knew the ropes.

The train had scarcely left the Gare du Nord when the two strangers began to share intimacies from their lives. Ian had been a prisoner of war for five years, captured by the Nazis in St Valery-en-Caux while serving as a divisional intelligence officer with the 51st Highland Division and sent to Rommel, a camp on the German–Polish border. It had been said that he tried to keep the hopes and spirits of his men alive, even though he knew their situation was a hopeless one, with many of his regiment disappearing on death marches and not returning. After the Allies liberated the camp Ian found his newfound freedom bewildering; he had also not seen a woman for five years and after a brief reconciliation with Louise, followed by the birth of their second son, Colin, in 1946, they went their separate ways.

Margaret proved to be a sympathetic listener and he expressed his regret at her divorce from Charlie, admitting that he followed her name in the newspapers. Ian's interest in Margaret's personal life was inspired by his first glimpse of her, over a decade before, when he saw her descend the staircase at the Cafe de Paris and turned to his wife, Janet, and said: 'There's the girl I'm going to marry someday.' The admission did not concern Margaret, despite being friends with Janet. It played to a role Margaret knew well, that of the belle of the ball – women wanted to be her, and men wanted to be with her – and rather than finding Ian's remark an insensitive one toward his wife, she was flattered. He also confided that he and his second wife, Louise, the mother of his two young sons, were estranged and that, although she was in love with an exiled Russian prince, she did not want a divorce.

The manner in which Ian spoke of his wives did not alarm Margaret, nor did she find his overt familiarity off-putting. She thought the attention he paid to her was genuine, and that her money had nothing to do with it. Although charming, there was an intensity that lurked beneath Ian's debonair persona; the same hedonistic mixture of fun and danger that Margaret had known during the war. She sensed he was a damaged person, and owing to his wartime experiences he had been left with deep psychological wounds, attributed to the shell shock he suffered after being captured and then imprisoned. Perhaps she thought she could ease his transition into civilian life, and he responded to the kindness she had shown him. When the train reached London she invited him to her home, and into her bed.

9

Crowning Mistake

In September 1949 Margaret and her children received an invitation from the Duke and Duchess of Sutherland[1] to stay at their family seat, Dunrobin Castle, in the Highlands of Scotland. The setting of Dunrobin might have been coincidental, for it was there that Margaret heard the news of Ian Campbell's succession to the dukedom of Argyll. Recalling their encounter on the Golden Arrow two years before, Margaret said: 'He'll make a very attractive duke.' And Clare Sutherland, also the custodian of an ancient Scottish title, remarked: 'So at last Ian has become a duke. He's been waiting for it for years.'

'Margaret had always been intrigued by the idea of being a duchess,' Charlie wrote in his memoirs, and it could explain her visits to Paris, which had become more frequent, with a view of encountering Ian. She did so, at a party in Paris given by a mutual friend, and she delighted in hearing, once again, about his unhappy marriage to Louise. Several times Ian had broached the idea of a divorce, and each time he was rebuffed. As the mother of Ian's two sons, effectively his heir and spare to the dukedom, Louise had become their trustee, a position which may have been compromised by Ian taking a new wife, who would then be his duchess. However Margaret's pursuit of Ian was done with the intention of marrying him, and Ian did not discourage her, for he was 'lazy, broke, and had expensive tastes befitting his station'.[2] In short, Louise, or 'Oui-Oui' as Ian called her, became an obstacle to their achieving happiness, and Margaret viewed her as her enemy, despite having never met her, and rechristened her 'Wee-Wee'.

There is no evidence to suggest Margaret knew of the darker side of Ian's character, or that she heeded any suggestions that he was to be avoided. The women in his life, and those who had fallen foul of his temper, perhaps did not speak openly about it at the time, as shame often silenced the recipient. His former wife, Janet Aitken, who was often in Margaret's company and had once been engaged to Bobbie Sweeny, described in her memoirs how she invented excuses for Ian's long disappearances and his erratic behaviour, and his treatment of her. To understand Ian's dual personality is to recognise his addictions: gambling – which, if such biological things can be proven, he inherited from his father – alcoholism and drug-taking, which might have been a coping mechanism for what he had experienced during the war. Gambling took precedence, however, and every penny he owned, including the £15,000 which he had inherited from his father, was squandered in French casinos. Rich women were a lifeline, and a means to support his addiction and pay his debts, which had amounted to over £200,000.

There was an air of desperation about Ian, revealed only to those with whom he was on intimate terms; he slept until noon, and despite his serving in the war and being a learned man, he was work-shy and all of his schemes foundered, including an aborted plan to run for parliament and a stint at the *Evening Standard* newspaper, which lasted a week. Sometimes Ian threatened to kill himself[3] in order to retrieve money out of others to pay his creditors, a combination of fear and shame, as he narrowly escaped being imprisoned due to unpaid debt. His own father had been sent to prison for the same reason. And now, having inherited a dukedom, he was bitterly disappointed when he learned the estate was worthless, as Niall Campbell had resented those who tried to interfere with his financial affairs and had once threatened the First Commissioner and Permanent Secretary of the Office of Works with imprisonment in the dungeon of Inveraray Castle. With the exception of his cousin's unpaid bills, totalling £82,000, there were death duties of £357,000, which brought Ian's inherited debt to around £2.5 million. With his yearly allowance of £1,000, he could not afford to pay back such vast sums, nor could he keep his own head above water, and Louise had no interest in settling the Argyll estate, as throughout their marriage he squandered everything but her American trust funds. Penniless as he was, his new titles – the 11th Duke of Argyll, Chief of Clan Campbell, Hereditary Master of the Royal Household in Scotland, Keeper of the Great Seal of Scotland, and Hereditary Keeper of the Royal Castles of Dunoon, Dunstaffrage, Tarbert, and Carrick – afforded him collateral and his quest to find a rich woman was easier than ever.

'I was so alone,' Margaret later wrote, 'and felt drawn towards this troubled man who had so much charm.'[4] Ian's so-called charm was in abundance, and in Margaret, he had found a woman not only connected to the international jet-set and with money to support them both, but who was also impressed by a title. There had been eligible men in her life before, though none were interested in marriage, and by her own admission, she was determined not to be a one-man woman. And Ian was equally determined that she would not cast her eyes elsewhere. In one another they found a common thread which bonded them together; they were each ruled by their consumptive natures, and sex and money would govern their lives, particularly Ian's. Mistaking sex for love, Margaret was flattered by the attention he paid to her, and in time she ignored those who warned her against him. In many ways Ian appealed to Margaret's naivete and had their early meetings not been so secretive, Helen might have said: 'Don't touch him. I don't like him. He's a crook.' Her friend Janet Aitken was well-versed in Ian's Dr Jekyll and Mr Hyde complex, and as with Margaret, she was at first taken in by his charm. The darker side to his character revealed itself on his honeymoon with Janet, when he took her to a Parisian brothel and told her 'she had a lot to learn'.[5] On another occasion, when they sailed to Jamaica, he stole Janet's jewellery and pawned it to pay his gambling debts. Later, when Janet thought him sincere in wanting to reconcile she agreed to go to his room at the Park Lane Hotel, whereupon he beat her up and broke her cheekbone and rib. Such rages came to dominate Ian's relationships with women; however, in the beginning, there was never any indication as to what lurked behind his charm offensive.

Although Margaret claimed her thoughts centred around Ian and his unhappiness, she was having her own casual affairs in London, or that is what they were rumoured to be. Alexis von Rosenberg, Baron de Redé, on whose arm she was often seen, was a scion of two of Eastern Europe's banking dynasties and a celebrated aesthete. In spite of his pedigree, he was impoverished, due to his father's ill-judged schemes and suicide, and in the 1930s he supported himself and his disabled sister by working in an antique shop in Los Angeles. At the age of 19, he became the live-in lover of Arturo Lopez-Willshaw, a married Chilean millionaire who settled $1 million on him. 'It was an unusual arrangement, but it worked,' he said.[6] Far more unusual would have been public knowledge of de Redé's living arrangements, as he and Arturo lived and travelled with Mrs Arturo Lopez-Willshaw, who played a part in the ménage à trois before decamping to Neuilly with her own lover. His friends, including Margaret, flocked to him because of his lavish tastes, evident in his style of dressing and his red and gold apartment in the Hôtel Lambert, a seventeenth-century mansion designed by Louis le Vau, the architect of Versailles.

In the New Year of 1950, Margaret gave a luncheon party for Alexis de Redé and Arturo Lopez-Willshaw. Adhering to her own rules of having more men than women, she realised she was a man short. By coincidence, or not, Ian was in London, and they had met at Claridge's Hotel the day before and she asked him to make up the numbers at her party. It was to be held on Friday 13 January, and Margaret, who was not superstitious regardless of her belief in psychics, did not think it an unlucky day or a bad omen. In years to come, she would realise that she was wrong.

★

During the first few months of 1950, Margaret made several visits to Paris to see Ian, and learning that Louise was having an affair of her own in Biarritz, she felt compelled more than ever to attach herself to him. She accepted an invitation to Barbara Hutton's ball, where the Maharajah and Maharanee of Jaipur were the guests of honour, and asked Ian to accompany her. A week later they went to the Travellers' Club ball, where the Duke and Duchess of Windsor were the star attraction. In her diary, dated 25 March 1950, Margaret wrote of a day she spent with Ian; they lunched at an old mill house in the French countryside, later that evening they dined at Maxim's, and afterward they went to the Lido nightclub.

Although Margaret claimed that Ian dominated her thoughts, he was not the only man with whom she was romantically involved. During her visits to Paris she was also seeing Roberto Caracciolo, the 11th Duke of San Vito, whose ancestors were the former royal family of Naples. Having served in many diplomatic posts – in 1935 Benito Mussolini appointed Roberto as the first Italian Consul to Los Angeles, as an attempt to establish 'emigrant enclaves as fugitive outposts of the once far-flung Roman imperium'[7] – his latest diplomatic post was in Paris. He was described as a 'rich, elegant bachelor ... [with] a magnificent castle on top of the island which he has made over into a weekend house'.[8] Like the Campbells of Scotland, Roberto's family were something of a clan, Italian style, and it was said 'Caracciolos and trash are never lacking in Naples'.[9] Of the two dukes, Roberto was in a position to give Margaret everything she wanted, but he treated her with an air of indifference, for he, too, was involved with other people.

When Margaret returned to London she found herself missing both Ian and Roberto, the latter having waved her off at Orly Airport. Acting on impulse she telegrammed both men, with the words: 'Bored and missing you. Wish you would come to London.' The first response came from Roberto, who declined her offer as he could not leave his office. Ian did not write back at all; instead, he arrived at Upper Grosvenor Street and surprised her. 'You must know why I have come,' he said. 'I'm here because of your cable, and I was very glad to get it.'[10] Eight days later Ian took Margaret to the Globe Theatre to see Christopher Fry's English adaptation of Jean Anouilh's comedy *L'invitation au château* (the English version was called *Ring Round the Moon*). It was a poignant title, for after the play and having waited twenty minutes to leave the box as the door had become stuck, Ian proposed to Margaret and she accepted. 'Please be sympathetic. Do stand by me this evening. Take my money,'[11] a line of dialogue from the play, could have applied to Margaret and Ian's dynamic. Afterward, they went to the 400 and danced until four o'clock in the morning. Recalling the happiness she had felt on that particular evening, she later wrote: 'If anyone had told me on that night that I was steering a course towards tragedy I would have thought them crazy.'[12]

Margaret did, however, ignore several bad omens throughout her relationship with Ian, which, in hindsight, she realised were a warning for what the future held. For now, she was content with the promise that, as soon as Ian's divorce from Louise was final, she would become his duchess. Ian's ambition to marry Margaret, and to wait for her, flattered her ego and clouded her judgement; she failed to realise that Louise had refused to divorce Ian on the grounds of her own adultery. Therefore Ian was courting Margaret in public to give his estranged wife grounds for a divorce, and thus naming Margaret in the petition. In turn, Margaret failed to recognise that she was being exploited for the benefit of others, as Ian made her feel that she was vital to his happiness. 'I noticed that the sadness had left Ian's eyes. He now looked happy,' she observed, after several months of their being together. This she attributed to the attention she paid him, and how she had given him hope for the future. She was right: he had captured her hook, line, and sinker.

The charm Ian had displayed towards Margaret was applied to her parents, whom he had met in their suite at the Dorchester shortly after their engagement. George and Helen appeared to like him, and, as Janet Aitken later said, when emotions were not involved he was 'interesting and likeable'. Helen, crippled with arthritis and in constant pain, perhaps took a vague interest in her daughter's suitor. And George, who shared much of Margaret's naivete, was impressed by Ian's title, his ancestral seat, and the promise that his daughter would become a duchess. He also appealed to their Scots heritage, as Clan Campbell was the oldest and largest in the Highlands. Further taking George into his confidence, Ian spoke of the financial situation regarding the Argyll estate and the condition of Inveraray Castle, whose roof he planned to remove to avoid further tax bills. George admired Ian's honesty, and, appointing himself a patron of Clan Campbell, he offered £25,000 to Ian and expected nothing in return, financially speaking.

Margaret had become emotionally involved in not only Ian's life but the future of the Argyll legacy, and the plan he had set in motion aboard the Golden Arrow was beginning to bear fruit. 'I think you had better come and see Inveraray for yourself. It is quite a task you will be facing,' Ian said to Margaret, before they left for Scotland. The remembrance of this particular visit was sanitised in Margaret's memoirs, for her first visit had taken place months before, in late March, when Ian had received news of a fire and invited her to accompany him to inspect the damage. It was a token request, for he knew Margaret harboured dreams of repairing the castle. They had travelled on the night train, and arrived at Arrochar the following morning, from where they motored over the Rest and Be Thankful Pass, and Margaret saw, for the first time, the beauty of Argyll. The Gothic revival architecture of Inveraray Castle greeted her at the end of a tree-lined avenue, surrounded by Loch Fyne, and a woodland that had been planted for Mary, Queen of Scots. The romanticism was not to last, for Margaret was not a countrywoman at heart, nor could she find contentment in such a remote place. Contradicting her first impression of Inveraray, James Lees-Milne thought the castle, which he had visited in the 1940s, 'a gaunt grey block ... built of ugly stone, which turns grey in the sunlight and black in the rain'.[13] For Margaret, she declared it was love at first sight.

On closer inspection of the castle, Margaret saw that the interior was run down and the gardens were overgrown, a visible reminder of Niall's neglect which had lasted for thirty years, as he lived there alone with his elderly butler and ghosts, and failed to notice any repairs or maintenance that needed to be done. It must have resembled James Lees-Milne's description of being 'grim and forbidding, like some hydropathic hotel'.[14] The electrical generator had stopped working on the day she arrived; perhaps it was another, if overlooked, omen. The fire, which had taken place inside a turret, had created a hole in the roof, letting rain in and damaging several family portraits. Although threatening to cause lasting damage if left untreated – several buckets were strategically placed to catch the rain – the biggest problem appeared to be dry rot which had crept through the rooms, and the thick layers of dust which coated the floors, paintings and antique armour. With an air of criticism, Margaret wondered how Louise had overlooked its housekeeping during the four months she had spent there. There was no such negativity directed at Ian, even though he had not visited in twenty years before inheriting the dukedom, along with a small staff including a cook and a secretary.

Armed with paraffin lamps and candles Margaret embarked on a tour of the castle. The eighty-eight rooms were filled with the academic papers and correspondence that Niall had collected over sixty years; his own letters to others were copied and added to the collection. To Margaret, it appeared as junk, and she recalled having to force open a door, as two four-poster beds, tins and boxes of papers had jammed it closed. Ian was far more sensitive to his cousin's idiosyncrasies and refused to burn the papers, as Margaret had suggested. Instead, he catalogued each one, a lengthy exercise which also revealed Niall's monastic existence which had intensified in the years before his death. There was treasure among the decay; Waterford glass and Crown Derby, Sèvres, Limoges and Meissen china in the servants' hall, a contrast to the glasses and plates from Woolworths in Niall's former living quarters. Many more pieces of valuable glass and china were uncovered in the attic and basement, with crystal stoppers for the decanters scattered throughout the house. The most valuable heirloom, a Louis Quinze desk, was to be sold to raise money for the estate. Margaret thought of her old friend, J. Paul Getty, one of the richest men in the world, and Ian set off for Rome to find him. It was a hopeless mission, for Getty could not be found and the desk remained unsold.

Although there was no further progress in the Argyll divorce, Margaret continued to fulfil her promise to help Ian restore Inveraray. From the library, the only habitable room in the house, she ordered him to recruit eight of his strongest men, and from there they would sort through Niall's belongings and genuine Argyll heirlooms. As her knowledge of antique furniture was scant, she and Ian devised a colour-coded system: red meant the item could be removed from the castle, green indicated it had to stay, and blue signified they were unsure. In truth, she disliked much of the furniture, especially the Chippendale in its original dark hues, as she and Helen had their own valuables coated in white paint, over twenty years ago, on the advice of Syrie Maugham. 'Those two weeks at Inveraray were the most physically exhausting I had ever known, and the happiest,' she recalled. 'For the first time in my life, I felt that I was helping someone to do a constructive and important job.' The feeling was enough to fend off criticism from members of Clan Campbell, who did not approve of Margaret's presence at Inveraray, because Ian had left his wife for her. There were rumours their eventual marriage would end badly.[15]

In London Margaret and Ian made their first public appearance as a couple at Clare Sutherland's annual ball, a fitting social debut as it was at the Sutherlands' home that Margaret learned of Ian's accession to the dukedom of Argyll. Their promenading around the ballrooms of Mayfair was to pay dividends, in Margaret's case, for after years of refusing to do so, Louise finally agreed to divorce Ian. Dismissing it as procrastination, Margaret originally thought Louise's reluctance to divorce Ian was an attempt to deprive him of happiness. However in January 1951 Louise finally agreed, and a petition for divorce was filed citing Ian's adultery, of which, in recent days, there was ample proof. Two months later Louise appeared at the Edinburgh Court of Session and produced evidence of Ian's adultery in the form of a guest book from a Sussex hotel. A Mr and Mrs Campbell were recorded, and she proved it was Ian's handwriting and that she had not accompanied him. Louise was finally worn down and a divorce was granted, which – unlike the situation under English law where a cooling off period is required – was effective from that day. Margaret and Ian had achieved what they wanted, though for different reasons. Louise was granted custody of their sons, Ian and Colin, and Margaret paid the boys' annual school fees of £1,000. As Ian had spent much of Louise's fortune, she was not in a position to decline Margaret's offer.

'Did he rob you?' Janet asked Louise, after her divorce from Ian.

'He took everything but my trust funds,' Louise replied.

And Margaret, with her rose-tinted spectacles and her father's millions, was to be next.

10

The Duchess

The last time Margaret had been set to marry a rich and titled man, she had let her father talk her out of it. Fulke Warwick shared many similarities with Ian; however, the latter was better at disguising his shortcomings. In the year that Margaret and Ian had known one another, he never uttered a cross word, and she thought him gentle and kind towards her and her children. Furthermore Ian encouraged her independence, apparent in his giving her a free hand with Inveraray. The change in his behaviour, so familiar with his former wives, revealed itself to Margaret a day after his divorce from Louise. Arriving at Upper Grosvenor Street, he appeared tense and bad-tempered, and before Margaret could say anything he launched into a verbal attack against Frances and Brian (now 13 and 10, the latter being at school in Gstaad), calling them spoiled brats and criticising how Margaret had brought them up. Then he vilified her father, her friends, and Margaret herself. She had no explanation for his behaviour, and he offered none. Instead, he departed and went to White's Club. This treatment of others was common towards those Ian felt superior to, or those from whom, on a rare occasion, he had nothing to gain. 'He was one of the coldest, nastiest men I've ever known,'[1] Ian's future son-in-law, Norman Mailer, said. The following morning Margaret asked Ian what had provoked his rage, and again he responded in a similar manner and remained in a bad temper for the next forty-eight hours. Their wedding was days away, and Margaret was having second thoughts. 'It seemed too late to back out,' she said. 'Or was it?'

The decision weighed heavily on Margaret's mind, and she knew her father would tell her to leave Ian and forget about the wedding and the promises she had made to him. She went to her parents' suite at the Dorchester, but could not muster the courage to knock on the door, even though she knew George was inside. Although she knew George prized her happiness above all else, she did not want to disappoint him as he had invested so much in Inveraray Castle. She also felt compelled to marry Ian, as he had given up custody of his sons for her. Or so he wanted her to believe; the truth was he never had much interest in raising his children. Nor did Ian have much interest in maintaining his chivalrous behaviour, and perhaps he did not have to. He had achieved what he set out to do; Margaret had willingly talked to her father and secured him £100,000 without asking for a penny in return. And, as she became further attached to Ian and Inveraray, she convinced George into parting with more money. 'We poured a great deal of money into the castle,' Margaret recalled, 'but my father never said a word about it. Nor did I. Because Ian was a very difficult man.'[2]

In return Margaret would receive nothing for her efforts, aside from a worthless piece of paper, which Ian had misled George into believing was a Deed of Gift, permitting Margaret to keep the valuable spoils of his inheritance – French furniture, paintings, and tapestries. 'All these belong to Margaret,' Ian often told visitors, and he pointed to their initials which he had painted on the ceiling of Inveraray in 1952. Neither George nor Margaret thought to consult a legal representative, thinking Ian was a man of honour befitting his rank. As such, they had no way of knowing that the Argyll estate was managed by trustees and that Ian was not in a position to sign over its contents or to make decisions on behalf of the estate. The sanctions were enforced by Ian's lack of interest in Inveraray, a place he had not visited in over twenty years, and the trustees' perception of him as a foreigner, as he was half-French and lived in France. They were equally suspicious of Margaret, for her own life was far removed from Scotland and its heritage. Unlike her future husband and his background she could, at least, claim to be 100 per cent Scots. Therefore Ian would profit regardless if Margaret married him or not. 'Now I'll get my bills paid,' he said to his friend, Bill Thornton.

On the eve of Margaret's wedding to Ian, she received a letter from Charlie Sweeny, its contents revealing that he still loved her and he warned her not to marry Ian. The latter sentiment was inspired by Charlie's visit to Louise, who told him of Ian's opportunistic ways and of his poor treatment of their sons; he never contributed a penny toward their upkeep, nor did he send his children a Christmas wire. 'I only hope you're not deluding yourself that Campbell is inspired by any great love, because he's not,'[3] Charlie wrote to Margaret, and he advised her not to have a child with Ian, for it would only serve as 'insurance for his old age'.[4] She appreciated her former husband's concern but thought it was a meaningless letter, as Charlie had written similar ones in the past. And she ignored the information Louise had shared with him, thinking it typical of an ex-wife to find faults with her ex-husband, and vice versa in Charlie's instance.

Margaret married Ian on 22 March 1951, at Caxton Hall. Far from the lavish display of her first wedding, she looked brittle in a simple grey chiffon dress and a cloche hat fashioned from lime-green feathers. George gave her away, and Helen was there, a rarity for she disliked being seen in public in her wheelchair. After a reception for eighty guests at Upper Grosvenor Street, Margaret and Ian caught a night train to Glasgow to begin their honeymoon at Inveraray Castle. Their arrival was signalled by Ian's personal piper, Duncan MacArthur, who played 'The

Campbells Are Coming', and Margaret appeared nervous when Ian carried her over the threshold and almost dropped her on the stone floor. 'I love coming home,' Ian told the local dignitaries who had gathered in the Great Hall. 'I always love coming back to Inveraray, but I can assure you that I have never loved it as much as I do this time.' Thinking his speech genuine, Margaret convinced herself that his recent behaviour was a minor setback, and now they were married he would revert to the charming, loving man he was before.

For the duration of the honeymoon, Margaret was dressed in workmen's overalls and tasked with putting her marital home in order. She began with the logistics of the castle, particularly the distance between the kitchen and dining room, as their meals always arrived cold. There was also Ian's preoccupation with various schemes to contend with; one of these was the search for the wreckage of the *Duque de Florencia*, a Spanish Armada galleon rumoured to be filled with £30 million of golden coins and a crown, sent by the pope. The investigation would cost £100,000, and once again Margaret was faced with asking George to give Ian money, with a promise of a financial return as soon as the treasure was found which, by salvage rights granted to Ian's ancestor by King James II, belonged to the Duchy of Argyll. Such was Ian's certainty in finding the treasure that he formed a diving company, Argest, and promised the frogmen divers a £200 bonus if they found it. The venture would last for five long and unsuccessful years, after which Margaret not only paid the famous diver Margaret Naylor to investigate the wreckage, but also the bill the Royal Navy sent Ian for its assistance in the project. In theory, Ian was correct that a shipwreck lay covered in silt beneath the shores of Tobermory Bay, but it was an Istrian-built merchantman called the *San Juan de Sicilia* – 'a much more mundane project'.[5]

After three weeks of living at Inveraray Castle, Margaret began to resent her surroundings; she was no further along in its restoration, she could not adapt to the isolation, and Ian's moods had become a pendulum of uncertainty. They went on an official honeymoon, albeit a belated one, driving to France and Madrid, and then on to Seville. Their last stop coincided with the *feria* after Easter and every hotel in Seville was fully booked except for the Hotel Madrid, where they took a basement room with a grille above their head offering a view of the pavement above. Ian found fault with the room and, owing to his title, thought he should be offered something grander. 'Sweetie, don't try that one,' Margaret said. 'In this town dukes are two-a-penny. If you want to get results just start crackling a few crisp dollars.'

The cause of Ian's moodiness, as Margaret was to discover when they returned home, arrived in the form of two writs, one of which he hid under a cushion in the library. Just as his two former wives had, Margaret began her married life to Ian by fending off his creditors. The first writ was from Worth, suing him for £4,000 – the cost of a mink coat, which he had bought Louise to celebrate his inheriting the dukedom. Unable to face the shame of Ian being publicly sued, Margaret confided in her father and he settled the debt. The second writ was from the Royal Navy, suing Ian for £3,000, for their assistance with the investigation of the *Duque de Florencia*. Months previously Margaret had asked about the navy's bill, and Ian lied and said there would be no cost; they were participating out of interest in the wreckage. She begrudgingly settled the latter debt; it was one thing to ask George for money, it was another matter when it came from her personal allowance. The money, she thought, could have been put to better use in restoring Inveraray Castle.

But what of Inveraray? There was a continuous stream of Whigham money being poured into the castle and yet it remained a white elephant on the shores of Loch Fyne. With their options (and budget) exhausted, the trustees were left with little choice but to sell the island of Tiree to meet the 10th duke's death duties. Furthermore, part of the Argyll estate in Inveraray was sold, and proposals were sent to shopkeepers to offer them an opportunity to buy the premises they rented. Several farms in Kintyre, which also belonged to the estate, were also sold for £200,000. It was a short-term solution and Ian lacked the business acumen for ensuring the estate could generate an income and eventually pay for itself. Margaret suggested they open Inveraray Castle to the public and charge a fee for guided tours; however, the trustees rejected her idea and thought it unrealistic. Margaret successfully contradicted their view, and reminded the trustees that times had moved on and the Duchy of Argyll no longer had the pre-war privileges of power and low taxation to keep its estate afloat; they could let the public in, or allow the castle to crumble around them. The last duchess to reside there was Princess Louise, who loathed the castle and took no interest in its upkeep. There had not been a permanent duchess in residence for several decades, and it could only benefit the estate that Margaret was an international celebrity who could attract tourists to western Scotland, an isolated spot in the days before commercial air travel.

In terms of Margaret's celebrity, the local tweed industry stood to profit from her name. She approached the Paris fashion houses on their behalf, namely Dior, Balmain, Molyneux, and Balenciaga, all of whom were interested in having their tweeds imported from Inveraray. However the orders never arrived and when Margaret enquired why, she learned that no one in Inveraray knew how to complete an export form and so they abandoned the idea of sending the tweed to Paris. Although the plan failed, it proved Margaret was serious about the islands' economy and she was invited by Lord Malcolm Douglas-Hamilton to become the London Appeals President of the Highland Fund, a scheme devised to repopulate the remote areas by loaning money to farmers and crofters to enable them to return to the Highlands and earn a living. Ian headed the committee, though he showed no interest in it, and it took Margaret ten days to persuade him to sign his name on the appeal leaflets.

Next, Margaret turned her attention to the town of Inveraray, which had been moved several miles from the castle in the 1770s to create a feeling of solitude. She was troubled by the town's lack of entertainment facilities, and she thought the mobile cinema which came once a fortnight and showed old films could be improved upon. So, having called a meeting with the town leaders, she proposed to turn the old drill hall into a 200-seat cinema, with films hired from London and shown four times a week. It was agreed on the terms that she financed the equipment herself and guaranteed any financial loss if it failed, but if it succeeded she promised it would become the town's property. Everyone smiled respectfully and went home certain that the idea would fail.[6]

In the first week of September, the Argyll Cinema officially opened with a showing of *On The Town*. For the launch Margaret enlisted help from Inveraray Castle's staff; she had the carpenter build a platform, the head gardener arranged floral displays for beneath the screen, and she borrowed tapestries and curtains from the castle to decorate the hall. She also hired Leon Berenthal, a wounded Polish soldier who had remained in Britain after the war, as its manager. 'The Duchess of Argyll knows the right people in Hollywood and Wardour Street. And that is why movies – her word – have come in a big way to this sleepy town,' wrote the *Daily Mirror*. Although the locals attended the cinema and screenings were often sold out, Margaret's taste in films did not match that of the townsfolk. 'We don't like the brash or brassy type of film,' remarked a local man, Mr MacBride. 'But there's no problem now. She's a real tonic to the town.'[7]

Encouraged by the success of the Argyll Cinema, Margaret turned her attention to preservationism. She paid for the repairing of the defunct public clock and rehung it on the church tower. Then she hoped to re-paint the Georgian town houses, which belonged to the Argyll estate, and install black window-boxes on the windowsills. However, the idea was rejected due to the estimated costs of £100,000. 'That's as far as I've got at the moment,' Margaret said, defeated by the setback. She was invited to become a member of the Inveraray Town Council, due to her regeneration of the town which earned her the respect of the locals, who agreed 'she has come to Inveraray like a touch of spring'.[8] Ian rejected the offer on Margaret's behalf, as he thought it beneath her.

★

It did not take long for disenchantment to set in and for Margaret to discover the true nature of the man she had married. After returning from their honeymoon in Spain, and in between Margaret's work for the town of Inveraray, she went to the London Clinic to have an operation on her sinus. 'This is going to be a bloody nuisance having to come up here every day. It's miles from the club,' Ian said, after Margaret came round from the anaesthetic. The club to which he referred was White's, a mere 2 miles away.

After Margaret's recovery she and Ian went abroad, but a change of scenery did little to lift his moods, and if anything it intensified his rages. In the Bahamas, they stayed with Olive Bailie, and it was there that others were made privy to the dynamics of their marriage. Margaret described Ian's behaviour as 'rude and sadistic', and two male houseguests challenged him. 'By now Ian had become very arrogant, and no one could mediate,' she recalled. They left Nassau for Havana, Cuba, to stay with friends of Ian. The location mattered little to Margaret, for she was distracted by Ian's conduct and was constantly apologising on his behalf. From Havana, they flew to Kingston, Jamaica, and it was there that she was forced to confront the passive (and enabling) part she played in a marriage that had become abusive. Their rows in Kingston had escalated from raised voices to physical violence. She recalled feeling 'acute embarrassment', a reaction inspired by Sir Robert having to rush into their bedroom to stop Ian from attacking Margaret. The swiftness in which Ian could change from an introverted, moody individual to exerting violence was related by Janet Aitken: 'Suddenly he was someone else, a man who kept shouting and hitting me, breaking a rib, a cheekbone, and bruising my whole body.'[9] Later Margaret would recall an incident when he had 'violently assaulted' her and 'caused her pain'.[10]

Rather than Margaret admitting her folly and cutting her losses, she attempted to justify Ian's behaviour. She thought his split personality could be attributed to his astrological sign. He was a Gemini, and she considered him to be 'two people within one body', and although the astrological sign is fabled for its duality, she refused to believe it could be psychological. It was George who confronted Margaret with the truth: 'Do you really not know what's causing the trouble? It's drink. I'm afraid you have married an alcoholic.' George also confided that whenever he saw Ian at White's he was seldom without a drink in his hand, regardless if it was morning or night. It seems contradictory that George had known of Ian's alcoholism and allowed Margaret to marry him, despite always wanting the best for her. Instead of challenging her father she accepted what he told her: 'Your only hope of saving your marriage is to get him off the bottle.' She also accepted that George, like herself, was often taken in by Ian's charm which 'he used to influence people all his life … even my father, who was such a clever man, was putty in his hands'.[11] Their mutual friend, Bill Thornton, echoed what George had told her; Ian was dependent on alcohol and began his day with a neat gin, often as early as ten o'clock in the morning. 'I felt almost relieved,' Margaret said; 'at least I now knew what I was facing.' She thought by monitoring Ian's drinking she could restore him to the charming man he was before their marriage, and she offered to convert her library at Upper Grosvenor Street into a replica of White's, so he could escape to a club-like atmosphere without leaving home. He rejected the idea, telling her that his purpose of going to White's was to escape her.

The complexities of Ian's personality were too complicated for Margaret to understand. He had begun to humiliate her in private and in front of their friends, and as a consequence her stammer had grown worse, making it impossible to defend herself or voice her opinions. 'He toyed with me as a cat plays with a mouse,' she recalled. 'Every time he sensed that I had come to the end of my tether, he would then choose to become his most agreeable self, ready to do anything to please me.'[12] At a ball given for his and Janet's daughter, Lady Jeanne Campbell, Ian danced with his first wife and ignored Margaret for the duration of the evening. Always so controlling of her image in public, Margaret could only watch as her husband charmed Janet, who had, once again, almost fallen under his spell. 'I saw Margaret's composure was beginning to wear thin … One moment she was standing in the doorway, glaring furiously, and then she was gone,' Janet wrote in her memoirs. Margaret later told Janet that she understood her predicament, but at the time she did not and their friendship came to an end.

Things did not improve when Margaret and Ian returned to Inveraray Castle and she tried to fulfil the role of stepmother to Ian's sons, Ian, the Marquis of Lorne, and Lord Colin Campbell. Devoted to their own mother, the boys had come to despise Margaret, as they felt she had influenced Ian's divorce from Louise. Margaret came to the conclusion the boys, Ian Lorne in particular, were being poisoned against her, and that Louise was responsible for the campaign of hatred. This conclusion was reached after Ian had apparently found letters from Louise to their sons, though Margaret did not consider if it was her husband who was planting seeds of discord. In an attempt to bond with her stepson, she took Ian Lorne for a drive and told him she realised he did not like her, and explained that Ian and Louise were leading separate lives before his father had met her. Perhaps Margaret wished the latter part of her sentiment to be true, as she was either oblivious to (or ignoring) the fact Ian had discarded Louise to pursue her. Then Margaret proposed she leave for London when the children came to Inveraray, so they could be alone with their father. 'That wouldn't be very nice of me, would it?' Ian Lorne said, and Margaret wrote in her memoirs that the boy had tears in his eyes. Although Margaret and Ian Lorne would never reach a truce, she attempted to understand his point of view; a difficult thing to do as, until then, she did not have to share her own father with anyone.

As a gesture of friendship to her stepchildren, Margaret bought them a spaniel puppy, possibly recalling how her father's gift of a dog had relieved the unhappiness she had felt at a similar age. She gave Frances a dachshund and Brian a labrador, and bought herself a poodle whom she called Gaston, and she also had two spaniels known as the 'Mayfair Boys'. This reflects a childlike view of the world, that surrounding the children and herself with dogs could provide comfort and companionship. For Margaret it was true: 'She certainly found solace with her animals,' recalled her friend, Brodrick Haldane. Her bond with animals was such that when Haldane referred to a set of poodles that she kept in her later years as 'the dogs', she said: 'Don't called them dogs. They're called Alphonse [and Louis]!'[13]

The animals and the children could not distract Margaret from the problems surrounding her. Ian had demanded she give up her London home and live permanently at Inveraray Castle, a strange request given his recent behaviour. Although she claimed to love the castle, she found its setting and the company stifling. At Upper Grosvenor Street she could lapse into her familiar pattern of entertaining friends and socialising at a moment's notice. It was a different lifestyle in the Highlands, receiving guests meant she had to plan in advance the logistics of their arrival and host them overnight, or for days. And, regardless of her interest in regenerating the town of Inveraray, the lives of the locals held no charm for her. The same could be said for Ian's pastimes of gardening, birdwatching and catching butterflies, perhaps Freudian in that he could capture a beautiful thing and kill it for pleasure. 'All you think about is poking about in your bloody garden,' said Margaret, disapprovingly. Her reaction was prompted by his neglect; he rarely spoke to her, and his attention was spent indulging in his hobbies and obsessing over the *Duque de Florencia* wreckage. The environment, though not what he was used to, was a welcomed alternative to his aimless life before the war and the bewildering freedom he felt after five years in a prisoner-of-war camp. 'On release from the [camp] he wandered around Europe, seeing people and places with no apparent plan,' Janet wrote in her memoirs. 'He had simply disappeared.'[14]

Given the unhappiness between Margaret and Ian, it might be ironic to suggest she had enabled a new sense of stability in his life, as it was her father's money that made it possible for him to have a home of his own. Although he was happy at Inveraray, she was not, and in demanding she give up Upper Grosvenor Street he was taking away her independence. They reached a compromise; Margaret would keep her London house as a base for when she was in town and spend the rest of the year at the castle. She also agreed to rename the property 'Argyll House', as Ian did not have an official London address, which insulted George as it was his name on the lease and his money paying the bills. Still, Ian was not satisfied with all Margaret and George had done for the Argyll estate, and, as though to validate his behaviour, he said: 'You have created nothing in your life. You have not even created a garden; you have only created yourself.'[15] The remark prompted tears from Margaret, a reaction that did nothing to discourage him. 'Ian had a markedly sadistic streak in his character. Things like this were done deliberately to hurt me, and hurt me they always did,' she wrote in her memoirs. 'I realise now that if I had not given him the satisfaction of knowing this, Ian would have been deprived of much pleasure.'[16]

★

In May 1953 Margaret and Ian went to London to prepare for the coronation of Queen Elizabeth II, which was to take place on 2 June. His remark that Margaret was the product of self-creation rung true, particularly in this official outing as a duchess, for she had no choice but to create an image for herself. The ninth Duchess of Argyll, Princess Louise, died in 1939 and her tenure as duchess and chatelaine of Inveraray had come to an end in 1914 following the death of her husband, John Campbell, the 9th duke. Owing to the lengthy period between Margaret and her predecessor (she did not consider her husband's previous wife a duchess), she had nothing, except for a title, to build upon. There were no duchess robes, as Princess Louise's robes were fashioned in royal purple and – as Margaret was not a princess or a member of the royal family – she was forbidden to wear them. As such she had to be fitted for her own robes of red velvet and white ermine, designed by Victor Stiebel, who also created the silver dress she wore underneath. There was no jewellery in the Argyll family, as Princess Louise had bequeathed her jewels to the Duke of Kent, and Margaret wore her own diamond tiara fashioned in the shape of clovers, a gift from her parents, and she borrowed a coronet from the Duchess of Sutherland, who owned two.

During the coronation ceremony Margaret and Ian were seated separately; she sat in the front row next to the Duchess of Portland, and Ian was placed next to the Duke of Rutland, who in a few years would become Margaret's son-in-law. The day, according to Margaret, had been perfect and since their arrival at Westminster Abbey, she felt secure in knowing Ian would be on his best behaviour. Her only concern had been that, owing to the advice she was given to chew Horlicks tablets to maintain her strength, the television cameras had captured her animated jaw. Afterward, Margaret and Ian went back to Upper Grosvenor Street, as being divorcees they could not attend court nor were they invited to the evening reception at Buckingham Palace.

Instead Margaret accepted an invitation from her friend Odette Massigli, wife of the French Ambassador to the United Kingdom. She thought it a far more exciting offer, as Odette was 'such a dream figure in London'[17] and friends thought her parties were 'tip-top'.[18] As Margaret dressed for the party, her enthusiasm dimmed when she noticed Ian becoming irate, a result of his heavy drinking after the coronation. She remained silent, as she often did when he became unreasonable, and assumed he would not cancel their invitation and offend Monsieur Massigli. Several nights previously Ian had expressed similar displeasure at having to attend a ball at Londonderry House. It was to be hosted by Perle Mesta, 'the hostess with the mostest', a former US Ambassador to Luxembourg and socialite whose reputation inspired Irving Berlin's musical *Call Me Madam*. Prior to their leaving, Margaret gave a dinner party for eighteen guests, and Ian, who had been at White's all day, returned home drunk and in a bad temper and came to the table wearing a grey flannel suit. After dinner he changed and accompanied Margaret to Londonderry House, his mood improved and he forgot his tantrum of only a few hours before. However, on the night of the Massigilis' ball, Ian was beyond the pale. The traffic contributed to his mood, and when the driver made a detour to avoid the crowds, Ian said: 'I'm not going to sit in this damned car any longer.' He opened the door and got out, leaving Margaret to go to the embassy alone. The same excuses were made, that Ian was suffering from a cold and was too sick to attend. Odette, like many of Margaret's friends and fellow hostesses, graciously accepted her explanation despite knowing it was a lie.

The most bizarre and humiliating incident, according to Margaret, was an invitation to a dinner dance given by the Duke and Duchess of Sutherland. She declined the invitation as such things did not amuse Ian and she did not want to risk another scene, but Ian decided he did want to go, as he had heard from friends what a good party it would be. No amount of reasoning would change his mind, and he did not care that Clare Sutherland would have to rearrange the table setting to accommodate himself and Margaret. As Clare's husband was a distant cousin of Ian and knew him well, she told Margaret she understood her predicament. The day arrived and an hour before they were due to leave Ian announced he was no longer going, and Margaret, once again, went alone and invented an excuse for her absent husband.

Ian's changes of heart, often at the last minute and without warning, had become a pattern. Although Margaret came to expect him to 'chuck' (her word) social engagements,[19] including not showing up to his own dinner parties, his absence made her feel less confident and inventing excuses had become second nature. The circles in which she moved were all too aware of Ian's behaviour, and of his vices, and while Margaret might have gained a title and a new social rank, they also knew her life was a sham.

★

When Inveraray Castle was first opened to the public on 25 April 1953, Margaret could, at last, fulfil her role as not only a duchess but also a hostess, albeit to tourists paying 2*s* 6*d* for the privilege of her company. It would serve as a temporary fix and she knew this herself. Now that the renovations were completed Ian no longer had any use for Margaret, nor did he express any gratitude for all she and her father had done. In hindsight, she remembered the opening day as 'glorious'; the weather was perfect, and the pipe band of the Argyll and Sutherland Highlanders played from a balcony as visitors toured the rooms, observing the historical artefacts on show. It was, perhaps, how she wished it to be.

Prior to the castle's official opening to the public, there was a party held the day before for 150 guests, the majority of whom were public bodies and representatives from tourist agencies. It was a formality which Margaret might have found dull yet necessary, and she did not expect anything out of the ordinary to happen.

Ian had certainly not prepared Margaret for the arrival of Louise and their son Lord Colin, nor did he mention that his daughter, Lady Jeanne, would be joining them, all three having sailed on the *Queen Mary* from New York. Far from being interested in the restoration of the castle, Louise wished to see her elder son, Ian Lorne, who was attending school at Glenalmond, Perthshire.

The visit, albeit a harmless one on Louise's part, irritated Margaret and she felt threatened by the presence of her husband's ex-wife and the children he shared from his two former marriages. Over dinner Louise shared the news that she was to be married, and her soon-to-be third husband was Robert Claremont Timpson, a New York stockbroker. Not only was Louise marrying a rich and successful man, albeit a titleless one, but she would be relocating to New York and living a life that Margaret had, perhaps, envisaged for herself. Although there would be an ocean between the two duchesses (Louise would lose her courtesy title when she remarried), Margaret's predecessor would continue to exert her influence over Inveraray Castle, as not only the trustee of the two sons she shared with Ian, but as the mother of the future Duke of Argyll. On the outside, Margaret expressed little to no feelings about Louise's visit and news: '[It] seemed to have no effect on Margaret, who, rather like a nurse, had cultivated an emotional detachment that enabled her to watch those around her either happy or in pain without feeling anything,' wrote Charles Castle.

This apparent coldness, though mistaken for indifference, might have been an act of self-preservation. It was apparent in photographs of Margaret and Ian, taken to promote Inveraray's tourist season, which ran from April to August. Dressed in a tweed jacket and Clan Campbell tartan she looked frail as she held on to his arm and they strolled across the daffodil lawn, with the castle looming in the background. The aura of disinterest, the vacant eyes and lantern jaw were reminiscent of her youth, in the days before her debutante season, when she was in the company of Helen. Margaret was unhappy then, and she was unhappy now.

11

Cat and Mouse

During the three years in which Margaret had been married to Ian, her life had been unpredictable and predominantly unhappy. Although there were fleeting moments of happiness and she began to view the extremities of his behaviour as cyclic, nevertheless she found him 'difficult to cope with'.[1] The opening of Inveraray Castle had offered Margaret false hope, as during the tourist season Ian found a purpose in his daily routine of greeting visitors and overseeing tours, and when they closed their doors in August he reverted to his habit of lying on the sofa for hours and chain-smoking cigarettes in a long holder. With nothing occupying his time he was once again drinking heavily and taking his frustrations out on Margaret. There were times when Margaret pitied Ian, particularly when it was announced that Queen Elizabeth, Prince Philip, and Princess Margaret would be visiting Iona, a Hebrides island that belonged to him, but that owing to his two divorces he could not accept the appointment of Lord Lieutenant of Argyll and could not receive the royal visitors. Ian was bitterly disappointed, Margaret even more so; she realised she had married a man who could give her a title and little else. Though, as patron of the Royal College of Midwives, she was present when the Queen Mother laid the foundation stone at the college's new premises on Mansfield Street.

For four months since the grand opening of Inveraray, Margaret tolerated Ian's behaviour and, having decided she could live with him no longer, she announced she was going to America to stay with friends. On the evening before she left they parted on bad terms, and the usual reasons were to blame. He had promised to take her to dinner, but when he came home from White's he announced she could dine alone and left without another word. The familiar feelings of anger and humiliation struck her; she was entertaining David Rose, head of Paramount Pictures in Britain, and he had witnessed their exchange and offered to take her out. They returned home after ten o'clock and Margaret was greeted by police and reporters, who informed her that a burglar had climbed up the scaffolding of an empty building next to her house, crawled along the roof and into her bedroom window. The burglar ransacked her wardrobes and dressing table, stealing over £6,000 worth of furs and jewellery, none of which were insured. They were never recovered, despite Margaret offering a reward. It was her maid, Kathleen Carpenter, who discovered the theft after she went upstairs to turn down Margaret's bed, and the butler, Leslie Duckworth, telephoned the police. Having noticed she arrived home with a man who was not her husband, reporters asked about Ian's whereabouts and Margaret lied and said he was at a business dinner. At that moment Ian appeared in the doorway of the upstairs library, visibly drunk, and fell down the stairs. The reporters helped him to his feet, and they promised Margaret there would be no mention of it in the next day's newspapers. For this, she was grateful, as it was not the first time they had agreed to protect Ian's dignity. The same could not be said, years later, when neither Ian nor the newspapers offered Margaret the same courtesy.

The following morning Margaret set sail on the *Queen Mary* for New York, where she spent ten days as the guest of the Broadway producer Gilbert Miller and his wife, Kitty, who was an art collector and philanthropist. Then she flew to South Carolina to stay with Benjamin and Carola Kittredge at their fabled plantation, Cypress Gardens, near Charleston, surrounded by a swamp, black waters and wisteria vines. Despite the Southern Gothic setting, Margaret was not wallowing in her own unhappiness; if anything, she made the most of her time away from Ian. She went to New Orleans and attended Mardi Gras in the company of the Duke and Duchess of Windsor, Sir Roger Makins, the British Ambassador to the United States, and senior officers from the Royal Navy. As was the tradition, Margaret was asked to curtsy to the queen of the carnival, a Kurri hospital worker named Miss Del Coleman, and she was happy to do so, as were the Windsors, but the American First Lady Bess Truman refused. During the celebrations, she accepted invitations to parties given by the Royal Navy, both ashore and on board their ship. The officer who, in her words, 'set most female hearts a-flutter', including her own, was Rear-Admiral Keith Campbell-Walter, father of the fashion model Fiona Campbell-Walter, to whom Charlie Sweeny was close before her marriage to Baron Hans Heinrich Thyssen. As many esteemed individuals were present at the naval parties, Margaret's presence was not considered improper, despite the fact that she was surrounded by men. She made no secret of her preference for male company, both socially and privately. 'Sometimes I feel I need a man so desperately that my body aches,'[2] she said.

While Margaret was happy away from her husband, Ian was equally happy away from his wife. Since his marriage, he had been conducting secret affairs with several mistresses, which Margaret suspected but of which had no proof. At that time, during the lowest ebb of her marriage, she would have begun divorce proceedings, for not only had her vanity suffered but her finances too, as George had closed his cheque-book to Ian. She also feared George would accuse her of squandering his money on mink coats and diamond bracelets for herself, and subsequently cut her off. So it was her responsibility to fund not only Ian's ill-advised schemes but his expensive tastes too, which included trips to Paris to have his kilts made by Lanvin.[3]

However, it was Ian who made the first move to accuse Margaret of adultery. Through social gossip, he came to suspect that she had installed a young lover in the mews cottage on the grounds of Upper Grosvenor Street, an arrangement that had been going on for six months. When he telephoned her from Inveraray, Margaret denied the claims that she had been unfaithful, and she justified the reasons as to why she was seen out and about with other men. 'But surely I'm allowed to have ... to have friends,' she stammered over the telephone, a clear sign of the distress he was causing her. 'How can you escort me yourself when you're stuck up at that dreary hole in Scotland for most of the time?'[4]

The man to whom Margaret had grown close was Sigismund von Braun, a German diplomat, and contrary to rumours he was not younger than her, and nor was he living in her mews cottage. It was a controversial move, for not only was Margaret effectively leading a separate life from her husband, but she was seeing a man who had once been a member of the Nazi Party, and whose brother, Wernher von Braun, invented the V-2 rocket which the Luftwaffe had used to bomb Britain during the war. Although von Braun had resigned his Nazi membership and assisted with the Nuremberg trials, he was, from Ian's point of view, the enemy. It was hardly surprising, given Ian's prisoner-of-war record, that he reacted badly when Margaret invited von Braun and his wife, Hildegard, to Inveraray Castle. It was a daring move for Margaret to devote all of her attention to von Braun, with whom she vanished for long walks, and to ignore Ian, who was left to entertain Hildegard. Described by his peers as 'a man of enormous charm and a real ladies' man', von Braun was in demand by Margaret and her ilk; he was also handsome, rich, and a threat to Ian's masculine pride. It was also then, during his first visit to Inveraray, that Ian realised the rumours of Margaret's infidelity were true.

Margaret and Ian continued to lead separate lives; she no longer went to Inveraray for long periods of time, and although he stayed at Upper Grosvenor Street during his visits to London he ignored her for the duration. Therefore it was interesting that they continued to holiday together, perhaps done on Margaret's behalf so they would not appear estranged and neither party would be tempted to enforce a legal separation. They each had something the other needed or wanted; Ian gave Margaret a title and social importance, and Margaret offered him a reliable source of income, even if George no longer wrote cheques for Inveraray. Although there had been moments when Margaret entertained the idea of a divorce, she had her children to think of, especially Frances whose coming out was drawing nearer. Not for a moment did she imagine that Ian was plotting to divorce her.

In February 1955, while Margaret and Ian were holidaying in Morocco, she received a cable from her father, informing her that Helen was seriously ill. During the last fifteen years of Helen's life, she had been confined to a wheelchair and suffered from chronic pain, a side-effect of rheumatoid arthritis, and for several months her condition had been deteriorating. Soon after Margaret returned to London, Helen fell into a coma and died. The death of her mother would mark a watershed moment in Margaret's life, though she did not realise it at the time, as they shared no great bond nor did she experience the depths of grief following her death. Throughout Margaret's childhood, Helen had always been an obstacle in the way of her happiness and she often bemoaned that her mother failed to understand her, or at least made no attempt to empathise with another person's struggles. In her memoirs, she wrote: 'Although my mother and I had not agreed on everything, I was proud of her as she was of me.' She imagined that her father, advancing in his seventies, would settle into widowhood and their relationship would continue as before.

Four days after Helen's death, Margaret accompanied Frances to Buckingham Palace for her presentation to Queen Elizabeth,

Prince Philip, the Duke and Duchess of Gloucester, and the Princess Royal. Gone were the extravagant displays of pageantry, which had come to an end in 1939; there were no strict dress codes, no Prince of Wales feathers, and Frances made her curtsey wearing a tea-length Norman Hartnell dress. There were whispers that Margaret, voted one of the best-dressed women in the world, looked uncharacteristically dowdy in a black suit and hat which, it was reported, she wore for a public occasion four years before. She was in mourning for Helen, as reflected in her clothing, but did not look out of place among the mothers in their afternoon frocks. However, Margaret felt uncomfortable among the new generation of debutantes and the lack of formality that had prevailed over her first season in 1930. 'As I once more entered the white and gold State ballroom it was brought home to me how the splendour of the 1930s had vanished forever,' she wrote in her memoirs. The young women of Frances's generation were far more cultured and independent than their mothers; many earned their own living as fashion models or as secretaries, and Frances herself had completed her education in Florence and Paris, and spoke fluent Italian and French. The lack of formality mirrored the shifting attitudes on social class and the significance of debutantes, as, by the 1950s, many were not of blue-blood stock but the product of rich parents, as Margaret herself had been.

In the summer of 1955, Margaret returned to her natural habitat of the Mayfair ballroom, albeit to supervise Frances's season and to revel in the glory of having a beautiful daughter who, like herself, would be named Debutante of the Year. There was a coming-out ball held for Frances at Claridge's Hotel, with dinner for 100 guests and a further 700 invited to the dance. The theme of the evening was pink, with the decor and food adhering to the colour scheme; salmon and prawns, strawberries and pink cream, and so forth. Ian was conveniently absent and Margaret made the excuse that he was too busy searching for the *Duque de*

Florencia to come to London. Still, she drew on her Scots heritage and her title, and an Inveraray piper, Ronnie McCallum, played Highland Reels; and the Deep River Boys, an American gospel group popular in the 1940s, were hired for the cabaret act. It was a successful season, marked by Frances falling in love with Charles Cadogan, Viscount Chelsea, the eldest son of the 7th Earl of Cadogan. However, the couple were forbidden to become engaged, as the Cadogans disapproved of Frances being a Roman Catholic, and a devout one too. 'It's their loss and not yours,'[5] Margaret said.

Although Margaret had successfully launched her daughter into society she had no intention of retiring from the spotlight and continued to be a popular figure at London parties and among the international jet-set. In August she was invited on a promotional cruise of the Greek islands, aboard Stavros Niarchos's yacht, *Achilleus*, a scheme organised by Queen Frederika to bring well-heeled tourists to Greece. Elsa Maxwell, the American gossip columnist and hostess, was charged with inviting 200 guests, among them duchesses, industrialists, film stars, opera singers and, in her words 'just plain socialites and only one journalist' – the journalist was Pierre Galante, editor of *Paris Match*, who was invited with his new wife, the Hollywood star Olivia de Havilland. As Ian was preoccupied with his shipwreck, Margaret assumed he would refuse to go, and was surprised when he said: 'I don't care who else is going. I'll be there with bells on.'[6] It was an optimistic start, and Margaret wrote to Elsa to ask if Frances and Brian could also join the cruise, perhaps thinking of Frances's success as a debutante and the eligible bachelors on board. A week before they were due to leave for Venice, from where they would board the ship, Ian announced he was no longer going. 'If you think I'm going with you on that cruise you must be out of your mind,'[7] he said.

Margaret and her children spent a week in Venice before boarding the *Achilleus* and making their first stop in Capri on their way to the Greek islands, where they were followed by Stavros Niarchos's yacht, *Creole,* and often invited aboard for caviar and champagne. 'We're going to see Greece and Greece is going to see us!' Elsa shouted to news reporters from the yacht, as it was loaded with fifty cases of champagne and 300 gift packages of powdered milk and confectionery, the latter produce to be given to poor Greek children. In Ian's absence, Margaret became reacquainted with Prince Aly Khan and Loelia, the Duchess of Westminster, who preferred the cruises from her halcyon days off the western coast of Scotland which were 'enlivened by harpooning basking sharks'.[8] It was the cultural experience Margaret had hoped it would be, and she and the children toured museums and palaces that were specially opened for the party. The highlight of the trip, for Margaret, was being presented to King Paul and Queen Frederika.

Three weeks later, Margaret, Frances, and Brian returned to London to find Ian waiting for them at the airport. It was an unexpected sight, as for the duration of the cruise, he had not bothered to write or cable Margaret. The reasons behind Ian's silence were soon made clear: Inveraray Castle was once again in financial trouble and, with the estate's debts amounting to £100,000 there was a possibility he would have to leave the castle. It was the first time Margaret refused to help; she did not dare ask George for money, a decision that Ian resented. She explained that her own finances, although substantially more than Ian's annual income of £1,500, could no longer keep the estate afloat, as she had to pay for her stepchildren's education, her own children's upkeep, the costs of running two houses and paying two sets of staff. True to form Ian managed to find the money without exerting too much effort. Mrs Eliza Sale, a woman neither Ian nor Margaret had ever met, claimed to be related to him through her father, a rich jeweller named Joseph McGregor Campbell, and to Ian she bequeathed £40,000 'to be used for the good of the Clan Campbell'. To further increase his income Ian lent his name to the Burlington

Hosiery Company, whose range of tartan socks were distributed in America and branded as 'Authentic Argylls'. Ian was said to have advised on the designs and he appeared in full-page advertisements, holding a pair of socks, with a label depicting his coat of arms and the Campbell family motto, 'forget not'.

Relieved of the financial burden of Inveraray and with Ian's ego boosted from his unexpected inheritance, Margaret focused on her life in London while he remained in Scotland. Drawing on her natural flair for publicity, she guided Frances's social career with the same attention she had given her own two decades before, and was surprised to learn of her daughter's secret charitable work in the East End. 'I could not help but contrast this with the butterfly existence my friends and I had led as debutantes,'[9] she said. To conclude Frances's first social season Margaret took her to New York in time for Christmas, after which she sent her to stay with friends in Palm Beach. As her daughter was half-American, and in many aristocratic circles America and its modernity were frowned upon, Margaret wanted Frances to have the best of both worlds when it came to choosing a husband. Margaret herself preferred the company of American men, thinking them more handsome and generous than their English counterparts.

It had been said that, when growing up, Frances often behaved as if she despised her mother.[10] On one occasion when Brodrick Haldane went to Inveraray to photograph the castle's exterior from the old road bridge beside Loch Fyne, Frances told him not to. 'Mummy says it doesn't look large enough from there,'[11] she remarked. However, it was not to suggest that Margaret was domineering in the way Helen had been throughout her childhood, as she was too self-involved to exert power over someone else. Elements of their personalities were similar, and like Margaret, outsiders were struck by Frances's composure, which they understood as lacking a sense of humour, or even unhappiness. 'She seldom laughed,'[12] it was said of Frances. 'She don't make many jokes, do she,'[13] another said of Margaret. With their moral compasses fixed in opposite directions mother and daughter, although alike in their popularity, were different in their principles. Margaret always wanted the best for Frances; she gave her a good education, bought her nice things, and ensured she had decent friends. After all, Margaret had grown up thinking money was the key to happiness.

*

In October 1956 Margaret was to suffer a bitter blow to her sense of security when she received a telephone call from George, who broke the news that he had secretly married Jane Corby at Caxton Hall earlier that morning. He purposely did not announce the marriage or invite Margaret, as he, in his own words, did not want to attract publicity. 'So don't feel hurt on that score,' George said, to justify not telling her. Although approaching her forty-fourth birthday Margaret never outgrew the dependency on her father, emotionally and financially. In many ways, she remained a child to him, and he was her constant protector. Although Helen had often caused them both much unhappiness, she could never compete with the bond Margaret shared with George. In her childlike way Margaret did not want to believe that her father had the capacity to love another woman, particularly one as young as his daughter, and she did not understand his need for companionship after the death of Helen.

In her memoirs, Margaret wrote of her regret in not staying with George after Helen's death, and she blamed Ian for her inability to care for her father. The sentiment was expressed with the benefit of hindsight, but it enforced her belief that Jane, whom she viewed as an opportunist, had taken advantage of a lonely man. But was this entirely true? It appeared Helen eventually came to learn of the affair between George and Jane, which began in 1947, and they often dined as a trio at the Whighams suite at the Dorchester. Margaret had met Jane on several occasions, and so she was not a stranger to her. Consumed by her own life she failed to acknowledge that Jane, a young woman with a daughter from her first marriage, was, in fact, her father's mistress, and there was a possibility that she did not care. As there was no security in being the other woman, Jane could have moved on and married another man, had marriage and money been her motives during the years in which Helen was alive. Margaret also failed to accept that her father was happy and that he, too, wanted her to be happy for him. A year later George would resign as chairman of Celanese, which after several takeovers and mergers eventually amalgamated with Courtauld, and settled in Cookham Dean, Berkshire. 'I have been pretty lonely and aimless since poor mummy died,'[14] he wrote to Margaret, hoping she would empathise with his predicament. Sensing how she would react, George explained 'there was not a trace of romance in the whole thing'[15] and he had married Jane as he needed someone to care for him in old age.

The words did little to reassure Margaret of her place in George's life. As a child Margaret never had to share her two most prized possessions: her teddy bears and her father. She would outgrow the former, discarding the bears for materialistic things, but she never lost the sense that her father belonged to her, and only her alone. 'I have always hated the word "my", and forbade the children ever to use it,' she wrote in her memoirs. The rule did not extend to George, and at the time she thought only of herself, and the threat of losing both her father and her inheritance added to her despair. She also knew her marriage to Ian was coming to an end. Lost for words, Margaret burst into tears, and asked: 'How could you do this to me, daddy?'

Slipstream

Although Margaret's marriage to Ian had been in decline for years there was one event that she viewed as a turning point. In the autumn of 1956, Ian developed influenza which, aside from the common symptoms, left him weakened and depressed. Thus he engaged the services of Dr John Petro, who prescribed him two blue pills, which Margaret discovered were 'purple hearts', or to use the medical term, drinamyl – half barbiturate, half amphetamine. In a short period of time, Ian became addicted to the pills and dependent on Petro, whom he thought 'the most able diagnostician in London'.[1] Regardless of Petro having an admirable medical record – during the war he had worked alongside Sir Alexander Fleming, administering penicillin to the troops – his unorthodox practice of meeting patients in teashops and the London underground earned him the nickname 'the junkies' friend'.

For weeks Margaret observed Ian's changing appearance as he ate little and lost weight, and she listened as he talked manically throughout the day and into the night, a reoccurring theme being his early childhood. After two months of tolerating Ian's erratic behaviour and incoherent ramblings, Margaret was surprised when he announced he was leaving her. 'By the time you get home this afternoon I shall be gone,' he said. She thought it an empty threat made under the influence of drugs, and when she returned home she discovered Ian had left and his whereabouts were unknown. Telephoning Inveraray Castle and White's was pointless, for nobody knew where Ian was, and she finally learned from a *Daily Express* columnist that he was staying at Claridge's under an assumed name. In an attempt to disguise any scandal, Margaret explained to the columnist that Ian was staying at the hotel while she had the house decorated, as he disliked the smell of paint. The columnist remained unconvinced and told her the news came from Ian's former secretary, as the head porter at Claridge's had seen her talking to reporters in the hallway.

The former secretary in question was Mrs Yvonne MacPherson, the widow of Brigadier Cluny MacPherson, who had been imprisoned with Ian during the war. After MacPherson's death in 1952, Yvonne was engaged by Ian as a full-time social secretary, and he also asked Margaret to hire her. His reason for doing so was admirable, as he wished to increase Yvonne's modest earnings from her late husband's pension. Another reason for Ian keeping Yvonne on long after her services were no longer required – which was not clear to Margaret until much later – was her loyalty to him and an apparent dislike of Margaret. Such feelings of admiration continued, despite Ian not having paid Yvonne's wages for six months, and Margaret was horrified to learn of this and paid the money owed to her. 'Another drain on my finances,' Margaret recalled, as it had been agreed beforehand that Ian would pay Yvonne for any work she did for him and Margaret would take care of the rest. However, after Frances came out in 1955 Margaret no longer required a full-time secretary and she offered to find Yvonne new employment, and by coincidence her friend, Maureen, Marchioness of Dufferin and Ava, needed a secretary.

During the time that Ian recovered from influenza and became addicted to drinamyl he resumed his working relationship with Yvonne. Or as Margaret put it, he was 'seeing quite a lot of Yvonne at the moment', implying that their involvement with one another ran deeper than employer and employee. She suspected Ian and Yvonne were conspiring against her. How? She was not sure. When she telephoned Ian's suite at Claridge's, to confront him about the press, he denied the suggestion that Yvonne had been involved. Then, ten minutes later, he rang back and asked Margaret to repeat her question, and she heard a faint click as though someone had picked up the extension telephone. The eavesdropper was Dr Petro, who had listened in on their conversation at Ian's request. Margaret thought it more than a coincidence that Petro had sided with Ian and Yvonne against her, as earlier in the day she had asked Petro to wean Ian off drinamyl and to convince him to return home. 'There is no need for me to repeat anything. You heard quite well what I said,' Margaret told Ian. She did not realise that her brief telephone exchange with Ian would have dangerous repercussions.

In the meantime Margaret and Ian continued to live separately, and he remained at Claridge's, running up bills and expecting her to pay them. Every day he went to Upper Grosvenor Street to collect his post and use the library without saying one word to her. Margaret was unhappy about it, but she did not reproach him. When she held a dinner party, four days after his initial departure, he turned up and embarrassed everyone by drinking too much and telling the Minister of Defence, Duncan Sandys, how to do his job. The following morning Ian announced he was going to Paris and ordered Margaret not to follow him; she agreed and begged him to stop taking the drinamyl. However, her family doctor, Ivor Griffiths, advised against this, as Ian would become ill and lapse into a deep depression. Instead she was advised to humour him, as though he were a child, and agree with everything he said. She had been doing little else for the past three months.

Margaret thought it a promising sign when a telegram arrived from Ian inviting her to join him at the Ritz Hotel in Paris. After her arrival she found a note from Ian in her suite, informing her that he was staying at the Travellers' Club and that she was to remain at the Ritz. It made no sense to Margaret, but she heeded Dr Griffiths's warning and did not question Ian's behaviour. Half an hour later Ian telephoned Margaret and asked her to dine with him, to which she agreed, and he appeared with his luggage and without an explanation moved into her suite. Recalling their reunion, Margaret wrote in her memoirs that Ian woke up one night and asked, 'Maggie, why did I ever go to Claridge's?' to which she responded, 'Because you were very ill, Ian.' However, Ian's memories of their Parisian reunion contradicted Margaret's, and he later confided that he had to put a bolt on his bedroom door to keep her out. At the Ritz, though, he, in his own words, 'succumbed to her charms'.[2] Their remembrances are reflective of their individual egos and how they wanted to preserve their vanity at any cost. Ian claimed Margaret was a nymphomaniac and that he found her too forceful to resist, despite loathing her at the time. And Margaret cited pity as the reason for her staying married to Ian.

It was Ian who took the initiative to end their marriage, a decision Margaret considered impulsive despite him plotting against her for years. The first sign was his handling of Yvonne MacPherson and their preoccupation with Margaret's query, asking whether or not she had spoken to the press. Margaret thought it a harmless question, but Ian and Yvonne viewed it as slander and they intended to hold her accountable for her actions and to sue for damages. They confronted Margaret in the drawing room of Upper Grosvenor Street while she was entertaining her friend and newest confidante, Magda Buchel, whom Ian disliked, or pretended that he did. Unbeknown to Margaret it was Ian who had invited Magda to 'drop in' and act as a witness for Yvonne, presumably for a percentage of the damages.[3] 'Margaret, here is Yvonne. I have brought her here to ask you to apologise to her and retract the statements you have made about her,' Ian reputedly said.[4] Margaret did not respond, instead she rose from her chair and walked out of the room, closing the door behind her. 'Come downstairs and stop acting like a coward. You're a yellow-belly,' Ian shouted as she walked away. To prevent Ian from making a scene in front of the servants and her children, Margaret returned to the drawing room. She answered his questions regarding Yvonne and her supposed accusations, explaining she had merely repeated what the columnist had told her, and she reminded Ian it was a private conversation that was not meant to be repeated. Margaret would later claim that Lord Rothermere, proprietor of the *Daily Mail*, confided that Yvonne had been 'on his books for years and got £20 every time she opened her mouth'.[5] Meanwhile, Yvonne was taking notes in shorthand and demanding an apology, which Margaret refused to give. Instead she ordered Yvonne to leave her house, and Magda followed her.

Ian's recent conduct did nothing to repel Margaret, and she thought 'evil influences' were to blame. They went on a motoring holiday to Tuscany, a disastrous suggestion on her part, as she sensed something was afoot and her instincts proved correct when she returned home to find a letter from Yvonne's solicitor, suing her for damages and the original figure of £600 eventually increased to £5,000. Ian feigned shock, a reaction purposely done to gain Margaret's trust, and he promised to convince Yvonne to drop the case, as she had no grounds to sue. However, he delivered the news that Yvonne 'had a bit between her teeth' and intended to proceed with the case.

On 1 November Yvonne issued a writ against Margaret for libel and slander. Contrary to Ian's opinion and Margaret's memories of the event, Yvonne did have a case. For, on 18 April 1957, Margaret had sent a bogus telegram to Ian, having telephoned it through from Inveraray post office, pretending it was sent from Yvonne:

> Rushing off for ten days leave but all is ready as we planned to tear strips off Margaret financially and otherwise. A million thanks for your love, support and invaluable information

without which I would be helpless. Happy Easter and then into battle side by side. Yvonne.

It was an impulsive thing to do, and it would have lasting ramifications for Margaret. It also marked the beginning of Margaret's friends abandoning her, beginning with Maureen, Marchioness of Dufferin and Ava, who continued to employ Yvonne, despite Margaret's warning that she was indiscreet. Later it became known that Maureen had encouraged Yvonne to sue Margaret and in doing so she guaranteed her legal costs.

Ian continued to correspond with Yvonne, and he insisted that Margaret apologise, something she refused to do. His disloyalty should not have surprised her, but it did. Furthermore Ian wrote to George and suggested that Margaret 'eat humble pie'. It was a gesture that infuriated George, for whether or not Margaret was wrong he would defend her against the 'despicable and cowardly' behaviour of her husband.[6] 'I deeply resent my daughter being accused of lying,'[7] George wrote to Ian, and he reminded him that for the past twenty-five years Margaret had been 'a very popular and respected member of London society'.[8] The latter sentiment was especially poignant, for Ian and Dr Petro were plotting to have Margaret certified as insane, claiming that her fall down a lift shaft had left her with brain damage. For the plan to succeed they needed Margaret's doctor, Ivor Griffiths, to sign a document, but he refused and warned her of their meddling. She refused to believe that Ian could be so cruel, and blamed the drinamyl for altering his personality.

Although Margaret's life was falling apart, she looked to the future and was living vicariously through Frances, who, at the age of 20, had become involved with Charles Manners, 10th Duke of Rutland, a divorcee eighteen years her senior and custodian of Belvior Castle. Margaret approved of Charles and thought him 'a catch' despite the age gap between himself and Frances, and his having a daughter only ten years her junior. However, Charlie

Sweeny did not echo Margaret's enthusiasm, and although he thought Charles a 'fine man',[9] he worried Frances was not improving her chances with eligible young men who wanted to marry her. Furthermore, the couple's different religious backgrounds troubled him, as Charles was a Protestant and there had not been a Catholic Duke of Rutland since the Reformation. 'I understand, daddy. I won't go out with him anymore,'[10] Frances said. But Margaret had other ideas.

In the winter of 1958 Margaret was surprised when Ian suggested they tour the Middle East, a place he had visited several years before. In the light of what had happened, it seemed preposterous that Ian would ask Margaret to go abroad and also, as he continued to take drinamyl, that she would agree to go with him. The aforementioned was related in her memoirs, but it wasn't true – it had been Margaret's idea[11] and an impromptu one too; she was desperate for Frances to marry a duke, and the trip, taking in Lebanon, Jordan, Iraq, Iran, and Israel, was a ploy to encourage the relationship between her daughter and the Duke of Rutland. 'I then thought of inviting a younger man to accompany us and to make the trip more amusing for Frances,' she wrote, keeping with the story that Ian was accompanying her. Apparently the 'lovesick' Charles 'jumped at the idea'.[12] Coincidently, or rather conveniently, Ian refused to go and Margaret cancelled his booking.

On 29 January 1958, Margaret, Frances, and Charles arrived at Heathrow Airport to board their flight to Beirut. As George Whigham had done, years before, when Margaret and Fulke Warwick were destined for England, she informed the press. Or, as she innocently wrote, 'A mother, a pretty daughter and an unattached duke was quite enough to start rumours of a romance.' There were no rumours; the fact was Charles loved Frances and wanted to marry her and she reciprocated his feelings. At the Accadia Hotel in Tel Aviv, the couple became engaged.

Margaret was ecstatic, Charlie less so; 'I was aware of the problems the marriage faced, and at one time I seriously considered preventing it, which I could have done quite easily.'[13] A few months later Charlie ignored his own advice and married Arden Snead, a successful American fashion model twenty-one years his junior; it was an impulsive proposal and an ill-matched marriage, which ended in divorce eight years later. 'Arden had a disposition which at best could be described as difficult,' he wrote, 'and a temper which, at its worst, could only be described as psychotic.'[14] However, Frances, unlike her father, approached her future marriage with a sense of pragmatism; she was aware of the religious difficulties she faced in marrying Charles, particularly when she received criticism from several Catholic bishops who disapproved of her marrying a divorced man. A compromise was reached and Charles agreed that their children would be raised Catholic until they came of age and could decide for themselves. They were married on 15 May 1958 at Caxton Hall, as Charles, being a divorcee, could not marry in an Anglican or Catholic church. Both Margaret and Frances wanted a church wedding, and Margaret compensated for this by giving a large reception at Claridge's which she co-hosted with Charlie, whom she was on better terms with than her present husband. As for Ian, he stepped into the role of bystander. Reflecting on her life, which had come full circle, Margaret wrote: 'I had become a duchess and mistress of an historic castle. My daughter had also married a duke. Life was apparently roses all the way.'

*

Margaret's outing as the mother of the bride was to serve as a prelude for reviving her public duties as a duchess. In August 1958 Ian was invited to visit the Argyll and Sutherland Highlanders in Cyprus, as requested by their colonel to boost morale. 'I dared him to leave me behind!' Margaret said, after Ian announced that her presence was not welcome. She went regardless of his wishes, and they stayed at Government House. The trip was blighted by his moodiness and her suffering an abscessed tooth, which was extracted by an army dentist.

Two months later Ian visited the Canadian Argyll and Sutherland Highlanders in Toronto, and again Margaret insisted on accompanying him regardless of whether he wanted her to. While she continued to blame Ian for spoiling their time together, she did not mention her own indiscretions which occurred more often than not. On the *Homeric*, she became infatuated with a young man who was travelling with his parents, and they had a brief affair. Surprisingly, Ian did not appear moved by her blatant adultery nor did he express any signs of jealousy or disappointment. After their engagement in Toronto, they flew to Boston and then on to New York, and Ian made arrangements to leave early, as he had a meeting in London, and he expected Margaret to accompany him. She decided to remain in New York with her young boyfriend, and when Ian remarked that she was making a fool of herself, she said: 'You're just a stupid, jealous old man.'

Returning to London in December Margaret learned that Frances was expecting her first child, and that Ian intended to spend Christmas without her, at the St James Club. The prospect of becoming a grandmother did little to quell her extramarital affairs, which she no longer hid from Ian. 'What was I supposed to do with you stuck ... stuck up at that damned castle all the time?' she retorted, her stammer emphasising how frightened she was by the scene. It was one thing to be seen with other men, it was another to be confronted for it by a man whose temper she feared.

In the New Year of 1959, Ian resumed his ducal travels and went to New Zealand and Australia to meet members of Clan Campbell. He and Margaret were barely on speaking terms, and yet she was determined to go and bought her own ticket, despite his wanting to go alone. The reasons for his intended solo tour became clear upon their arrival at the Australia Hotel and her friend, Sir Frank Packer, asked why she and Ian had come to

Australia. 'To visit the Campbells,' Margaret said. She learned that the main reason for his visit was to raise money for Inveraray Castle, and the people whose hospitality they were accepting were also being asked to donate money. In public, they played their respective parts and were received by Colonel and Mrs Eric Campbell at their historic home, Yuemburra, in New South Wales, and for the remainder of the six-week tour they also visited Victoria, Queensland and South Australia.

It was in Sydney that the saga of their marriage reached its penultimate conclusion when Ian, looking for a comb on Margaret's dressing table, noticed her red leather engagement diary for 1956–59. He glanced at it, and among the notes of her travel arrangements and cheques he saw the names of half a dozen men, all of whom Margaret was meeting. It might have appeared harmless, for her duties as a duchess saw her meet with chairmen and other male officials, but the unusual format of her diary gave Ian reasons to think otherwise. She was fastidious about recording her daily life, and each page was divided into four sections, giving the same days of the month for four years, allowing her to compare what she had done on that day the year before and so forth – or to confuse prying eyes. 'What are you doing with my property? Give it to me,' Margaret said, as she tried to retrieve the diary from his grip. He accused her of adultery and she did not deny it. The following morning Ian flew home, leaving Margaret to make her own travel arrangements. 'That trip to Australia was an absolutely wonderful trip. Really royal, and the last time we were together as man and wife,' she recalled. She thought it a turning point in her relationship with Ian, that at last he was taking his role seriously, and had stopped drinking as much. 'I was pretty happy about him, and then *bang*.'[15]

It seems astonishing that Margaret failed to realise the severity of the situation with Ian. Rather than flying home from Australia and confronting the problem, she went to New York and stayed with friends. While there, she met with her father who confided that he, too, was experiencing marital discord with Jane. As George was now in his eightieth year, Margaret was concerned for his well-being and he eventually moved into a mews cottage on the grounds of Upper Grosvenor Street, where Jane sporadically visited him. During Margaret's absence, Ian searched through her private belongings, hoping to find evidence of her adultery. In her desk drawer he found diaries, and with the help of a locksmith he broke into a locked cupboard and stole her letters. Behind a bookcase, he discovered more letters and two of her four-year diaries for 1948–51 and 1952–55. A manilla envelope addressed to Margaret caught his attention; inside were two sets of notes and a sheet of white paper folded around several Polaroid photographs. Aside from the diaries and letters, which provided ominous evidence in her dealings with other men, the photographs would seal her fate. In two of the images, Margaret and a man appeared naked; the man's identity was concealed as he was photographed from the neck down, and although her back was turned to the camera she could be identified by her signature hairstyle and three-strand pearl necklace. Although Ian was relieved to have found concrete proof of Margaret's infidelities and equally shocked at the images of her performing a sex act on another man, it was a further piece of evidence that served to infuriate him. Among her things, he came across sheets of hotel writing paper with words cut out from letters written by Louise and arranged as to suggest she was questioning the paternity of her two sons with Ian. He removed his findings to a safety box until he could present them to his solicitor, and before filing for divorce he knew he needed one further piece of evidence: her 1955–59 diary.

Margaret remained oblivious to Ian's intention to divorce her. Some might have called her naive, even stupid, but she was pre-occupied with her own plan of deception. In her desperation to have a child with Ian, she came up with the idea to fake a pregnancy and adopt a newborn baby boy and pass it off as his son and heir. It explains why she went to the trouble of forging letters and pretending they were from Louise, to discredit Ian's two sons and their rights of succession as his heirs. Margaret was already the mother of a duchess, her grandson would become the Duke of Rutland, and she wanted a son who would inherit the dukedom of Argyll, thus securing a return on the money she and her father had paid into Ian's estate. To achieve her ambition Margaret asked her friend, Diana Wolkowicki, to go to Venice and from there to use her Polish contacts to find a baby, or, rather, buy a baby and bring it back to England. In the meantime Margaret padded her stomach and hinted to others that she was pregnant, though the news failed to reach Ian or perhaps she was purposely keeping it from him. Either way, Diana had little faith in the plan and she dismissed Margaret with, 'Don't be stupid, dear.'

Unlike Margaret's false pregnancy, the forged letters were a work in progress before Ian had found the blueprints. At the time he refrained from confronting Margaret, as he was waiting for her to tangle herself up in lies. The only sign that something was afoot was her discovery of the missing letters and diaries, and much to Ian's surprise she admitted to having a brief affair with one man. As she refused to name the man in question, Ian drew his own conclusion that it was Sigismund von Braun. Then Margaret walked into Ian's trap, as he knew she would. After a trip to Paris, she gave him two sheets of hotel writing paper, containing extracts of the forged letters which she claimed to have found in Paris. It was a fanciful story; the gist being that a friend had shown Margaret the letters, and noticing that they contained damning information about Ian and his children, she asked to read them alone, whereupon she copied fragments from the letters. Margaret produced a poison-pen letter, written in the same handwriting as the ones she had previously shown Ian, which read: 'Hoping that this will help a very good woman to reveal the lies of a very evil one.' Another letter arrived a few days later, following the theme of the last one: 'I am old and of poor health, but I do not like to see anyone living a lie.' Frances received a similar letter and gave it to Margaret, who then passed it on to Ian. 'I believe that in her muddled, desperate way Margaret had only been trying to seek some sort of revenge on Ian when he made it clear he was starting divorce proceedings,'[16] Brodrick Haldane wrote. Desperate as she might have been, the letters were composed before Margaret realised Ian was filing for divorce.

Ian was determined to expose Margaret as the author of the forged letters and recruited Scotland Yard to help. He also informed Louise of the lies that were being circulated about their sons. This contradicts Margaret's statement that Ian looked grey with worry, and that he begged her not to reveal the contents of the letters or the rumours surrounding his sons. If he gave her the impression that he was worried it could have been a ploy to nurture within her a false sense of power and therefore encourage her reckless behaviour. Years later Margaret would claim she knew private information about her stepsons' paternity, as Ian had confided in both herself and George. 'It's a *dreadful* thing to say against children,' she said, though it did not prevent her from referring to Ian Lorne and Colin Campbell as 'bastards'. Louise was determined to stop Margaret, whose claims fell under slander and libel, an action that she believed was influenced by the Yvonne McPherson case, the outcome of which was yet to be decided. A writ from Louise arrived on the day Margaret's first grandchild, David, Marquis of Granby, was born. 'Good God,' Margaret said, 'how much more of this am I going to have?'

As the dates for the court hearings were yet to be announced, Margaret believed it gave her time to win Ian back. 'He knew I adored him. Knew I was an idiot,' she said. She also believed she was beyond reproach, and given her title, social influence, and her money, that no one would dare cross her. George shared her point of view and never told her that the court cases would have ramifications; he only advised her to prepare for a barrage of negative publicity. What was written in the newspapers became an extension of Margaret's reality; apparent when she made her scrapbooks, which she said were for her grandchildren, and bypassed the news clippings on her marital troubles and legal issues. Ian knew that Margaret was frightened by the consequences and so he manipulated the situation for his own gain, telling her if she agreed to the injunction he would abandon his plans to divorce her. She agreed to his conditions and went to her solicitors and asked to sign the papers for the injunction, which they advised against as it meant she had admitted to slandering Ian's sons. The legal technicalities no longer mattered to Margaret; she only wanted her husband back. They spent two nights at the Ritz Hotel in Paris, and then he vanished.

The court hearing for Louise's injunction toward Margaret was heard at Oxford, as Ian did not want the press reporting on the story, fearing it would tarnish his sons' reputation and the Duchy of Argyll. It was a brief hearing, and Margaret signed the injunction and paid £10,000 in damages and costs, of which Louise received £7,000. Afterward, Margaret went to stay with Jack and Drue Heinz in the south of France, which she realised was a mistake as she was miserable and in tears most of the time. Ian and his daughter, Jeanne, were also in the south of France, and they brought with them the injunction Margaret had signed and were passing it around at dinner parties. Ironically it was Louise who spoke to the press, and Ian invited Peter Baker from the *Daily Express* to have a drink with him – a ruse, for his main objection was to show Baker the injunction and encourage him to write about it. Baker refused, thinking the legal element too dangerous, and informed Margaret about it.

A month later Margaret decided to change the locks on her front door and asked her secretary, Diana Crossland, to make the necessary arrangements with a locksmith. The information was passed on to Ian, and he later admitted that Diana, who had previously worked for him, was the culprit. Ian telephoned his daughter, Jeanne, and spoke of his intention to raid Margaret's house for the missing diary – the one whose contents he had glimpsed in Australia. Ian and Jeanne entered the house at six o'clock in the morning, using the latch key Ian had kept, and they climbed the two flights of stairs to Margaret's bedroom and found her asleep. They crept downstairs and ransacked the study, and failing to find what they were looking for, they returned to her bedroom. The noise had awoken Margaret, and as she switched on the bedside lamp she saw two figures walking toward her from the bathroom. Although paralysed by fear she managed to ask Ian what he wanted, and she told Jeanne to get out. Jeanne rushed to Margaret's bedside and held her down, while Ian took the diary from her bedside table. When recalling the story Margaret often mixed Ian and Jeanne up, and who held her down and who stole the diary, and so forth. The content was much the same; she had been robbed and there was nothing she could do about it, as by law Ian had the right to enter his wife's home. 'It was a horrible experience,' Margaret wrote in her memoirs, 'and the next day I suffered from delayed shock.'

The experience did little to warn Margaret to keep her distance from Ian, and she asked their mutual friend, Bill Thornton, to talk to him. Thornton reminded Ian that he, too, had had affairs and as such he was in no position to hold Margaret accountable for her indiscretions. It was not Margaret's affairs that motivated Ian to seek a divorce, but the forged letters and her discrediting the paternity of his children which, he thought, made her a dangerous liability. Margaret thought Ian's reaction meant he had something to hide, though the injunction prevented her from pursuing her theory. In due course Ian visited Upper Grosvenor Street to inform Margaret that his divorce petition was being sent by his legal advisers to the Court of Session in Edinburgh. Losing her temper, Margaret told him to take his divorce petition and leave. 'I blew the chance to get him back. It was my fault,' she said. 'I blew it. I just blew it.'[17]

Ian had no intention of returning to Margaret, and although they both knew a divorce was on the horizon, he wanted to seek revenge first. He went to Louise and told her that Margaret had broken the injunction by speaking of their sons to Bill Thornton. Despite Margaret denying the accusation and Thornton declining to get involved, Louise's lawyers sent an application to Mr Justice Paull for Margaret's committal to prison. Margaret was frightened of the outcome and knew if Louise's case was successful she could face imprisonment at Holloway, and so she attempted to leave the country and go to Switzerland. 'I won't have that silly girl in the house!'[18] said Mary Chevreau d'Antraigues, a friend of Helen and George, when Margaret telephoned to ask if she could stay with her. The hearing took place on 20 December 1959 in Mr Justice Paull's private chamber at the High Court; the press and public were forbidden to attend and were only permitted to enter when the verdict was read. It had gone in Margaret's favour, though she remained fearful of the injunction and of Ian setting her up. 'I believe in British justice,'[19] she said, pleading her innocence. A reporter asked if Margaret was 'happy or happier'? Glancing at her solicitor, Mr Cecil Jobson, she answered: 'I think I am happy. I can say that, can't I?'

The words Margaret uttered to the press had little meaning. She was far from happy, and the final nail in the coffin of her marriage to Ian came in the form of an interdict that banned her from entering Inveraray Castle. As so much of her father's money had gone into restoring the castle she felt she had a right to enter her marital home and she ignored Ian's warning not to visit. Months before the interdict was enforced and against Ian's wishes, Margaret visited the castle with her father and stepmother and thought something was amiss when Ian and Jane disappeared on long walks and she privately concluded they were having an affair. When they left for London, Jane said to Ian's chauffeur: 'Remember Peach, you take your orders from the duke now, not from the duchess.'

On another occasion Margaret had telephoned a servant in advance and informed them she would be visiting the castle and, as Ian was abroad, they were not to tell him. Two days after arriving, she sent for a locksmith from Glasgow to open Ian's study door, whereupon she stole an oil painting, photographs, and two boomerangs. She also broke several of Ian's favourite gramophone records, which he thought was done out of spite. A short time later Margaret told Ian she planned to take up residence at Inveraray, and he reminded her that she was banned from the castle. Undeterred, she sent a telegram:

Arriving at castle for lunch on Saturday 19th with my father and Donald Nicholl. Another couple arriving for dinner and weekend. Please inform staff and tell MacDonald to make sure my bedroom is quite ready. Give my fondest love and a big kiss to Colin.

It was then, after Margaret ignored Ian's verbal warnings not to visit Inveraray, that he successfully applied for the interdict, which was granted by Lord Wheatley and pinned to the wall of the Edinburgh High Court.

Margaret was given one day lasting from dawn to dusk to retrieve her personal belongings from Inveraray Castle. She was also going to identify the various heirlooms that were given to her in Ian's Deed of Gift, which she had marked with green labels during their restoration of the castle. Arriving with her maid and lawyers Margaret was besieged by reporters who had decamped to the town of Inveraray, and when she had breakfast at the George Hotel she was approached by townsfolk, who remained fond of her. She was surprisingly calm, the effect of a benzedrine tablet which she had taken to prevent her from breaking down. It worked, for when Ian greeted her in his usual cold and curt manner she smiled and proceeded to follow her lawyers, identifying the items which she believed were hers. Walking through the State rooms she said, 'That is mine … that belongs to me,' and so forth. As dusk fell over Loch Fyne, Margaret left

Inveraray for the last time, watched by Ian and his heir; the two men who harboured so much bitterness toward her, and who knew that she was entitled to nothing under their roof.

It was then, after Margaret's lawyers applied to the Scottish courts for the heirlooms laid out in the Deed of Gift, that she learned it was a worthless piece of paper. The items did not belong to Ian, as he had mortgaged them in 1949 to provide himself with an annual income of £1,000. It was then that she realised she had been cheated of what was rightfully hers, and that her marriage was built on a lie. 'My husband was terribly persuasive,' Margaret said, 'as all crooks are.'[20]

Treachery

On Margaret's nineteenth birthday, held at the Embassy Club, an astrologer had predicted her future. 'I see happiness, laughter … much love,' he said. 'But beware! There is danger.'

'Danger from what?' Margaret asked.

'Treachery. You will be betrayed by the people you trust.'

Thirty years had passed and the premonition would soon come to light.

In the present time, Margaret continued to count her father as her strongest, and only, ally. They were both experiencing the collapse of their respective marriages and the retaliation from their spouses. And, while Margaret knew Ian was seeking his own revenge against her, she, too, fought back with the same underhanded tactics she had used before. As it had done on previous occasions, it backfired. She accused Jane of having an affair with Ian, and although she wanted to destroy her stepmother's reputation – she never forgave her for marrying George – she also wanted to discredit Ian, who had since filed his petition for divorce.

Margaret hired private detectives to follow Jane, hoping she could find evidence of adultery or misconstrue the information to make it seem so. The traps set for Jane were far from subtle; they began with a letter sent by a stranger inviting her to join them in their hotel room at the Dorchester, which she declined. On another occasion, Jane's brother, Leslie Corby, was offered £5,000 to sign a statement declaring that his sister had committed adultery with Ian. After telephoning the police Jane learned it was Margaret who had hired the detectives and when she approached George about it, he did not appear surprised and nor did he offer to stop Margaret, as he, too, suspected she was being unfaithful. Jane retaliated by accusing Margaret of trying to ruin her marriage to George, and, as she implied, a fight broke out between the couple and she was left with a bruised fist and a black eye, which she said George had given her for speaking badly of his daughter. Instead of consulting with lawyers, Jane spoke to the press, which prompted George to announce that Margaret had not 'in any way tried to upset or interfere' with his marriage. 'My only wish was that Jane should make my father happy for the last years of his life,' Margaret wrote. 'Sadly, this was not the case.'[1] A few months later George asked Jane to sign a deed of separation and gave her £20,000 for doing so; he also promised to make frequent visits to their marital home and to give her more money. Although Jane felt like his mistress rather than his wife she agreed to his conditions, as she thought it a meaningless gesture done to appease Margaret.

In the New Year of 1960, Margaret and George left for a four-month holiday at his home on Cable Beach in the Bahamas. It was a bittersweet period for Margaret, for while she had her father all to herself she also learned he had throat cancer. They returned to Upper Grosvenor Street, and a short time later Jane sent her solicitor over with a writ; she was suing George for a divorce on the grounds of cruelty. However, after learning of his terminal illness, she offered to withdraw the petition, but he declined as he wanted to fight her allegations. Two weeks later George was admitted to the London Clinic, and Margaret refused to tell Jane of his whereabouts, or that he was in a coma and dying.

On the evening of 6 November, Margaret dined with a psychic friend, who said: 'Listen to the bells. Don't you hear them?' Margaret could hear nothing. 'All the bells in a church on the Clyde are ringing for your father, and all his family are waiting for him, especially your mother.' The psychic world had always fascinated Margaret, and she came to depend on clairvoyants and mediums during her lengthy divorce battle with Ian. Eva Petulengro, a renowned psychic who had made her name at Brighton Pier, was engaged by Margaret to come to her home and do a reading. 'She was like a cross between a high-class whore and the wicked witch who gave Snow White the apple,'[2] Petulengro recalled, though the contents of her predictions for Margaret remained private. Margaret would call on Petulengro several times and thought of her as an adviser for her problems, although whether or not she listened to the advice is debatable. Their relationship came to an end when, according to Petulengro, Margaret attempted to seduce her in the drawing room by wearing a see-through negligee and saying, 'Come on, Eva.'[3] The recollection is the first to suggest Margaret was bisexual, as, particularly in her later years, she was known to favour younger men;[4] a pastime that brought both success and failure, and placed her sexual preferences on a spectrum that offered no ambiguity.

Margaret took heed of the psychic who predicted George would not live long and summoned her chauffeur to drive her to the London Clinic. Jane had arrived before Margaret, although she was forbidden to enter the room by the nurse in charge, and recalled being pushed aside by Margaret and told to get out. Moments later Margaret emitted a loud shriek, and Jane knew that George was dead. 'You will never see my father, alive or dead,' Margaret reputedly said to Jane, before leaving with her chauffeur. A few days later Margaret dispatched her father's solicitor with a letter informing Jane she was not welcome at the funeral, but she attended with her brother and sat in the widow's pew. Nor was Jane entitled to anything from George's estate, as she had signed a deed of separation and received a £20,000 settlement. Although Jane accepted that George had written her out of his will, she fought for her right to inherit his Cable Beach house, as under a Bahamian dower law a widow is entitled to her late husband's property. Margaret contested Jane's claim, resulting in a legal battle that continued for fifteen years and eventually ruled in Jane's favour.

★

Prior to Margaret and Ian's divorce hearing the court cases that were to follow offered a sense of what was yet to come. The first occurred when Margaret was in the Bahamas, and in her absence her lawyers settled the case against Lady Jeanne Campbell. She was suing her estranged stepdaughter for damages relating to trespassing into Upper Grosvenor Street with Ian, when they had pinned her to the bed and stolen her diary. It was settled out of court and a substantial sum was paid to Margaret.

The swiftness of the case against Jeanne, and it having gone in Margaret's favour, had perhaps given her false hope. The Yvonne MacPherson case, which had dragged on for three years, was finally heard on 2 May 1960, at the Queen's Bench Division. Mr Gilbert Beyfus QC represented Yvonne; he was an elderly man and terminally ill, and, according to Margaret, 'this was his last case and he was clearly determined to make the very most of it'. Prone to melodramatic speeches, Mr Beyfus told the jury of the differences between the women, drawing on their physical appearances: 'Mrs MacPherson is a comparatively humble person. The duchess is a far more dazzling figure … the possessor of great wealth and great beauty, and who has become, and is, a poisonous liar.'

Ian testified against Margaret, and when cross-examined he admitted to giving Yvonne confidential documents with a view of their contents being 'useful to her in an action against my wife'. He read from a letter, dated March 1957 and sent from

Sienna during a holiday with Margaret: 'My dear, Yvonne, you were right. M took the bait and relayed the message within hours.' M was shorthand for Margaret, and in the letter, Ian had also called her 'Satan', though he admitted he could not recall what the bait was. It was hardly surprising to Margaret that her husband had betrayed her, as she knew of his involvement with Yvonne from the beginning. However, the evidence that was given by her friends Magda Buchel and Diana Wolkowicki came as a shock, and their testimonies served to influence the jury.

Magda confirmed she had been privy to Margaret's slanderous remarks about Yvonne, and that she had advised Margaret to stop it, as it would get her into trouble. Furthermore, Ian said he advised Margaret to listen to Magda, but Margaret said: 'I don't listen to anybody.' Diana testified that Margaret had telephoned her in the spring of 1959, asking her to make a false statement claiming they had spoken on the telephone on 18 April 1957. The date was a significant one, for it was the day Margaret had sent the bogus telegram to herself. 'I have no reason to be here. I don't like it,'[5] Diana said. 'But I can't go through life having it on my conscience that a perfect stranger suffered because I gave false evidence.' After she had given evidence Diana went to her seat and broke down in tears. Dr Petro was then questioned about a telephone conversation he had heard between Margaret and Ian, in which she reputedly accused Yvonne of leaking information to the press. Years later, when Dr Petro's own misdoings came to light and he was imprisoned for prescribing illegal drugs, Margaret felt triumphant: 'I could not be sorry that the law caught up with him.'[6]

As the hearing drew to a close Mr Beyfus asked the jury, 'What sort of punishment ought to fall on a woman who has been so wicked as the duchess has been in the case?'[7] The jury delivered the verdict that Margaret had slandered Yvonne four times and libelled her once, and she was forced to pay £7,000 in damages and £3,000 in costs. Despite Margaret refusing to apologise and claiming she would fight Yvonne, she declined to step into the witness box or to say one word in her own defence. 'That evidence was to the effect that the duchess admitted sending a faked and forged telegram and in order to escape the consequences had committed perjury,'[8] Mr Beyfus said. Indeed Margaret had signed an affidavit swearing that she had not sent the telegram to Ian, a deceitful and illegal gesture done to protect her own interests and 'because everyone was ganging up on her and she had to fight back'.[9] But Margaret blamed Ian for her silence, as his testimony against her destroyed any fight she had left. 'I realised at last,' she said, 'I had been married for nine years to a man who had the devil in him.'[10]

A month later Ian's divorce petition was adjourned for twenty-eight days by Lord Wheatley QC in the Edinburgh Court of Session, due to his allegations about Margaret and the adultery she was said to have committed between 1955 and 1959. Ian claimed she had had affairs with three men but her lawyer, Mr C.E. Jauncey, emphasised that Ian could name only two. And so Ian also listed the pornographic photographs of Margaret and 'the headless man' as further evidence of her adultery. 'I shall spare her the indignities of what those photographs depict,' Lord Wheatley said at the time. 'In them, the persons were indulging themselves in a gross form of a sexual relationship.' Owing to the delay, and Margaret realising the evidence was stacked against her, she decided to cross-petition Ian and attempted to divorce him by naming her stepmother as a co-respondent. Both Ian and Jane denied the allegations of adultery, and she ordered her lawyers to sue Margaret for libel. Ian also tried to file a claim, but as he had lived with Margaret during the rumoured affair with Jane, he had no grounds to sue.

After Margaret filed her petition for divorce she left for a tour of South America, stopping first in New York to see her son, who was working there, and to meet with her trustee, Sir Charles Russell. 'I have always believed that travel is the best tonic when one is worried or upset,' she wrote in her memoirs, 'it inevitably takes your mind off your problems.' In New York Margaret's problems were intensified when she was telephoned by a hire-car company, offering her low rates in exchange for using her name for publicity purposes. She thought the black Cadillac that had been put at her disposal was old and dirty, and as a result, she used it three times before seeking other arrangements. The car, owned by an undertaker, had been bugged by Horace Schmahl, a lawyer and private investigator known as 'America's premier snoop', who had been hired by Ian's legal team to eavesdrop on Margaret's private conversations. However, in New York there was – and still is – a 'one-party law which forbids the wire-tapping and eavesdropping of private conversations'. Schmahl was arrested and pleaded not guilty, and was released on bail of £357. Despite this, Margaret sued him for £178,000 in damages, but the New York Supreme Court found him not guilty, as the tape recordings did not 'contain anything a bit embarrassing to the duchess'. Instead, it was Margaret who had to pay costs, amounting to £1,070.

Margaret's legal problems continued, and in the spring of 1962, she received a letter from Lord Wheatley, of the Edinburgh Court of Session, asking her to provide further substantial evidence of the alleged adultery between Ian and Jane. Having failed to do so, Margaret dropped her divorce action against Ian, as she said a vital witness who did not reside in the British Isles could not be relied on to attend the hearing in Edinburgh. Her lawyers learned of her decision moments before the court hearing on 29 May. It was, she said, 'naturally a great disappointment to me and to the people who have helped me'. In retaliation Jane ordered her lawyers to sue Margaret for libel, and to claim damages for:

Conspiracy to prefer and sustain by illegal means a false and malicious charge of adultery against her, to suborn and bribe a person, or persons, to give false proceedings based on such charge, to pervert by illegal means the course of justice in such proceedings and to injure her thereby.[11]

The case was settled a year later, in a hearing that took three minutes to rule in Jane's favour, and Margaret, who was absent, was ordered to pay £25,000 in damages, as well as costs. However it would seem Margaret was correct in her accusations, as years later Jane admitted to having an affair with Ian, though she emphasised it was after his divorce.

★

From 1956 until 1962 Margaret's life had been dominated by legal issues, and she was both the perpetrator and victim of costly lawsuits, particularly in her underhanded tactics to gather evidence against Ian. Although she was being sued for divorce on the grounds of adultery, which she denied, she was casting around for her next husband. Upon hearing that her friend Ian, the 13th Duke of Bedford, had become engaged to Nicole Schneider, Margaret sent him a cable, asking: 'Why have her when you can have me?'[12] Presumably Ian Bedford declined Margaret's offer, for during that period she met William 'Bill' Harrington Lyons, a rich American living in London and working as a sales director for Pan Am airlines, and the two began a clandestine affair. The secrecy was for both of their sakes, as Bill was married to a woman he described as emotionally unstable and who often threatened suicide when the topic of a separation presented itself. Many of Margaret's friends thought Bill was a nice, dependable man, content with standing aside and letting her star shine, but wary of forming attachments to others. Was it his unavailability that had attracted her to him, and would later inspire feelings of marriage? For although Margaret would soon be available to remarry, she enjoyed her courtesy title of duchess and would not have easily given it up. Bill, on his part, viewed their affair as a pleasant respite during a difficult period in his marriage, but he had no intentions of divorcing his wife. As for Margaret, she considered him her third husband.

Margaret and Bill travelled the world together and spent much of their time in Paris, away from the British press, who followed the scandal she had courted in recent years and the farcical undertones of the Argyll divorce. Interestingly, from 1963, Betty Kenward, the author of 'Jennifer's Diary', a social column that appeared in *Tatler*, and then *Queen*, took a stance against reporting on Margaret and blacklisted her from the magazine. Therefore in Bill, Margaret had an ally and thought he had been 'sent from heaven at the moment I needed him',[13] as he, being the son of a lawyer, advised her to defend herself and fight Ian's accusations, despite her daughter and friends wanting her to maintain a dignified silence. 'That was the most important consideration of all,' she said of protecting her children, 'but at the same time, a tremendous handicap.'[14]

*

After three and a half years of setbacks and postponements, the divorce hearing began at the Edinburgh Court of Session. Presiding over the case was Lord Wheatley, a Jesuit-educated Roman Catholic and a member of Clan Campbell on his mother's side, renowned for delivering harsh sentences for crimes involving sex. George Emslie QC represented Ian, and Walter Fraser QC acted on behalf of Margaret. The small courtroom was packed to capacity with individuals from the British and foreign presses sitting in the area normally reserved for the jury, and only twenty-three members of the public were admitted to the gallery. Ian was the first to give evidence, which he did while seated, as his counsel asked for him to be pardoned on medical grounds. He was cross-examined for five hours, with Mr Fraser objecting to Margaret's diary being used as evidence on the grounds of confidentiality, but Lord Wheatley rejected this and the diary was to remain the focal point of the hearing. When it was time for Margaret to be cross-examined by Mr Emslie, who swished his robes and shouted questions at her, she asked if it was necessary as she was neither deaf nor accustomed to being spoken to in such a manner. Lord Wheatley ordered Mr Emslie to lower his voice, and he adopted a gentle, differential approach which gave Margaret a false sense of security and encouraged her to make indiscreet remarks that destroyed her credibility. Her time in the box amounted to thirteen hours, and not once did she ask to sit or was offered a seat, unlike Ian. Recalling her time in the box, Margaret wrote in her memoirs that she did not stammer – her speech was clear, having been driven by anger – and she defended her right to keep a private diary and to protect its contents from public consumption.

In Margaret's latter diary, covering the period 1954–59, the letter 'B' appeared throughout, and Ian believed it stood for Sigismund von Braun. Contradicting Ian's system for identifying the men with whom Margaret had had affairs was the absence of a 'J' or a 'C', as he had also accused her of sleeping with John Cohane and Peter Combe. Therefore it was a small victory for Margaret when Lord Wheatley thought the diaries useful in establishing a timeline of her social activities (an *aide memoire*, as he called it) but lacking in substantial evidence regarding her infidelities. However, Lord Wheatley reminded the jury that it did not diminish the fact that Margaret had committed adultery, and that Ian, as her husband and with access to her home which he had once shared, was within his right to take such personal items to use as evidence. Referring to the latter diary, Lord Wheatley said: 'There was a deliberate raid on her house during the time they were living apart to recover that diary. The pursuer thought it would be useful to him as evidence of her infidelity.' In a final conclusion Lord Wheatley decided the diary should be submitted as evidence, as it reinforced his theory that it served as a guide to Margaret's wrongdoings, which he supported with her personal letters from Sigismund von Braun and John Cohane.

Of the three men named only Peter Combe denied the allegation of adultery and defended himself against Ian. And, of the three men, Margaret admitted to having an affair with von Braun, which she claimed happened between 1946 and 1947 and ended in 1950, before she married Ian. 'She seemed to think association with a married man, or indeed adultery with a married man, was not a serious breach of the moral code if the man was not happy with his wife,' Lord Wheatley said. Contradicting Margaret's admission, Ian suggested that telegrams and letters, often signed 'Sigis', were exchanged between Margaret and von Braun in 1956, and that she had written 'there are ghosts all around me'. Admitting to using the phrase in a telegram, Margaret also said it was an expression used by both herself and Ian, but offered no explanation as to what it meant. She might have attributed it to Inveraray Castle, renowned for its supernatural activity, or that Ian's staff were discreetly watching her and reporting back to him. As Margaret's letters from von Braun were not dated – she had accused Ian of tearing off the top parts of the letters – there was no proof they had an affair during her marriage. Furthermore, as Ian continued to live with Margaret until 1959, Lord Wheatley was satisfied he knew of her involvement with von Braun and had condoned it. Ian, on his part, said he was 'so shattered at finding the letters that everything else was excluded from [my] mind'. Satisfied that Ian was the victim in the marriage, Lord Wheatley drew on another theory, which implied 'there might be special circumstances for condonation constituting a general forgiveness of adultery with men unknown to her husband, such as the case of a wife who had embarked on a life of prostitution'.[15]

It was Margaret's diaries which fuelled the speculation that she had been unfaithful during the latter part of her marriage. Although at first glance they revealed little by way of Margaret's adulterous affairs, Ian concluded that she used the cryptic symbol of v to record when she had sexual intercourse. In her own defence, Margaret offered no explanation as to what v represented, except to deny his claims. However, Lord Wheatley read from one of John Cohane's letters to Margaret, which he said confirmed Ian's findings: 'I have thought of a number of highly intriguing things we might do, or that I might do to you.'[16] And, having had a brief sexual affair with Cohane in New York, Margaret was eager to continue it in Paris, evident from his letter: 'I am completely frustrated as to how we can get together. I would like to be with you in Paris – what a titillating idea – but I just can't get away.' In a diary entry, dated 13 January, Margaret wrote 'Jackie 9–10'. Both Lord Wheatley and Ian agreed that it suggested a tryst with Cohane, and the former was appalled that the two had supposedly met for intercourse in the morning; the early hour was emphasised to remind the jury of Margaret's promiscuity.

Although Cohane, a self-confessed 'wolf', did not deny his attraction to Margaret, his evidence did not correspond with her testament. It was noted they had met at a party in New York on 10 January 1956; Cohane said there were fifty guests present, Margaret claimed there were 200. At the party, he recalled Margaret was introduced to him by her former name, Mrs Sweeny, which Lord Wheatley doubted as 'no New York hostess would miss the opportunity of introducing a duchess to her guests'. He admitted to propositioning Margaret, as he was 'anxious to pursue the chastity of the woman', and that he had tried to 'date' her for lunch and dinner. As Cohane's letters to Margaret had indicated, they did have a brief affair, though Margaret said their meetings were platonic and occurred over the course of three days during her visit to New York with Frances. She admitted to inviting him to her suite, which she shared with Frances, and they had a drink and the following day he drove her to the airport. 'Not exactly a heavy romance,' Margaret said. However Cohane's memory of their time together differed from Margaret's: 'I never knew that such a short acquaintance could keep a hot flame burning so high for so long,' he wrote.

The third and most recent allegation of adultery was directed at Peter Combe, a former press officer for the Savoy Hotel and a man twelve years Margaret's junior. As Margaret knew his mother, Lady Moira Combe, she claimed their friendship was platonic and that he often escorted her to social gatherings after she and Ian had separated. On the evening of 13 July 1960, private detectives noted Combe's arrival by car at Upper Grosvenor Street; he entered the house and a moment later came out, and brought three dogs inside with him. Later in the evening Margaret and Combe went to the 400 nightclub and returned at 1.25 in the morning; he walked the dogs and left two hours later. The reason for his staying so long, Margaret explained, was due to the dogs making a mess of the house, which she and Combe tidied, and then had a nightcap. Dismissing her statement, Lord Wheatley found it difficult to believe that three dogs would have had the run of the house and that Margaret herself would clean up their mess when she had servants to attend to 'such an unpleasant chore'.[17] Furthermore on 23–25 September Ian accused Margaret and Combe of going to Spain, which they both denied and then admitted to being true, as she wished to buy land, though when questioned she could not remember the exact location, or her reasons for doing so. Margaret admitted Combe had access to her hotel room, as they often met there for a glass of champagne, but Lord Wheatley was convinced they had shared a bed. Therefore he ruled that Margaret and Combe did have an affair, and she was found guilty of committing adultery.

The final proof of Margaret's adultery, as Lord Wheatley reminded the jury, was the pornographic images in which she appeared. It was rumoured there were thirteen Polaroids in total, involving Margaret and two men, though on separate occasions. Denying that she was the woman in the photograph, Margaret recounted a social gathering in New York, towards the end of her marriage, when Ian exhibited pornographic postcards from his collection. 'I was horrified,'[18] she said, and recalled that her friends put on their coats and left. 'I can only deplore his taste and standards of value,' Lord Wheatley remarked. However Lord Wheatley concluded that such photographs, as in the ones taken of Margaret, would belong to a woman with a sex perversion, rather than a man with a similar interest. It was one thing for Ian to be intrigued by pornography and to exhibit his collection of postcards and photographs, but it was another thing for Margaret to depict what was usually reserved for such images.

At first, Margaret denied that she was the woman in the photograph, saying that it came from Ian's pornography collection, as he had similar images with the couples' heads cut off. On closer inspection, the woman was proven to be Margaret, identified from the back by her signature hairstyle and three-strand pearl necklace which had a diamond clap and was bought from Asprey. Finally admitting it was her, she also claimed the man was Ian, and that he had borrowed a Polaroid camera to specifically take the photographs. As the man was captured from the neck down, the only way Ian could prove it was not him was to have a medical examination, and 'he had to live with the humiliation of publicly declaring his lesser dimensions'.[19]

The identity of the headless man remained a topic of much speculation. Ian believed it to be Sigismund von Braun, others thought it could be either the Hollywood actor Douglas Fairbanks Jr, or Duncan Sandys, the Minister of Defence and Winston Churchill's son-in-law. After it became known that Sandys was attached to the scandal he offered the Prime Minister, Harold MacMillan, his resignation but it was refused. 'I was amazed that the Conservative Government could be so fragile as to be shaken by mere unsubstantiated rumour,' Margaret recalled in her memoirs. Although Sandys had wished to save his political party the embarrassment of being associated with the Argyll divorce and the rumours it spawned, he was not the headless man, for during the war he had stepped on a mine and underwent an operation to mend his legs, which had left him with scars. Whether Margaret meant to or not, she made a comment which intensified the rumours, stating that the only Polaroid camera in the country at the time had belonged to the Minister of Defence. Thus, she directed the suspicion to Sandys, who then admitted to being sexually involved with Margaret, even if he was not the man in the photograph. The same could be said for Fairbanks Jr, who was a frequent guest at Upper Grosvenor Street, and who 'was very busy with the girls'.[20] Fairbanks Jr rejected the theory that he was the man in the photograph, and he often threatened to sue if anyone said otherwise. 'But Fairbanks was the ultimate sexual swordsman,' his mistress, Christine Keeler, wrote. 'He wanted it all the time and in the circles I moved in there was never any doubt that he was the man in the photograph.'[21] Having lived and worked in Hollywood, and as a prominent player in the cinema industry, Fairbanks Jr possibly owned a Polaroid camera[22] and had brought it with him to England. Therefore he was an obvious choice, but having received a special knighthood and with a successful acting career, would he have risked it all by leaving incriminating photographs in Margaret's possession?

Both Duncan Sandys and Douglas Fairbanks Jr were accustomed to getting their own way with women and were aggressive in their propositions. Moira Lister, an actress who was close to Margaret, and who had worked with Fairbanks Jr and knew Sandys, recalled: 'After we had been in the taxi for about two minutes, [Sandys] lept on me, and I started struggling. And then I thought, Thank God it's a taxi and nobody knows it is me … It wasn't too long a drive and I was able to get away from him.' Under ordinary circumstances, Margaret, who was also sexually aggressive, welcomed such advances, though it was a consensual encounter. Her friend Barbara Cartland said:

> Every man wanted to go to bed with her and she wanted to go to bed with every man. And why not? There's nothing wrong with that. She did go from man to man. She didn't have love affairs which lasted a long time. I think men found her rather boring after a time.[23]

The Polaroid photographs, like the symbols in her diaries, were perhaps used out of context. Margaret never revealed who the headless man was, and in recent years it had been suggested it was Bill Lyons. For this to be true, the dates of Margaret's first meeting with Bill and their subsequent affair would have to be contradicted, as she met him in 1961 and Ian found the Polaroids in 1959. Was she hiding the fact that she and Bill were involved before 1959, thus protecting her own image and version of the truth, for in her memoirs she pleaded innocent to everything Ian had accused her of? Bill was, as she wrote, 'the one man, ironically, whom my husband might have named in the divorce, but never did'. Was this a hint at who the headless man was, or merely an absent-minded remark? 'It was clear, as a seasoned liar, she was unchanged in her private whitewash campaign,' Charles Castle wrote of Margaret's sanitised version of the truth. Her writing of her affair during the divorce proceedings could have been a jibe at Ian, for as superior as he behaved and the power he exerted over her, he did not know of Bill.

Had Ian been aware of Bill, he could have bypassed a lengthy divorce case and named one man in the suit. That was not Ian's style, as he enjoyed watching Margaret suffer. 'Ian was like a spider,' she said; he had merely set the traps and she had walked into them. There was also the fact that Bill never came to Upper Grosvenor Street, as Margaret could not risk a private detective noting his visits or a member of her staff betraying her, as two of her secretaries had previously done. There was one thing that could not be misconstrued and that was the setting of the photograph, taken with the self-timer in her art deco bathroom, its mirrored wall displayed clearly even if Margaret's likeness was blurred. In his pursuit of evidence, Ian listed the numerous men Margaret associated with, and with whom he thought she had had an affair. Of the eighty-eight suspects, all taken from Margaret's dinner party guest lists, Ian deduced the man in the photograph was Sigismund von Braun. The conclusion had been reached, not by an in-depth investigation, but by two factors: the commercial release of the Polaroid camera and the timing of Margaret's association with von Braun. Margaret never disclosed the identity of the headless man. As with Ian's list of the men she reputedly had affairs with, and knowing that he was wrong, her concealing who the man was might have given her a sense of control.

There was a possibility that Ian's findings were wrong, as the first Polaroid camera was made available in America in 1948, and Margaret happened to be there at the time and could have easily bought one, or had one sent to London. What Ian and the jury did not know was that during Margaret's romance with Joe Thomas, beginning in 1947 and ending in 1948 after he married Poppi de Salis, the two of them had taken explicit Polaroid photographs. The setting was a balcony in London, possibly Upper Grosvenor Street, and two of the prints were in Joe's possession and possibly never saw the light of day. They were discovered by Joe's 12-year-old son, Michael, while he was looking through his father's bureau and noticed a brown envelope. 'One was of a good-looking woman with dark hair and a confident gaze; the other was of my father. Both were what is today delicately described as "full frontal". Nothing left to the imagination.'[24] Could the photographs Ian had previously found behind a bookcase at Upper Grosvenor Street have been taken in 1948 and hidden there by Margaret who, over the years, had forgotten about their existence? Had she been in the habit of taking sexually explicit photographs with the men in her life then surely Ian would have had similar photographs and could have framed her as early as 1955, when their marital problems first arose, and without the effort of ransacking her house for evidence.

Ian was granted a divorce on the grounds of Margaret's adultery with Peter Combe, though she continued to deny having an affair with him and he echoed her sentiments. 'I have absolutely nothing to say,' said Combe, 'if I had anything to say at all it would be full of four-letter words.'[25] The 50,000-word judgement took three hours and ten minutes to read, with Lord Wheatley relishing the theatrics and pausing several times to sip from a glass of water. It was a treatise of a warring couple, a he-said-she-said account of an embittered marriage, recalling Ian's drinking, Margaret's socialising, their joint accusations of adultery, and how Ian had gained his evidence and achieved the upper hand over Margaret. In the final damning verdict, Lord Wheatley declared Margaret was 'a highly-sexed woman who had ceased to be satisfied with normal relations and had started to indulge in what I can only describe as disgusting sexual activities to gratify a basic sexual appetite'. Margaret, when asked of her views on Lord Wheatley, said: 'God knows he was an old bastard.'[26]

On the day the verdict was to be heard Margaret was in Paris with Bill. Far from a defeatist move, it provides an insight into her character; as with most things, she did not consider the consequences or that they could be far-reaching. She expected to win, and had bought a new red feathered hat to celebrate; by contrast, Ian was planning a celebratory bonfire with his servants at Inveraray. 'It couldn't be much worse,' her lawyer said over the telephone. 'I've never in my life heard such a cruel judgement.' As Margaret listened to a summary of Lord Wheatley's verdict she knew her world was disintegrating around her. Although her reputation never recovered, she evoked admiration from the women in the public gallery, who wrote to express their 'admiration for your courage in standing in the witness box and speaking so eloquently and bravely in your own defence … You touched our hearts. We have watched and listened with sincere sympathy for you'.

Margaret was guilty of committing adultery, the same way that Ian, too, was guilty of it. For the past two years, Ian had been involved with Mathilda Mortimer, an American divorcee over twenty years his junior, whom he married on 15 June 1963, three weeks after his divorce from Margaret was finalised. As Margaret's financial situation was healthier than Ian's she was ordered to pay seven-eighths of the costs, and in turn, he had to pay one-eighth. 'I feel that as a woman,' she said, 'I have the right to defend my fair name without having to pay vast costs.'[27] At £50,000 it made records for being the costliest bill in Scottish legal history.

The divorce did not signal the end of Margaret's legal problems. In June 1963 the headless man photographs were re-examined by Master of the Rolls, Lord Denning, who had been asked by Harold MacMillan to investigate an affair between John Profumo, the Secretary of State for War, and Christine Keeler, a showgirl, who was also involved with Yevgeny Ivanov, naval attaché to the Russian Embassy. Coincidentally, or not, Keeler had been introduced to the Establishment by the society osteopath, Dr Stephen Ward, at Cliveden, once the setting of Margaret's adolescent shame. Due to the allegations that Margaret had had an affair with Duncan Sandys, and due to her friendships with high-ranking Cabinet ministers, she was deemed a potential security risk. Lord Denning sent for the Argyll divorce papers and asked to interview Margaret, which she agreed to on the condition he came to her house and their conversation remained confidential. Their exchange was an informative one, as far as Margaret's knowledge of social gossip was concerned, but as Lord Wheatley had previously attested, her version of events could not be trusted. Viewing it as something of a respite to her own troubles, Margaret wrote to a friend that 'they all ought to thank God' for the Profumo scandal, as it 'gave people something else to think about'.[28]

It was the explicit photographs of Margaret and the headless man that Denning took an interest in, and the fact that they were taken with a Polaroid camera; he questioned if such a piece of equipment could be used to undermine the British Government. Using the piece of paper the photographs were wrapped in, Denning studied the handwriting, written entirely in capital letters, and asked the suspected men to visit his chambers and sign their name upon arriving. At first glance Sandys's handwriting did not match, and he had also agreed to have a medical examination to prove his innocence, as Ian had done months before. Then Fairbanks Jr arrived and signed his name, and his handwriting matched what was written on the paper, and Denning was confident he had solved the headless man mystery. 'The writing was exactly the same so I was able to say who it was,' Denning said. However, it could have been a coincidence, for there was a possibility the author of the suggestive captions was not the figure in the photograph, and Keeler, who was having an affair with Fairbanks Jr, said he denied any involvement. Although Denning was certain of his findings he did not pursue the matter, despite Keeler being cast as a Mata Hari figure. If Margaret's sex life had made legal history in Scotland and shocked a nation between 1959 and 1963, then it was Keeler's two-timing of a British politician and a Soviet diplomat that brought down the Establishment. Harold MacMillan resigned as Prime Minister, John Profumo left government, Stephen Ward committed suicide, and Keeler, much like Margaret though without the security of a trust fund, was forced into a shame-ridden exile. Failing to understand the severity of Lord Denning's enquiry, Margaret referred to it as 'the minor incident'.

Something which Margaret did not view as a minor incident was Ian's intention to serialise his memoirs in *The People* newspaper. He also sold the rights to publish his and Margaret's private letters and a report on her physical and psychological health, reputedly forged by Dr Petro. The first article, published on 15 November 1964, detailed Ian's life with Margaret, offering glimpses of her temperament and the fragility of her ego, which he thought was propped up by her own self-importance. He described her haughtiness when they were out in public; her dislike of his familiarity with shopkeepers and waiters, of whom she classed as 'small people'. And he wrote of her obsession with fame, and how if a morning newspaper failed to mention her name in the social columns she would become upset, or if they wrote something unfavourable she would hit him over the head, ordering him to wake up and demand that he sue the reporter.

Margaret appealed to the Chancery Court judge, Mr Justice Ungoed-Thomas, for an *ex-partie* injunction to prevent Ian from publishing intimate details of their married life, which her solicitor, Sir Andrew Clarke, called 'a scurrilous and vindictive attack'. In Margaret's statement, she said: 'During a number of years before our marriage began to deteriorate my ex-husband and I had a very close and intimate relationship in which we freely discussed with each other many things of an entirely private nature.'[29] A writ was sent to Oldhams Press, publisher of *The People*, and its editor R. Stuart Campbell was ordered to send Ian's articles to Margaret's solicitor, who found the contents in 'breach of marital confidence'.[30] The application for an injunction was heard on 17 November and was granted a month later, on the grounds that 'a relationship more intimate can hardly be conceived of than the relationship based upon mutual trust and confidences between husband and wife'. Of the six articles that were to be serialised only four were permitted to be published, as they did not infringe on Margaret's privacy. The judgement became known as the Argyll Law.

During the years that Ian sought revenge on Margaret and in his final triumph over her in the divorce court, he had compromised the most precious thing to her: her public image. But it would seem that Margaret would have the last laugh, for after Ian's attempt to reveal the secrets of their marriage, the committee members of White's Club decided his behaviour was in bad taste and they voted him out. The chairman, Mr David Stacey, wrote to Ian and invited him to resign before they expelled him, and with a heavy heart, he chose the former. 'It must have been a bitter moment for him,' Margaret said, without an ounce of sympathy. 'I can still remember the day in 1950 when he nervously paced up and down the library at Inveraray waiting to hear if he had been elected as a member.'[31] She had lost the battle, but won the war.

14

'Here Comes a Brand
New Woman'

After the curtain drew to a close on the Argyll saga, Ian and
Margaret went their separate ways. There was a newfound element of stability in Ian's life, inspired by his fourth wife, Mathilda,
whose interests in philosophy and politics were a contrast to his
hedonistic past. Although Ian and his wife were to suffer the loss
of a child, when their baby daughter was born in 1968 and lived
for only a few days, he eventually found peace during the last
years of his life in France. Margaret, too, was eager to move on
from her marriage to Ian, and she declared: 'I don't want people
to think that even after the divorce I spent all my time in the law
courts. That was bad enough. I want them to think, *here comes a
brand new woman.*' It was a contradictory thing to say, and typical
of Margaret, for she did not change her way of life and broke
twenty of her father's trusts to ensure she received her inheritance, estimated at £2 million, in full.

Life, however, continued to change around Margaret. By the
mid-1960s Margaret's relationship with Frances had become
strained, which many believed to have been the consequence
of her forged letters denouncing Ian's sons as illegitimate and

the lies she had told, resulting in numerous libel suits. Although Frances had attracted unwanted attention in her marrying a non-Catholic and a divorcee, she was a private individual who did not court publicity. Nor did Frances want her children to be associated with Margaret's behaviour and the scandal that seemed to follow her; therefore they did not have a relationship with their grandmother. 'I can't imagine not wanting to meet your grandmother once, bad or good, can you?' Margaret remarked. 'There's no great story behind it,' said a source who was close to both women. 'Margaret was a nightmare of embarrassment to her daughter. It's as simple as that. Frances is a staunch Catholic and a very private person, and she couldn't stand all that ghastly publicity anymore.'[1] And so mother and daughter were to become estranged for several decades. They reputedly encountered one another at a cocktail party, and Margaret tapped Frances on the shoulder and said, 'Hello, I'm your mother,' to which Frances replied, 'I remember,' and turned away.

There were no such ill feelings between Margaret and Brian, who was said to be 'one of her stoutest defenders'.[2] In the spring of 1965 Brian was involved in a car accident and Margaret cut short her trip to Paris and flew to New York to be at his bedside. 'This, of course, made my blood run cold,' she recalled in her memoirs, after she learned that Brian's Porsche motor-car was hit by a lorry towing a pantechnicon, and that he was almost crushed to death. Having undergone several operations to repair his 'smashed right side', he left hospital months later and went to London to recuperate at Margaret's house before returning to New York in the New Year of 1966.

After Brian's recovery, Margaret began an extensive period of travelling. 'Luckily I have no fear of travelling alone – in fact, I would much prefer to be on my own than with an irritating companion,' she said.[3] It appeared she had no choice but to travel alone as, on a trip to Egypt the previous year, Bill Lyons was photographed next to her at the airport and his name and profession were also printed.

It was hardly the air of discretion he wished to maintain, and perhaps Margaret thought history might repeat itself in Cairo and he would propose, as Fulke Warwick had done decades before. On her latter solo trip, she flew to Los Angeles and was entertained by George Getty, son of her friend J. Paul Getty, a man ten years her junior and with whom it was rumoured she was having an affair. 'I have known the duchess for some time,' George Getty said. 'There is no question of a marriage at present. I'm still married, although legally separated.'[4] From Los Angeles, Margaret went to Mexico City, and on to Buenos Aries, Chile, and Guatemala, where she discovered a minor revolution and an election were taking place. She also went to South America, visiting the countries she did not see on her 1961 tour. The three-month trip concluded in Houston, Texas, where she was received by her friends Riccy and Luba di Portanova, leaders of Texan society, who treated her like royalty and arranged for her to see the secret Gemini spaceship control centre at Clearlake City and to meet its astronauts, including Neil Armstrong. At the end of Margaret's stay, the mayor of Houston presented her with the Freedom of the City, an honour given 'only to rather special people'. The mayor said: 'The duchess's arrival created a fantastic stir here. Her impact was bigger than the Beatles. We feel that to give her the freedom of our city was the least we could do to show our admiration.'

After travelling around the Americas Margaret embarked on a tour of the East, stopping first in Ceylon, and enjoying a ceremonious welcome, as Lord Mountbatten was also on the flight and the well-wishers had turned out to see him. In her memoirs, she rattled off a few anecdotes about her travels; the people she had met ('I met the Prime Minister Dudley Senanayake and many of the Government officials'), the places she had seen ('I saw the Caves of Ellora and Ajanta … I went to Agra to see the Taj Mahal'), but it was nothing compared to her experiences of the late 1940s, after her divorce from Charlie Sweeny, when she travelled alone and fell in love, and regained her independence.

Although Margaret protested that she was not running away from her problems, she knew she needed to create distance between herself and Bill, as he kept leaving her to return to his wife. 'He didn't have the courage to, you know, get out,' Margaret said. In fact, she thought Bill had no moral courage at all, and his indecisiveness prompted her to feel insecure, not in his love for her, but of his permanency in her life. During her stay in Cambodia, she could no longer bear the feelings of loneliness and displacement, and she flew home to confront Bill, only to discover he was no longer on the scene. Having spent six years with Margaret, travelling the world and advising her during her divorce from Ian, Bill left her a note, thanking her for their time together. 'I would have married him within five minutes if he had been free,' Margaret said. They never saw one another again.

*

For the first time in years, Margaret's private life was comparatively quiet. She turned her attention to good deeds, an indication of the caring side to her personality that many of her admirers spoke of. The first of several causes was the Bleakholt Animal Sanctuary in Lancashire, whose appeal she found in her wastepaper basket, and the photographs of the many animals who faced euthanasia touched her heart. All her life Margaret was an animal lover; as a child, she had dreamed of living in a house surrounded by kennels and stables for old and abandoned animals. Now, at the age of 56, her ambition was to be realised in the form of becoming the patron and president of the sanctuary after she paid off its debts of £9,000 and founded an Appeals Committee to raise money for its upkeep. It was far from self-glorification, as many believed it to be after the press photographed Margaret at the sanctuary and wrote of her work there, for she took a genuine interest in the animals' welfare and was instrumental in turning around the fortunes of the sanctuary. Years later, when she reflected on her work with Bleakholt, she called it 'an act of God'.

Margaret's next endeavour would attract controversy and place her at the centre of yet another scandal. In 1968 she decided to adopt a child, a term she preferred to use despite there being no legal arrangement between herself and the parents. There was no rational explanation for this – even Margaret herself said it was a childhood dream, much like her stables of animals, and she wanted to care for 'six starving orphans'. As she was in her late fifties she rejected her original idea of adopting an orphan from India, as she was 'not prepared to have the whole nursery business again'.

It was Margaret's friend Father Andrew, a former chaplain to the Archbishop of Canterbury, who suggested she choose an English child and pay for their schooling and expenses until they came of age. The idea appealed to her, as she could take an interest in a child without the responsibility of parenting them. So, she approached Philip Rutter, the headmaster of Kinwarton House, a private preparatory school in Worcestershire, whom she knew as he had formerly invited her to become a patron of the school. 'Look out for a boy who is poor, and intelligent,' Margaret ordered Father Andrew and Philip Rutter. After her search rendered fruitless, Rutter told Margaret of a teacher at his school, a Mrs Jean Gardner, who was the mother of two young boys at a state school, and who was struggling to make ends meet on her teaching wage and elderly husband's pension. Although Margaret's original plan was to find one boy, she met the brothers, Jamie and Richard, aged 9 and 7 respectively, and thought them 'terribly sweet, well mannered, dear little boys'. An informal agreement was drafted by Margaret's solicitors and it was decided that she would oversee the children's education at Kinwarton House and pay for any expenses relating to their well-being until they were 21. She asked Jamie and Richard to call her 'Aunt Margaret', and it was agreed they would go to London during the school holidays and stay with her. 'Who pays the piper calls the tune,' their father, Howard Gardner, said, though he dismissed any suggestion that he and his wife benefited financially from the arrangement. 'The duchess has been a fairy godmother in this,' he told the *Daily Mirror*.

However, Worcestershire County Council and senior governors of Kinwarton House opposed Margaret's adoption of the Gardner boys and the unwanted press attention it brought to the school. She accused the chair of the governors of Kinwarton of making defamatory comments regarding her character, and tried to sue, but was unsuccessful as nothing could be proved. Questions were raised in the House of Commons by Leo Abse, a Labour representative for Pontypool, about Margaret's suitability as a mother figure, due to her age, marital status, and the scandal that followed her in recent years. There was also the conflicting interest that Philip Rutter played, as both headmaster of the school and his role as an intermediary in a third-party adoption. An appeal was made to Margaret Thatcher, the Minister of Education, to investigate the so-called adoption. 'They must have thought I was an axe-murderess,' Margaret said, thinking the enquiry unnecessary. She failed to understand the situation from an outsider's perspective, that a headmaster could source two children for a rich and influential woman, and by coincidence those children would be enrolled at his fee-paying school. If money was not Rutter's motivation, then his admiration for Margaret was, as he was captivated by her celebrity, and applauded her decision to adopt the Gardner boys.

It then became clear that Margaret had not adopted Jamie and Richard, as she had previously stated, and that no substantial legal agreement existed, except for a contract that forbade the Gardners from speaking to the newspapers. The latter was done to protect Margaret's image, as many believed she had bought the children off of their struggling parents. 'I drink Scotch instead of beer,' Mr Gardner had told a *Daily Mirror* journalist, who had caught him off-guard at a pub, before the stipulation of not talking to the press was enforced. Margaret did not adhere to her rule and she gave several interviews to the press. 'I don't expect to love them immediately,' she said of the children. 'You don't love people just like that. You grow to love them. I'm sure I'll grow to love these boys, and they may return my affection.' The statement attracted criticism, particularly in Jean Rook's column for the *Daily Express*: 'It's all too glossy. It's all too like popping into Harrods and choosing a couple of ornaments that'll look good either side of your Adam fireplace.' Fearing that outsiders would think Jamie and Richard were her illegitimate grandsons, Margaret explained why she had used the term adopt rather than sponsor, which she said was an American term and, as such, she did not feel comfortable applying it to her situation. Thus many were misled in their estimation that Margaret had taken on the parental responsibility of the children.

Although many doubted Margaret's motives she upheld her part of the agreement, though she ended it when Jamie and Richard turned 16 rather than 21, as, years later, she encountered monetary problems. She paid for their schooling and during the holidays they visited her in London for outings to the theatres and museums. 'Thank you for the lovely time we had,' Jamie wrote to her, 'I enjoyed it all very much, especially going to Harrods and choosing my bicycle.' Despite what her naysayers thought of her, the Gardner boys had known only kindness from Margaret and continued to speak highly of her after the arrangement ended. On her part, she was realistic about her role in their lives, saying that 'after they reach the age of twenty-one, I end'. In her contradictory way, she wanted to involve herself in a financial way, without forming an emotional attachment.

*

Although Margaret despised Ian for the pain he had caused her, she continued to gravitate toward the Argyll legacy. In 1968 her attention was piqued by a newspaper article reporting on the Labour government's intention to disband the Argyll and Sutherland Highlanders for economic reasons. Although military history was not high on Margaret's list of interests, she contacted Lieutenant-Colonel Colin Mitchell, who was involved in a campaign entitled Save the Argylls. Known as 'Mad Mitch' because 'he was a compulsive rebel who did mad things'; in 1967 he led the Argyll and Sutherland Highlanders into Aden, accompanied by fifteen regimental bagpipers playing 'Scotland the Brave', and while reoccupying Crater, a district in Aden City that was under British rule, he used the Chartered Bank building as his headquarters, with snipers on the roof, shooting at Arab militants. 'It was like shooting grouse,' Mad Mitch said, 'a brace here and a brace there.'[5] The campaign did not want money but a million signatures protesting the disbandment, and Margaret, who drew on her Scots heritage, offered to help. It also satisfied her ego that Ian declined to become involved with the campaign, regardless of having served with the regiment during the Second World War. 'I was amazed at how empty Ian's life must have become,'[6] she said of his lack of patriotism.

Placing an advertisement in *The Times* and the *Daily Telegraph*, Margaret invited the public to sign the petition and, if they wished to do so, they could find her at Scotch House, a shop in Knightsbridge, on 1 August from eleven in the morning until five in the afternoon. In her memoirs, she feigned surprise when news reporters and television cameras arrived on the day to film her entering Scotch House and meeting the public, who appeared in their droves. The Queen Mother's piper, Major Leslie de Laspee, signalled Margaret's arrival with 'The Campbells Are Coming'. It was part of a strategic publicity campaign, invented by Margaret and Mad Mitch, both natural publicists who attracted attention, whether good or bad. 'They were terrified of him. They were terrified of me. They were terrified of us both,' she recalled. She held a luncheon for Mad

Mitch and invited fifty of her friends, among them Max Aitken and Vere Harmsworth, both successors to their fathers' newspapers. Then she had an idea to approach the Commonwealth for signatures, and she telephoned the Associated Press and asked them to run articles in their countries' newspapers. That, too, proved successful but Margaret wanted to create more publicity. She appealed to the Scots in America, and a number of signatures were collected in St Andrews Clubs and Thistle Clubs and sent to her in London. Comparing her success as a theatrical show, she said: 'You must draw the curtain down.'

The petition ended at Christmas, and twenty-two whisky cartons were sent from Scotland to London, filled with signatures and escorted by four army generals. Margaret was at Euston Station to greet the train, which had broken down en route and arrived an hour late. 'We had a hilarious time,' she said, an ironic statement for someone accused of having no sense of humour. During the delay on the tracks, the army generals had got drunk, and they off-loaded the whisky cartons to the strains of 'Glendaruel Highlanders' by a piper who was also drunk. The cartons were taken to the Houses of Parliament and locked in a vault, before the petition was officially made. Arriving to watch the scene, Margaret and Mad Mitch listened to the cheers from the Conservatives and boos from Labour as boxes were presented before the Speaker of the House. The Prime Minister, Harold Wilson, was defeated and agreed the Argyll and Sutherland Highlanders could remain. 'Ian should have done something for the regiment, for God's sake,' Margaret said. 'He should have done what I did.'[7]

★

Ian was never far from Margaret's thoughts and, as throughout their marriage, she entertained the idea that his hatred toward her was inspired by love. 'I don't think Ian ever loved anybody the way he loved me,' she remarked. In her mind, love was tangled up with jealousy and irrationality, and she often confused sex with love, and vice versa. There were times when Margaret was motivated by revenge, particularly when she learned Ian and his wife were living in Paris and he had become a tax exile, though he was eager to reinstate his membership at White's Club. She telephoned her male friends who were also members of the club and blocked Ian's request. Years had passed since the divorce and within that period, Margaret and Ian were to meet only once and by coincidence, at the Ritz Hotel in Paris, where they briefly locked eyes with one another and, after a moment of recognition, looked away. She never saw him again.

In 1973 Ian suffered a stroke in France and was flown to the Western General Hospital in Edinburgh. A Scottish Labour Member of Parliament protested the notion that Ian could live as a tax exile abroad and return to Scotland to use the National Health Service. However, Ian's son, the Marquis of Lorne, argued that his family had paid sufficient taxes throughout the years and therefore Ian was within his rights to use the state's healthcare. After the controversial argument, Ian was transferred to the Royal Scottish Nursing Home, where he died a short while later. Margaret followed the status of Ian's health with keen interest, and on the morning of his death she claimed she awoke early and telephoned the nursing home, to be told that he had died at five o'clock that morning. 'Apparently he died alone, so I may have been the first person to hear of his death,' she wrote. Afterwards, Margaret gave a dinner party to celebrate, not Ian's death, but the strange sense of freedom she had felt from him dying. Now she thought she could speak freely of their time together without the fear of being sued.

'Why exactly did we fail, Ian and I? What poisoned our life together?' Margaret asked. As with many aspects of her life, she did not understand what she had done wrong, or the part she played. 'Unfortunately I am only too aware that I am still the same gullible, impulsive, over-optimistic "Dumb Bunny", and I have given up hopes of any improvement.'[8]

Old Foe

As the 1970s progressed Margaret was faced with a new predicament: she was running out of money. 'None of our generation expected to live for so long,' her friend, Brodrick Haldane, said. 'Furthermore it was unthinkable she should attempt to change her lifestyle.' During one of her few money-saving schemes Margaret travelled second class instead of first, an experience she did not wish to repeat. 'I don't think I'll do that again,' she said. 'There were children in the carriage.'[1] She stopped her financial arrangement with Jamie and Richard Gardner, as she could no longer afford their school fees, but paid for their education until they were 16. Although the boys were grateful for the opportunities Margaret had given them Jamie, in particular, thought she was naive in her plan for their futures. 'I think she probably thought there wasn't much point in boys like us going on to university,' he said. The truth was, she could no longer support them.

In an attempt to remedy her financial situation Margaret accepted an advance of £22,000 to write her autobiography, *Forget Not*, its title a translation of the Argyll family motto, *Ne Obliviscaris*. Written by three ghostwriters, Margaret's sanitised version of her life story sold poorly upon its release in 1975. The reviews were equally dismal, with Alistair Forbes writing: 'Her father may have been able to give her some fine earrings, but nothing to put between them.' Restricted by legalities and the fear of being sued, Margaret revealed little about her divorce from Ian and she did not mention the explicit Polaroid photographs. There was a time when being a social pariah was a commodity, and now, as she approached old age in a world that had been enlivened by the 'permissive society', she was a figure from the past. 'That tart Margaret Argyll',[2] as she was unkindly called, appeared as a Norma Desmond character, clinging to forgotten splendour.

The scandal that was airbrushed from Margaret's memoirs was lurking behind the scenes, and like an old foe it had found her at her lowest ebb. Several years previously she had agreed to sell her memoirs to the *Sunday Pictorial* for £55,000, then a considerable amount for a newspaper serialisation, and one that did not include the infamous diaries or reveal the identity of the headless man. After its publication Lord Hailsham denounced Margaret in the House of Lords, calling her 'an affront to a Christian country', and Lord Francis Williams attacked her adulterous marriage to Ian in an article in the *New Statesman*. Margaret retaliated by airing her views in the *Sunday Mirror*, hinting that their lordships had no business talking about her marriage to Ian, despite her submitting her life story into the public domain. Ian, it should be noted, did not sue or serve her with an injunction, as she had done when he serialised his own memoirs in *The People*. The fee of £55,000 was reduced to £20,000 after paying her agent's commission and tax, and she sued her solicitor, Oscar Beuselinck, for wrongly advising her on tax matters. An action was presented to the High Court for the recovery of her tax and costs, as she felt her memoirs were personal property and should therefore be exempt from taxation. She also made enquiries about Beuselinck and his suitability as a solicitor, prompting Beuselinck to counter-sue on the grounds of defamation. The judge, Mr Justice Megarry, dismissed Margaret's case as 'silly' and ordered her to pay costs of £13,940.

There appeared to be no end to Margaret's misfortunes. Another instance of bad luck was the lease of her house, which was coming to an end; in recent years she had struggled with its upkeep. She came up with the idea to open her home three times a week to the paying public, an enterprise that was managed by Vincent Shaw, a successful theatrical agent and impresario whose clients included the singer Kathy Kirby and Sooty the puppet. Hoping to attract rich American tourists in groups of thirty at a time, Margaret set the fee at £7.50, which included a tour given by her butler and a glass of champagne with her afterwards in the panelled dining room or, weather permitting, the garden. Ever the star, Margaret planned to greet her guests on the staircase, wearing a couture gown, a white fox fur stole, and her signature three-strand pearl necklace. 'We all have to change our way of life these days,' she said of the venture; 'even duchesses feel the draught.'

Days before the official opening Margaret invited the press and several distinguished guests for a private tour. A few ambassadors accepted her invitation, but the Americans she hoped to attract had declined. 'It is not every day that Margaret, Duchess of Argyll invites me into her bedroom,' Paul Callan of the *Daily Mirror* wrote. 'What an old-fashioned bedroom,' the Conservative politician, Norman St John-Stevas, remarked. Duncan Sandys, a politician familiar with the rooms of her house, left before the tour commenced. Norman Hartnell, the man Margaret claimed to have made famous, said: 'Actually I was taken around one of the greatest houses in Britain only yesterday – the Queen showed me around Windsor Castle.'[3] Hartnell's comment echoed the sentiments of those who thought Margaret opening her home was a foolish decision; 'Her house does not have a £7.50 pulling power.'[4] Margaret disagreed. 'Intelligent people will want to see an interesting and historic house lived in by its owner. It's quite unusual for tourists to meet English people and see inside homes like this one.'[5]

It was a bitter result for Margaret, as four decades before she had attracted the public in their droves and was the belle of the ball wherever she went, and she never lost sight of the fact she had been a star. Brodrick Haldane recalled an occasion when she visited him in Edinburgh and he suggested they go for a walk. 'I can't,' she said. 'I haven't got the right clothes with me, and they might see me.' However, times had moved on, and although Margaret attracted headlines whether good or bad, the public did not turn out to tour her house. Tickets sales were poor, and she had no choice but to abandon her venture.

Life in London was no longer appealing and Margaret considered moving to America, a country she thought 'vital, exciting, warm-hearted'. A contrast to her current life and the feeling of displacement she felt in the modern world. 'I don't think anybody has real style or class anymore. Everyone's gotten old and fat,' she said in an interview with the *New York Times*. The plan to move to America did not materialise, and although the reasons are unknown, it can be assumed the main reason was financial. It was rumoured she would marry J. Paul Getty, a lifelong friend who had wanted to marry her in the 1940s, but he had recently become involved with Lady Ursula D'Abo, her friend and by coincidence her son-in-law's sister. However Getty vowed to never marry again, having been forewarned by a gypsy that he would die soon after, and Margaret was content with their arrangement of her hosting his parties at Sutton Place and entertaining his American friends when they came to London.

For a short period, Margaret could sustain a semblance of her old life. Having exhausted her options in increasing her income, she admitted defeat and did not renew the lease of Upper Grosvenor Street, but she would not change her way of life, despite the circumstances. In 1978 she approached Lord Forte, chairman of Trust House Forte, which owned 600 hotels, including the Grosvenor House Hotel, and negotiated a yearly rent of £20,000 for a two-bedroom penthouse apartment on the eighth floor. The reduced fee was given to her as Lord Forte thought her celebrity would add a touch of glamour to his hotel. She brought with her a maid, two poodles, and a few pieces of antique furniture. The second bedroom was converted into a dressing room and filled wall to wall with her couture gowns, kept in individual plastic covers, René Mancini shoes, silk underwear which she kept in satin envelopes and monogrammed with her initials and duchess's coronet, and forty hairpieces on wooden stands.

Although Grosvenor House was a luxurious setting it was clear that Margaret was living in reduced circumstances. She continued to hold court with gossip columnists, though it often backfired. Peter Tory went to interview her at her suite and wrote of the rickety plumbing ('a sound that resembled Niagara'), which echoed through Margaret's fireplace. 'How dare you,' Margaret said, after seeing Tory at a literary reception, 'write in your paper that you can hear men urinating in my fireplace.'[6] She also continued with her entrepreneurial scheme of opening her home, in this instance her suite, to the public and hosted cocktail parties for an admission fee of £15.95 per person, which included a glass of Buck's Fizz and clients could pay extra for a signed copy of her autobiography. There were dinner parties for friends, though on a smaller scale than her parties at Upper Grosvenor Street, and the guests were predominantly young men, homosexual, and enthralled by her pariah status. She sometimes mingled with the hotel guests and became offended if they failed to address her as 'Your Grace' or grant her the respect she thought she deserved as a duchess, albeit a divorced one.

The staff were also reluctant to bow to Margaret's demands, and on one occasion while watching a firework display, her hairpiece slipped from her natural hairline and an indiscreet waiter shouted, 'Your Grace, your wig is walking.' It was perhaps a cruel thing to do, but her behaviour did not endear her to the staff. Many thought Margaret rude and entitled, and few considered the predicament she was in and the stress it had caused her. Having grown up in a world where social hierarchies were paramount, and having been the star of the show for so long, she failed to acknowledge that such barriers were outdated. Rebelling against her behaviour, the hotel staff began to call her 'Mrs Argyll', which rattled her self-confidence and taught her a lesson in good manners, at her own expense. She agreed to be nicer to the staff, having been unaware that she was at fault, and their formality was restored. Despite a few thinking Margaret 'damn rude' and 'such a bitch',[7] those who were privy to her private self thought she was 'a remarkable, formidable, sweet, kind woman, with a very dry sense of humour'.[8] Her friend Virginia Cherrill, said: 'Margaret was not an especially intelligent woman. But you know, I never could help liking her, and she did say the funniest things.'[9]

Along with Margaret's domestic problems, there was a scandal which she was unaware of until a detective brought it to her attention. From 1976 until 1984, a middle-aged woman named Barbara Hendry posed as the illegitimate daughter of Margaret and Ian Campbell, claiming her birth was the consequence of a secret affair in the 1930s. The guise was an elaborate one, with Hendry cultivating an identity far removed from her Gorbals upbringing: she called herself the Contessa de Leone, spoke with a refined Swiss accent, and said she was raised by her grandmother in Switzerland. Her victims were an elderly couple, Edward and Joan Warner, who, over four years, gave her £50,000 which she promised to repay as soon as she could access her £6.5 million trust fund. To gain their trust Hendry spoke of shopping excursions with Margaret and recalled how her cami-knickers had fallen down in front of American soldiers who responded by whistling, prompting her to ask: 'Have you lost your dog or something?'[10] Thinking the story of Hendry's parentage could be true, the detective constable, Kim Booth, who was working on the case travelled to Grosvenor House to interview Margaret, whom he found 'quite chatty' when she understood the severity of the case, though at first, she had been dismissive of the fraudster, and she showed him her photo albums and gave him a copy of *Forget Not*, which he later discovered was signed 'To Mr Walden, October 1979'.[11] Eventually, Hendry was arrested and sentenced to four years in prison, having previously served fifteen months for a similar crime. Speaking to the press, Margaret said: 'People should learn to grow up and not be taken in by strangers.'[12]

★

During Margaret's later years at the hotel her most difficult relationships were with her live-in maids. The first, Edith Springett, who had replaced Kathleen Carpenter, would serve her for ten turbulent years. Whereas Carpenter was passive, Springett was a decade older than Margaret and challenged her when domestic issues arose, or when she felt her mistress was being imperious. Their rows were volatile, with Springett throwing a plate of biscuits at a guest and verbally attacking Margaret for her sexual indiscretions; among her favourite insults was to call her 'a silly old bitch' and 'a Mayfair whore'. Such insults were reserved for when Margaret had guests to dinner, during which Springett would stand behind her and give 'knowing winks'.[13] Letters were dispatched from Margaret's solicitors, Radcliffe and Co., asking Springett to desist from calling her names. It did little to discourage Springett's behaviour, and an incident saw Margaret finding her face down on the floor, having consumed too much whisky. Springett claimed she had suffered a heart attack, and other sources listed a broken leg. Either way, it had been Margaret's bedroom floor and Margaret's whisky, and Springett, in her late eighties, was dismissed soon after. Elderly, unemployed and homeless, Springett was placed in temporary accommodation at the Adam Rondale Hotel, until the City of Westminster Homeless Persons

Unit found her a flat in St John's Wood, where she died a short time later.

Although Springett had caused Margaret emotional distress, her next maid, Samira Elaadouli, would be accused of committing 'a grave breach of trust'.[14] The 25-year-old Elaadouli was employed by Margaret as a personal maid and given 'pocket money' (Margaret's words) of £50 per week, £20 of which was to pay for English lessons. 'To live in a five star flat, with your own room and bath and everything done for you? It is ample,' Margaret said, when asked if her payment was sufficient for the duties expected of Elaadouli. It was contradicted by Elaadouli, who claimed Margaret treated her poodles better than she treated her staff. Recalling Margaret's fondness for animals, and not necessarily people, Charles Castle wrote: 'She leaned down ... scooped [the dog] up and caressed it lovingly. This gesture illustrated an element of tenderness and caring, hitherto alien to her nature.'

However, Margaret was old and frail, and her friends believed the new maid had 'taken her for a ride'. This accusation was the result of a £6,000 telephone bill, run up by Elaadouli, who placed daily calls from Margaret's private line and the hotel switchboard to her family in Morocco and the Ivory Coast. Having not given Elaadouli permission to make outgoing telephone calls, Margaret dismissed her and contacted the police. A case was presented before Southwark Crown Court, in which Elaadouli said Margaret had given her permission but could not remember as she drank a tumbler of whisky in the evenings and was often forgetful. There had been rumours that Margaret was a heavy drinker, with whisky being her preferred tipple, but the contents of her ten-ounce tumbler was cold consommé. 'Oh no, not drunkenness, I can't stand it,' Margaret responded angrily, and she dismissed any notion that she was forgetful. The judge ruled in Margaret's favour and Elaadouli was given a year's suspended sentence, though Margaret was responsible for paying the telephone bill. It was to be her last visit to the courtrooms, a public arena she had known too well, and, as was a familiar theme with all of her cases, the financial implications were severe.

By then Margaret had exhausted her trust funds, and her entrepreneurial schemes did not pay off. She spoke of challenging her father's Nassau trusts, but nothing became of it, partly because Jane Whigham was entitled to George's Bahamian estate under a dower law. A financial opportunity presented itself in the form of a television role in a soap opera produced by Park Productions, entitled *The Legacy*, in which Margaret would appear as herself in a storyline that centred around an infamous woman. As with many of her schemes, however, it faltered before it began; Margaret would not be defeated and she demanded remuneration for the time she spent rehearsing her role. She went to Park Productions' office in central London and announced, 'I am sorry, gentlemen, I have come for my money,' and sat down and refused to move until they wrote a cheque for £10,000, the sum she was contracted to be paid. It was to be her last triumph.

The symbolic gesture of taking what was rightfully hers was to be a small victory for Margaret, but it was not enough to sustain her. After a decade of living at Grosvenor House she could no longer afford the rent on her apartment, so she moved to a smaller room and remained there for a few years. She earned a modest income by writing a gossip column for *Tatler*, entitled 'Stepping out with Margaret Argyll', which was eventually reduced from two pages to a small corner in the magazine, ending after two years as she struggled to spell the names of those on whom she reported.

It became clear that Margaret's mind was failing and she was placed under a Court of Protection Order, as she could no longer handle her affairs. She was also £26,000 overdrawn with Barclay's Bank, and they were suing her for non-payment. To his credit, Lord Forte, owner of the Grosvenor House Hotel, never evicted Margaret nor did he pursue the unpaid rent, but he could no longer keep her as a long-term resident, as his shareholders were expecting to see profits and he was losing money. Several years before, when Margaret realised her inheritance would not last, she arranged for Jamie Gardner to take a position at the hotel as a trainee manager. 'I think she probably thought that I would end up as managing director and look after her there,' he said. With her usual naivete, the plan seemed realistic to her, but in reality, it did not work. She finally left the hotel in 1990, through the side door to avoid the waiting press.

Although much of Margaret's future looked uncertain, this marked a period of reconciliation between herself and Frances, who, along with Brian, paid her bills and found her accommodation. After leaving Grosvenor House Margaret rented a self-contained flat from her friend, Lady d'Avigdor-Goldsmid (née Rose Bingham), but it was an unsuitable arrangement for she required a live-in nurse and maid, and the premises were too small. Frances and Brian then moved her to St George's Nursing Home in Pimlico, where Loelia, Duchess of Westminster had died a few months before, and the actress Evelyn Laye had recently moved in. There was a small room with a linoleum floor[15] and bars on the window, and, perhaps alien to Margaret, she had to share a bathroom with other residents. She had some comforts at hand: her pet poodle, Louis, who was ill and nervously chewed her wig,[16] three photographs of her father and her children, and a tray with her cosmetics laid out.

Despite Margaret's reduced circumstances her appearance never suffered. Every day she dressed in couture clothes, applied her make-up, and someone came to arrange her hair in its signature upswept style, propped up with a hairpiece. She seemed content in her own world, sitting in the entrance hall, watching visitors come and go. When a self-contained flat became available in another wing it was declined, as she enjoyed people-watching, even if she was unaware of her surroundings. A friend telephoned, hoping to visit Margaret, but she said: 'I can't see you now. I'm on the *Queen Elizabeth* and we're still three days from Southampton.' Perhaps the pain of the last few years had left her, and in her mind, she had reverted to her heyday, when the world was at her feet.

Until the day of Margaret's death, 25 July 1993, the standards of her youth remained, and when luncheon was served at twelve o'clock she refused to eat it. Only servants ate at midday, Margaret said, and she defiantly waited until one o'clock, by which time the food was cold. Until the end, she could, at least, take satisfaction in knowing she had the last word.

Notes

Chapter 1: Careless People

1. 'I was a luxury they could not afford,' Campbell, Margaret, *Forget Not* (London: W.H. Allen, 1975) p. 13.
2. Ibid., p. 3.
3. Ibid.
4. Also referred to as The Broome.
5. Margaret wrote that it was an Australian banking crisis; however, that occurred in 1893, long after David was forced to economise.
6. *The Edinburgh Gazette*, 5 June 1896.
7. Described as the 'Brilliant Whigham Brothers', they were: Sir Robert Whigham, a distinguished soldier who served in the Nile expedition of 1898, the Second Boer War, and in the First World War, who was knighted for his bravery; Jim Whigham, an author, magazine editor and amateur golfer; Gilbert Whigham, director of Burma Oil and British Petroleum; Charles Whigham, director of Morgan, Grenfall and Company; and Walter Whigham, chairman of Robert Fleming and Company, and director of the Bank of England. Among the daughters born to David and Ellen Whigham were Sybil and Molly, both distinguished golfers in the 1900s.
8. Approximately £550,000 in today's money, according to the Bank of England inflation calculator.
9. Records show that George Whigham arrived in Key West, Florida, on 21 January 1913, en route to Havana, Cuba.
10. Margaret wrote that her parents returned to Scotland, but shipping registers contradict this.

11. Scotland Births and Baptisms, 1564–1950.

12. 'It is the lowest of the slum class.' Breitenbach, Esther, *A Documentary History, 1780–1914* (Edinburgh: Edinburgh University Press, 2013), p. 99.

13. On the subject of family names it seemed they were often recycled, as Douglas Hannay was named after his paternal grandmother (in the seventeenth and eighteenth centuries Douglas was a female name) and it is interesting that Jim's daughter was named Sybil, presumably after his and George's sister, Sybil Harriet Whigham, who was a champion golfer.

14. Margaret called her mother 'fey', as in the Scots definition of believing in superstitions and appearing otherworldly.

15. Passenger lists leaving UK 1890–1960. Margaret wrote in her memoirs that she sailed on the *Lusitania*. Shipping lists show this not to be true, although her father sailed on the *Lusitania* to New York in 1911.

16. Helen listed Cuba as the country of her intended future residence. New York Passenger Lists and Arrivals 1911–12.

17. In shipping registers George Whigham's profession was listed as 'engineer' and 'banker', and then 'president'.

18. He was sympathetic to the suffrage movement; he also promoted socialism and was an early advocate of what became the Easter Rising, leading to Home Rule in southern Ireland. Hartley, Stephen, *The Irish Question as a Problem in British Foreign Policy 1914–18* (Basingstoke: Palgrave MacMillan, 1987), p. 56.

19. Castle, Charles, *The Duchess Who Dared* (London: Sidgwick and Jackson, 1994), p. 11.

20. 'Six out of ten left-handed children who had been taught to use the right hand were practically cured,' *Sunderland Daily Echo and Shipping Gazette*, 8 December 1913.

21. *Dundee Courier*, 21 June 1910.

22. *Liverpool Daily Post*, 2 October 1916.
    Lionel Logue was an amateur actor and elocution teacher. His self-taught methods relating to speech therapy were put into practice with First World War veterans. A deeply religious man, he left his native Australia for England, as he thought it God's will, and discovered his calling in speech therapy. His number of wealthy clients subsidised the treatment of his poor ones.

23. Castle, *The Duchess Who Dared*, p. 9.

24. Possibly Stramonium, said to cure neurological disorders; in recent years research has proven it can improve stammering.

25. 'Glasses are very disfiguring to women and girls.' Sherrow, Victoria, *For Appearance's Sake: The Historical Encyclopedia of Good Looks, Beauty*

and Grooming (Westport, CT: Greenwood Publishing Group, 2001), p. 108.

26. Shipping records show they often sailed without their servants, therefore Margaret was in the care of her parents and not servants.

27. UK Outward Passenger Lists, 22 September 1919.

28. UK Inward Passenger Lists, May 1920.

29. Ibid.

30. Miss Sarah Thordielle, born in the West Indies. 1891 Scotland census.

31. It appears Helen fired Margaret's nurse, Anne, who had travelled to England from New York with the family, for she does not return with them, and Winifred is listed as the nurse. UK Outward Passenger Lists, October 1920.

32. Campbell, *Forget Not*, p. 20.

33. Menzies, Grant-Hayer, *Mrs Ziegfeld: The Public and Private Lives of Billie Burke* (Jefferson, NC: McFarland, 2016), p. 98.

34. Divorce Court File: 5494. John Edward Addinsell vs Muriel Addinsell and George Hay Whigham. National Archives, Kew. Ref J77/2091/5494.

35. Campbell, *Forget Not*, p. 18.

36. As per the Scottish census forms detailing the servants (including a governess) in the Hannay household, Helen's lack of education was not due to her parents withholding one.

37. Castle, *The Duchess Who Dared*, p. 11.

38. Ibid.

39. Waugh, Evelyn, *Vile Bodies* (London: Penguin Classics, 2000), p. 76.

40. Brilliant Chang was sentenced to fourteen months in prison for supplying cocaine to the actress Violet Payne. After his prison sentence he was deported. Payne herself was given three months' hard labour for possession.

Chapter 2: An English Girlhood

1. Jan Struther's memories of Miss Wolff. By kind permission of the Estate of Jan Struther.

2. Colt, George Howe, *Town and Country*, 20 July 2017.

3. Grosvenor, Loelia, *Grace and Favour* (London: Weidenfeld and Nicholson, 1961), p. 79.

4. Haldane, Brodrick, *Time Exposure* (London: Arcadia, 1999), p. 116.

5. Campbell, *Forget Not*, p. 21.

6. Mortimer, Penelope, *The Pumpkin Eater* (New York: McGraw-Hill, 1962), p.147.

7. 'I wish to God she had shut up.' Castle, *The Duchess Who Dared*, p. 12.
8. Campbell, *Forget Not*, p. 12.
9. *The Western Australian*, 5 February 1936.
10. *The Advertiser*, 5 February 1936.
11. Kennedy, Carol, *Mayfair: A Social History* (London: Hutchinson, 1986), p. 211.
12. Grosvenor, *Grace and Favour*, p. 74.
13. 'Every night she clasped each of us to her bosom and, smelling heavily of lavender-water, placed a bristly kiss on our brow. This was the moment for whispered confidences.' Ibid, p. 75.
14. Ibid.
15. Campbell, *Forget Not*, p. 29.
16. Fox, James, *Five Sisters: The Langhornes of Virginia* (London: Simon and Schuster, 2000), p. 336.
17. Ibid.
18. Campbell, *Forget Not*, p. 19.
19. 'It was as if he'd been shooting cocaine. It was something extremely immoral.' Fox, *Five Sisters*, p. 334.
20. Constance Markievicz was the first woman elected to parliament, but as she was an Irish Republican she did not take her seat.
21. Lord, Graham, *Niv: The Authorised Biography* (London: Orion, 2003), p. 36.
22. Michael Thornton to author.
23. Elizabeth Green, family cook. Michael Thornton to author.
24. 'Consider it a rumour.' David Niven Jr to author. However, Niven Jr claimed he did not know of his father's involvement with Margaret, even though it was mentioned in David Niven's authorised biography.
25. In Diana Petre's memoir she wrote of her mother's unwanted pregnancy. 'She had gone to a gynaecologist, faked certain symptoms and asked him to perform a curettage. When she came round from the anaesthetic, he said: "You lied to me, don't ever come to me again."' *The Secret Orchard of Roger Ackerley* (London: Slightly Foxed, 2016), p. 174.
26. Campbell, *Forget Not*, p. 34.
27. *New York Times*, 7 December 1975.
28. Ibid.

Chapter 3: The Season

1. As Margaret's birthday was in December, it was decided to launch her in the summer before her eighteenth birthday rather than waiting until

the year after, when she would be closer to 19. It allowed her to have two seasons while still the traditional age of debutante.

2. '… applications for presentation had to reach the Lord Chamberlain [in] the first post yesterday.' *Dundee Courier*, 2 January 1930.

3. Campbell, *Forget Not*, p. 34.

4. 'I helped to make Norman Hartnell and Victor Stiebel. They were beginners from Cambridge and then both go to Bruton Street in London. And I was in *everything, everywhere*.' Castle, *The Duchess Who Dared*, p. 17.

5. Many aristocratic parents would not let their children dine with them until they were 18. In some families such as Lord and Lady Londonderry's, the children, if they were permitted to come to the dining room, had to sit at a children's dining table until they were of age.

6. 'The 1930 debutante is a most surprising person! Having become so sophisticated that the elder generation finds it hard to keep pace with her.' *Belfast Newsletter*, 6 June 1930.

7. 'Debutantes are really very fortunate this season, for fashions are prettier than they have been for a long time, and seem to have been designed especially for youthful wearers.' *Folkestone, Hythe, Sandgate and Cheriton Herald*, 14 June 1930.

8. *Sheffield Daily Telegraph*, 29 May 1930.

9. Ibid.

10. 'All those marvellous tiaras just looked as if they'd been painted in charcoal.' De Courcy, Anne, *Debs at War* (London: Hachette, 2012) p. 47.

11. Ellen Murray Whigham hunted until her eighties, despite breaking her pelvis in a riding accident in her seventies. She lived until the age of 99.

12. *Daily Express*, 17 June 1927.

13. 5 February 1930.

14. *Morecambe Guardian*, 20 June 1930; *Essex Newsman*, 21 June 1930; *Londonderry Sentinel*, 21 June 1930.

15. Castle, *The Duchess Who Dared*, p. 15.

16. Horn, Pamela, *Country House Society: The Private Lives of England's Upper Class After the First World War* (Stroud: Amberley, 2013).

17. *Sheffield Daily Telegraph*, 29 May 1930.

18. The Prince of Wales preferred short presentations. During his brief reign as King Edward VIII he went to Scotland to oversee presentations at court. Halfway through he got his aide to announce that the rest 'could consider themselves presented', and he left for the golf course. De Courcy, *Debs at War*, p. 50.

19. 'Fourteen American debutantes who came over this year to make their curtsey to the king and queen will return home disappointed.' *Sheffield Independent*, 28 May 1930.

20. Castle, *The Duchess Who Dared*, p. 16.

21. Aly Khan's first wife, Joan Guinness (née Yarde–Buller) converted to Islam and was given the name Tajuddawlah. Their sons were therefore brought up as Muslims, and the eldest succeeded the Aga Khan. His second wife, Hollywood star Rita Hayworth, did not convert to his faith and refused $1million to raise their daughter, Princess Yasmine, as a Muslim.

22. Campbell, *Forget Not*, p. 43.

23. Ibid.

24. Jenkins, Alan, *The Thirties* (New York: Stein and Day, 1976), p. 24.

25. Philip Mould and Company.

26. *The Evening News*, 16 May 1938.

27. Castle, *The Duchess Who Dared*, p. 11.

28. Ibid., p. 20.

29. Ibid.

30. *The Telegraph*, 8 April 1933.

31. 'Everybody has been anxious to find the pretty French wife of the Aga Khan, but she very wisely returned to France … I think she would almost certainly have been mobbed, for the excitement was intense.' *Belfast Newsletter*, 6 June 1930.

32. *Leeds Mercury*, 4 March 1932.

33. Castle, *The Duchess Who Dared*, p. 20.

34. *The Telegraph*, 8 April 1933.

35. Kennedy, *Mayfair: A Social History*, p. 209.

36. Campbell, *Forget Not*, p. 46.

37. *The Chichester Observer*, 11 November 1931.

38. *The Bystander*, 11 November 1931.

39. *Tatler*, 15 October 1930.

40. *The Sketch*, 25 January 1933.

41. *The Sketch*, 2 September 1931.

42. *The Bystander*, 11 November 1931.

43. Castle, *The Duchess Who Dared*, p. 20.

44. Baker, Rob, *High Buildings, Low Morals: Another Sideways Look at Twentieth Century London* (Stroud: Amberley, 2017).

45. Castle, *The Duchess Who Dared*, p. 17.

46. Campbell, *Forget Not*, p. 61.

47. Archived at the British Film Institute.

48. Barbara named her son after Glen Kidston.

49. *Larne Times*, 9 May 1931.

50. Fitzgerald, F. Scott, *The Great Gatsby* (Ware, Herts.: Wordsworth Editions, 1994), p. 114.
51. '[I] was so terribly international.' Campbell, *Forget Not*, p. 19.
52. Kotowski, Mariuzs, *Pola Negri: Hollywood's First Femme Fatale* (Lexington, KY: University Press of Kentucky, 2014), p. 161.
53. Ibid.
54. *Larne Times*, 9 May 1931.
55. Campbell, *Forget Not*, p.52.
56. Ibid., p.53.
57. *Portsmouth Evening News*, 6 April 1931.
58. Campbell, *Forget Not*, p. 53.
59. Ibid., p.54.
60. Ibid.
61. Ibid.
62. Ibid.
63. *Taunton Courier and Western Advertiser*, 13 May 1931.
64. *Lancashire Evening Post*, 5 May 1931.
65. Campbell, *Forget Not*, p. 55.
66. *Lancashire Evening Post*, 5 May 1931.
67. Campbell, *Forget Not*, p. 57.
68. Ibid.
69. *Daily Mirror*, 6 May 1931.
70. Campbell, *Forget Not*, p. 58.
71. Sweeny, Charles, *Sweeny* (Canterbury: Harrop Press, 1990), p. 60.
72. Ibid., p. 61.
73. Ibid.
74. Ibid.
75. McKibbin, Ross, *Classes and Cultures:1918–1951* (Oxford: Oxford University Press, 2000), p. 29.
76. 'Margaret Whigham had many fond farewells to say before she sailed for Egypt.' *The Bystander*, 23 December 1931.
77. Ibid.

Chapter 4: Fate

1. Campbell, *Forget Not*, p. 61.
2. Chisholm, Anne and Davie, Michael, *Beaverbrook: A Life* (London: Hutchinson, 1992), p. 314.
3. Ibid., p. 315.
4. Ibid.
5. *Aberdeen Press and Journal*, 2 November 1931.

6. Castle, *The Duchess Who Dared*, p. 22.
7. Sweeny, *Sweeny*, p. 62.
8. Campbell, *Forget Not*, p. 66.
9. *Edinburgh Evening News*, 31 March 1932.
10. *Dundee Evening Telegraph*, 11 March 1932.
11. Campbell, *Forget Not*, p. 67.
12. Castle, *The Duchess Who Dared*, p. 23.
13. *Gloucester Citizen*, 19 March 1932.
14. Castle, *The Duchess Who Dared*, p. 23.
15. Campbell, *Forget Not*, p. 68.
16. *Nottingham Journal*, 31 March 1932.
17. *The Advertiser*, 1 July 1932.
18. *Taunton Courier and Western Advertiser*, 6 April 1932.
19. Campbell, *Forget Not*, p. 69.
20. *Birmingham Daily Gazette*, 14 May 1932.
21. Castle, *The Duchess Who Dared*, p. 23.
22. Sweeny, *Sweeny*, p. 63.
23. Castle, *The Duchess Who Dared*, p. 23.
24. Campbell, *Forget Not*, p. 69.
25. Sweeny, *Sweeny*, p. 6.
26. Twice he was thrown out of Westpoint; he fought in revolutions against three dictators; he was a decorated officer in the French Foreign Legion and the US Army during the First World War; a brigadier-general in the Polish–Soviet War and a military adviser in the Greco–Turkish War; he led a flying squadron in Morocco's Rif War; advised Loyalists in the Spanish Civil War; and spied for French Intelligence during WWII. Synopsis from Roberts, Charley and Hess, Charles P., *Charles Sweeny: The Man Who Inspired Hemingway* (Jefferson, NC: McFarland, 2017).
27. Castle, *The Duchess Who Dared*, p. 25.
28. Sweeny, *Sweeny*, p. 11.
29. Castle, *The Duchess Who Dared*, p. 28.
30. Sweeny, *Sweeny*, p. 66.
31. 'In her book she quite wrongly claims the credit for Larry Adler's first appearance in London. It was, in fact, my father Robert Sweeny who gave our engagement party.' *Daily Express*, 15 February 1977.
32. Sweeny, *Sweeny*, p. 67.
33. Campbell, *Forget Not*, p. 71.
34. Stonor, Julia Camoys, *Sherman's Wife* (Abingdon, Oxon: Desert Hearts, 2006), p. 256.
35. Sweeny, *Sweeny*, p. 67.
36. *Gloucestershire Citizen*, 2 February 1933.
37. *Dundee Evening Telegraph*, 17 February 1933.

38. *Dundee Courier*, 5 January 1933.
39. Ibid.
40. Campbell, *Forget Not*, p. 73.

Chapter 5: Mrs Sweeny

1. *Birmingham Gazette*, 22 February 1933.
2. *The Bystander*, 27 December 1933.
3. *The Journal*, 22 February 1933.
4. *Sheffield Independent*, 22 February 1933.
5. News footage from the wedding showed Margaret and Charlie walk-ing to their car, followed by ushers carrying her train and a policeman escorting them. It also showed Margaret and Charlie getting into the car and driving off. The young man in question was not captured on film, but a reporter recalled seeing him standing among the crowds and weeping.
6. Campbell, *Forget Not*, p. 75.
7. *Nottingham Evening Post,* 23 February 1933.
8. Campbell, *Forget Not*, p. 76.
9. Ibid.
10. *News of the World*, 19 May 1963.
11. Castle, *The Duchess Who Dared*, p. 28.
12. *News of the World*, 19 May 1963.
13. Sweeny, *Sweeny*, p. 74.
14. An antidote to Marie Stopes's *Married Love*, Mary Borden's book focused on practical matters such as living together, budget problems, the question of children, and mutual independence within the mar-riage. 'A sane book … [which] has a very general and universal appeal' (*Kirkus Reviews*).
15. *Sunday Times*, 2 July 1933.
16. *Western Daily Press*, 5 April 1933.
17. *Dundee Evening Telegraph*, 5 April 1933.
18. Ibid.
19. *Table Talk*, 30 March 1933.
20. Castle, *The Duchess Who Dared*, p. 29.
21. Campbell, *Forget Not*, p. 77.
22. Castle, *The Duchess Who Dared*, p. 26.
23. *The Daily News*, 12 April 1934.
24. *Gloucestershire Echo*, 17 February 1934.
25. Campbell, *Forget Not*, p. 81.
26. *Birmingham Daily Gazette*, 20 March 1934.

27. 'I loved it, even if I was classed with a piece of cheese.' *Daily Express*, 27 April 1953.

28. Campbell, *Forget Not*, p. 82.

29. *Leeds Mercury*, 12 June 1934.

30. Sweeny, *Sweeny*, p. 76.

31. 'I mean, it wasn't very cruel but it wasn't very kind either and I was miserable. I was very much in love with him.' Castle, *The Duchess Who Dared*, p. 27.

32. *The Bystander*, 4 December 1934.

33. Argyll, Margaret Duchess of, *My Dinner Party Book* (London: Ward Lock, 1986), p. 9.

34. Ibid., p. 39.

35. Castle, *The Duchess Who Dared*, p. 27.

36. *Sydney Morning Herald*, 14 January 1937.

37. *The Mail,* 27 July 1935.

38. Campbell, *Forget Not*, p. 90.

39. In Charles Sweeny's autobiography he wrote of being noticed by a golfing scout but his mother had other ideas, and decided the family should leave New York and move to Europe.

40. Campbell, *Forget Not*, p. 90.

41. Ibid.

42. Ibid.

Chapter 6: Idols of Consumption

1. *Shepton Mallet Journal*, 8 October 1937.

2. Count John McCormack begged Theresa to go on tour with himself and Chauncey Olcott, first tenor of the New York Opera.

3. Castle, *The Duchess Who Dared*, p. 112.

4. Sweeny, *Sweeny*, p. 66.

5. Ibid., p. 21.

6. Campbell, *Forget Not*, p. 87.

7. Sweeny, *Sweeny*, p. 111.

8. Campbell, *Forget Not*, p. 88.

9. Ibid.

10. Sweeny, *Sweeny*, p. 112.

11. *The West Australian*, 9 November 1937.

12. Campbell, *Forget Not*, p. 93.

13. 'It was a stroke of genius on the part of whoever first thought of getting young and attractive matrons like Mrs Charles Sweeny to act as chairman for various charity functions.' *The Bystander*, 25 November 1936.

14. Sweeny, *Sweeny*, p. 115.

15. Campbell, *Forget Not*, p. 90.

16. Ibid.

17. Sweeny, *Sweeny*, p. 110.

18. *The Sketch*, 28 July 1937.

19. *The Sketch*, 27 October 1937.

20. *Shepton Mallet Journal*, 9 July 1937.

21. Sweeny, *Sweeny*, p. 106.

22. 'Although a magnet for tourists from all over the world, Budapest has for several years been known to its own people as The City of Suicides. Budapest suffered badly after the war and has received unpleasant publicity from the number of cases of self-destruction occurring every year within its boundaries. Some of them are alleged to have been inspired by the Budapest song, "Gloomy Sunday", but be that as it may, the suicide rate in Budapest is definitely high. The favorite method adopted by most Budapest melancholics in drowning, and patrol boats are stationed along the boundary near the bridges to rescue citizens who seek consolation in the dark waters of the Danube.' *Sunday Times*, 17 October 1937.

23. *Daily Herald*, 9 May 1934.

24. Sweeny, *Sweeny*, p. 318.

25. Castle, *The Duchess Who Dared*, p. 11.

26. In Charlie's memoirs he also did not mention the birth of their still-born daughter, and so it would seem natural he would also bypass this troubling incident for Margaret.

27. Castle, *The Duchess Who Dared*, p. 27.

28. Ibid., p. 28.

29. *Warwick and Warwickshire Advertiser and Leamington Gazette*, 19 February 1938.

30. *Daily Mirror*, 12 February 1938.

31. *The Sketch*, 8 June 1938.

32. Sweeny, *Sweeny*, p. 119.

33. Ibid., p. 117.

34. Later, a German refugee came to the Marks's flat and, as he had no money, he offered to sell them a Renoir painting which he had smuggled out of Germany. He was offered £6,000 for it, and although it was worth much more, he accepted.

35. 'I hated leaving America, and I would have been sadder still had I known that it would be seven years before I was able to go there again, in spite of Chamberlain's promise of "peace in our time".' Campbell, *Forget Not*, p. 95.

Chapter 7: War

1. *Liverpool Daily Post*, 8 April 1940.
2. *Sunday Pictorial*, 26 November 1939.
3. Castle, *The Duchess Who Dared*, p. 30.
4. Campbell, *Forget Not*, p. 97.
5. Ibid.
6. Ibid.
7. Bell, Quentin, *Bloomsbury Recalled* (New York: Colombia University Press, 1997), p.136.
8. Christabel was responsible for revealing the identity of her father's chief suspect, M.J. Druitt, when she gave Daniel Faron a piece of paper from her father's case files and asked that he keep the identity a secret, as Druitt might have had relatives who were still living. Hainsworth, J.J., *Jack the Ripper: Case Solved, 1891* (Jefferson, NC: McFarland, 2015), p. 189.
9. 'To me, the mutilated bodies looked just like broken dolls.' Farson, Daniel, *Never a Normal Man* (London: Harper Collins, 1997), p. 268.
10. As a young woman she had asked, during a luncheon given for her mother's friends, why Oscar Wilde had been imprisoned. The question remained unanswered. So, before she married at the age of 19, she made a list 'Things I want to know when I marry', one being 'why did Oscar Wilde go to prison?' and, one night while in bed with her new husband, she asked him (www.Clan Macnaughton.net).
11. Castle, *The Duchess Who Dared*, p. 31.
12. Ibid.
13. Ibid.
14. Weideger, Paula, *Gilding the Acorn: Behind the Facade of the National Trust* (London: Simon and Schuster, 1994), p. 213.
15. 'As for Charlie, he was never well. He always had ulcers and just wouldn't do on a front line.' Castle, *The Duchess Who Dared*, p. 33.
16. Campbell, *Forget Not*, p. 103.
17. Castle, *The Duchess Who Dared*, p. 33.
18. Campbell, *Forget Not*, p. 103.
19. Letter from Eric Siepmann to Mary Wesley, 15 July 1945. Marnham, Patrick (ed.), *Darling Pol: Letters of Mary Wesley and Eric Siepmann 1944–1967* (London: Harvill Secker, 2017), p. 83.
20. 'And so with me. Colonel T. had been just as unable to satisfy Margaret's ego as I had.' Sweeny, *Sweeny*, p. 178.
21. Ibid.
22. *New York Times*, 7 December 1975.
23. Sweeny, *Sweeny*, p. 178.

24. Although her father did not survive his elder brother, the Earl of Sondes, who died without an heir, Isabel was permitted to use the prefix of Lady before her name, as her father was the son of an earl and was in line of inheriting the earldom of Sondes. The title passed to her brother.
25. Sweeny, *Sweeny*, p. 316.
26. Ibid., p. 219.
27. Ibid., p. 226.
28. Castle, *The Duchess Who Dared*, p. 36.

Chapter 8: The Golden Age

1. *Daily Mirror*, 24 May 1947.
2. Summer, Julie, *Stranger in the House: Women's Stories of Men Returning from the Second World War* (London: Simon and Schuster, 2009), p. 163.
3. When Margaret gave parties for Frances and Brian she seated the invited children and their nannies together, and they were placed at the table according to rank. Argyll, *My Dinner Party Book*, p. 39.
4. *Sunday Mail*, 4 May 1947.
5. *New York Times*, 2 January 1974.
6. Hoving, Thomas, *Making the Mummies Dance: Inside the Metropolitan Museum of Art* (New York: Simon and Schuster, 1994), p. 118.
7. Ibid., p. 117.
8. Castle, *The Duchess Who Dared*, p. 36.
9. Argyll, *My Dinner Party Book*, p. 38.
10. Campbell, *Forget Not*, p. 115.
11. Michael Thomas to author.
12. Ibid.
13. Argyll, *My Dinner Party Book*, p. 39.
14. *Daily Express*, 14 November 1994.
15. *Washington Post*, 19 July 1977.
16. Lister, Moira, *Daily Express*, 15 November 1994.
17. *Daily Express*, 15 November 1994.
18. Ibid.
19. Campbell, *Forget Not*, p. 119.
20. Aitken-Kidd, Janet, *The Beaverbrook Girl* (London: Collins, 1987), p. 140.
21. Ibid., p. 103.

Chapter 9: Crowning Mistake

1. Clare Sutherland, the duke's third wife, was a common feature in the gossip columns. An unforgotten incident occurred in 1948, on a trip to Palm Beach, when Clare refused to give precedence to the Duchess of Windsor, which prompted a legal debate on whether or not antiquated titles should be ranked higher than newer ones. Wallis, as the wife of the brother of a sovereign, was given precedence over other duchesses, but Clare won the popularity vote and gained many admirers after she challenged the former Mrs Simpson.
2. Castle, *The Duchess Who Dared*, p. 38.
3. 'He turned away abruptly, opened a drawer and took out a revolver … God he was serious!' Aitken-Kidd, *The Beaverbrook Girl*, p. 108.
4. Campbell, *Forget Not*, p. 119.
5. Aitken-Kidd, *The Beaverbrook Girl*, p. 101.
6. *New York Times*, 10 March 2005.
7. Barkan, Robert Elliot, *From All Points: America's Immigrant West, 1870s–1952* (Indiana: Indiana University Press, 2007) p. 312.
8. Baldridge, Letitia, *Roman Candle* (New York: Houghton Mifflin, 1956), p. 236.
9. Caracciolo, Carlo, *Vanity Fair,* December 2009.
10. Campbell, *Forget Not*, p. 120.
11. Anouilh, Jean, *Ring Round the Moon* (New York: Dramatists Play Service, 1952), p. 69.
12. Campbell, *Forget Not*, p. 120.
13. Bloch, Michael, *James Lees-Milne Diaries: 1942–54* (London: John Murray, 2007).
14. Ibid.
15. '"Keep clear," said my mother. "It'll end badly." "How could it end badly?" I protested.' Haldane, *Time Exposure*, p. 113.

Chapter 10: The Duchess

1. Lennon, Michael, *Norman Mailer: A Double Life* (New York: Simon and Schuster, 2013) p. 309.
2. Castle, *The Duchess Who Dared*, p. 43.
3. Campbell, *Forget Not*, p. 126.
4. Ibid.
5. *Daily Express*, 24 August 1982.
6. *Daily Mirror*, 6 June 1952.
7. Ibid.

8. Ibid.
9. Aitken-Kidd, *The Beaverbrook Girl*, p. 111.
10. *Evening Express*, 13 October 1959.
11. Castle, *The Duchess Who Dared*, p. 51.
12. Ibid.
13. Haldane, *Time Exposure*, p. 116.
14. Aitken-Kidd, *The Beaverbrook Girl*, p. 200.
15. Haldane, *Time Exposure*, p. 115.
16. Campbell, *Forget Not*, p. 141.
17. Mosley, Charlotte (ed.), *Love from Nancy: The Letters of Nancy Mitford* (London: Houghton Mifflin, 1993), p. 165.
18. Lehmann, John, *The Ample Proposition* (London: Eyre and Spottiswood, 1966), p. 94.
19. He did, however, attend Le Bal du Siècle in Venice, a costume ball hosted by Charles Beistegui, for which Ian dressed as a Georgian gentleman and Margaret an angel.

Chapter 11: Cat and Mouse

1. Campbell, *Forget Not*, p. 138.
2. Confided to her friend, Riccy di Portanova. Castle, *The Duchess Who Dared*, p. 127.
3. 'It will probably be the costliest kilt ever made …' *Daily Mirror*, 8 November 1956.
4. Castle, *The Duchess Who Dared*, p. 52.
5. Campbell, *Forget Not*, p. 140.
6. Castle, *The Duchess Who Dared*, p. 55.
7. Campbell, *Forget Not*, p. 141.
8. Grosvenor, *Grace and Favour*, p. 223.
9. Campbell, *Forget Not*, p. 140.
10. Haldane, *Time Exposure*, p. 121.
11. Ibid.
12. Ibid.
13. Lord Wimborne, *The Independent*, 28 July 1993.
14. Campbell, *Forget Not*, p. 147.
15. Ibid.

Chapter 12: Slipstream

1. Davenport-Hines, Richard, *Oblivion: A Social History of Drugs* (London: Hachette, 2012), p. 196.
2. *News of the World*, 12 May 1963.
3. Magda Buchel was a calculating woman and motivated by money. In 1949 Magda had sued Mr Henry 'Atte' Persse, a horse trainer, the Earl of Sutton, and a steward of the Jockey Club after she claimed the earl's horse had kicked and injured her at an Ascot race.
4. As recalled by Magda Buchel. *Birmingham Post*, 4 May 1960.
5. Ibid.
6. Campbell, *Forget Not*, p. 154.
7. Ibid.
8. Ibid.
9. Sweeny, *Sweeny*, p. 317.
10. Ibid.
11. Ibid., p. 318.
12. Campbell, *Forget Not*, p. 158.
13. Sweeny, *Sweeny*, p. 318.
14. Ibid., p. 347.
15. Castle, *The Duchess Who Dared*, p. 61.
16. Haldane, *Time Exposure*, p. 117.
17. Castle, *The Duchess Who Dared*, p. 70.
18. Haldane, *Time Exposure*, p. 117.
19. *Daily Mirror*, 22 December 1959.
20. Castle, *The Duchess Who Dared*, p. 68.

Chapter 13: Treachery

1. Campbell, *Forget Not*, p. 147.
2. Petulengro, Eva, *Caravans and Wedding Bands* (London: Pan Macmillan, 2012), p. 199.
3. Ibid.
4. 'When I was about nineteen I had a weird encounter with her just outside St George's Hanover Square when she, rather terrifyingly, gave me the eye. Needless to say there was no future in it and I, terrified, ran a mile!' Nicholas Maxwell to author.
5. *Birmingham Post*, 4 May 1960.
6. Campbell, *Forget Not*, p. 151.
7. *Daily Mirror*, 4 May 1960.
8. *Birmingham Post*, 4 May 1960.

9. Ibid.
10. Campbell, *Forget Not*, p. 181.
11. *Daily Express*, 22 October 1964.
12. Interview with Nicole, Duchess of Bedford. *Sydney Morning Herald*, 20 September 2012.
13. Castle, *The Duchess Who Dared*, p. 109.
14. Campbell, *Forget Not*, p. 194.
15. *The Telegraph, Bonker, Bounder, Beggarman, Thief: A Compendium of Rogues, Villains and Scandals* (London: Aurum Press, 2016).
16. Ibid.
17. Ibid.
18. Campbell, *Forget Not*, p. 170.
19. Castle, *The Duchess Who Dared*, p. 109.
20. Comment made by actress Moira Lister, as recorded in Castle, *The Duchess Who Dared*, p. 103.
21. Keeler, Christine, *Secrets and Lies: The Real Story of Political Scandal that Mesmerised the World* (London: John Blake, 2014).
22. 'When Fairbanks was in action a camera was never far away.' Ibid.
23. *The Independent*, 31 July 1993.
24. Michael Thomas to author.
25. *Daily Mirror*, 9 May 1963.
26. Castle, *The Duchess Who Dared*, p. 1.
27. *Daily Mirror*, 15 May 1963.
28. Seymour, Miranda, *Chaplin's Girl: The Life and Loves of Virginia Cherrill* (London: Simon and Schuster, 2010), p. 176.
29. Duchess of Argyll versus Duke of Argyll, 1964, p. 8.
30. Ibid., p.6.
31. Campbell, *Forget Not*, p. 203.

Chapter 14: 'Here Comes a Brand New Woman'

1. *Vanity Fair*, 1986.
2. 'Actually, Brian Sweeny has been one of her stoutest defenders and says that she was a good mother, by the standards of her time.' *Vanity Fair*, 1993.
3. Campbell, *Forget Not*, p. 211.
4. *Daily Express*, 3 January 1967.
5. *BBC News*, 1 December 2007.
6. Campbell, *Forget Not*, p. 223.
7. Castle, *The Duchess Who Dared*, p. 132.
8. Campbell, *Forget Not*, p. 241.

Chapter 15: Old Foe

1. Haldane, *Time Exposure*, p. 117.
2. Wells, Gully, *The House in France: A Memoir* (London: Bloomsbury, 2012), p. 70.
3. *Daily Mirror*, 10 April 1975.
4. *Australian Women's Weekly*, 11 June 1975.
5. Ibid.
6. *Daily Express*, 3 August 1993.
7. Beverley Jackson to author.
8. Allan Warren to author.
9. Seymour, *Chaplin's Girl: The Life and Loves of Virginia Cherrill*, p. 176.
10. *Daily Record*, 3 April 1985.
11. Kim Booth to author. Further information can be found in Booth's book, *A Cruel Deception*.
12. *The Lincolnshire Echo*, 3 April 1985.
13. *Daily Express*, 13 June 1988.
14. Judge Anwyl-Davies ruling, as reported in the *Daily Express*, 11 May 1989.
15. Allan Warren to author.
16. Ibid.

Bibliography

Aitken-Kidd, Janet, *The Beaverbrook Girl* (London: Collins, 1987)

Anouilh, Jean, *Ring Round the Moon* (New York: Dramatists Play Service, 1952)

Argyll, Margaret Duchess of, *My Dinner Party Book* (London: Ward Lock, 1986)

Baker, Rob, *High Buildings, Low Morals: Another Sideways Look at Twentieth Century London* (Stroud: Amberley, 2017)

Baldridge, Letitia, *Roman Candle* (New York: Houghton Mifflin, 1956)

Barkan, Robert Elliot, *From All Points: America's Immigrant West, 1870s–1952* (Bloomington, IN: Indiana University Press, 2007)

Bell, Quentin, *Bloomsbury Recalled* (New York: Colombia University Press, 1997)

Bloch, Michael, *James Lees-Milne Diaries*: *1942–54* (London: John Murray, 2007)

Booth, Kim, *A Cruel Deception* (Independently Published, 2019)

Breitenbach, Esther, *A Documentary History, 1780–1914* (Edinburgh: Edinburgh University Press, 2013)

Campbell, Margaret: *Forget Not* (London: W.H. Allen, 1975)

Castle, Charles, *The Duchess Who Dared* (London: Sidgwick and Jackson, 1994)

Chisholm, Anne and Davie, Michael, *Beaverbrook: A Life* (London: Hutchinson, 1992)

Davenport-Hines, Richard, *Oblivion: A Social History of Drugs* (London: Hachette, 2012)

De Courcy, Anne, *Debs at War* (London: Hachette, 2012)

Farson, Daniel, *Never a Normal Man* (London: Harper Collins, 1997)

Fitzgerald, F. Scott, *The Great Gatsby* (Ware, Herts.: Wordsworth Editions, 1994)

Fox, James, *Five Sisters: The Langhornes of Virginia* (London: Simon and Schuster, 2000)

Grosvenor, Loelia, *Grace and Favour* (London: Weidenfeld and Nicholson, 1961)

Hainsworth, J.J., *Jack the Ripper: Case Solved, 1891* (Jefferson, NC: McFarland, 2015)

Haldane, Brodrick, *Time Exposure* (London: Arcadia, 1999)

Hartley, Stephen, *The Irish Question as a Problem in British Foreign Policy 1914–18* (Basingstoke: Palgrave MacMillan, 1987)

Horn, Pamela, *Country House Society: The Private Lives of England's Upper Class After the First World War* (Stroud: Amberley, 2013)

Hoving, Thomas, *Making the Mummies Dance: Inside the Metropolitan Museum of Art* (New York: Simon and Schuster, 1994)

Jenkins, Alan, *The Thirties* (New York: Stein and Day, 1976)

Keeler, Christine, *Secrets and Lies: The Real Story of Political Scandal that Mesmerised the World* (London: John Blake, 2014)

Kennedy, Carol, *Mayfair: A Social History* (London: Hutchinson, 1986)

Kotowski, Mariuzs, *Pola Negri: Hollywood's First Femme Fatale* (Lexington, KY: University Press of Kentucky, 2014)

Lehmann, John, *The Ample Proposition* (London: Eyre and Spottiswood, 1966)

Lennon, Michael, *Norman Mailer: A Double Life* (New York: Simon and Schuster, 2013)

Lord, Graham, *Niv: The Authorised Biography* (London: Orion, 2003)

Marnham, Patrick (ed.), *Darling Pol: Letters of Mary Wesley and Eric Siepmann 1944–1967* (London: Harvill Secker, 2017)

McKibbin, Ross, *Classes and Cultures: 1918–1951* (Oxford: Oxford University Press, 2000)

Menzies, Grant-Hayer, *Mrs Ziegfeld: The Public and Private Lives of Billie Burke* (Jefferson, NC: McFarland, 2016)

Mortimer, Penelope, *The Pumpkin Eater* (New York: McGraw-Hill, 1962)

Mosley, Charlotte (ed.), *Love from Nancy: The Letters of Nancy Mitford* (London: Houghton Mifflin, 1993)

Petre, Diana, *The Secret Orchard of Roger Ackerley* (London: Slightly Foxed, 2016)

Petulengro, Eva, *Caravans and Wedding Bands* (London: Pan Macmillan, 2012)

Seymour, Miranda, *Chaplin's Girl: The Life and Loves of Virginia Cherrill* (London: Simon and Schuster, 2010)

Sherrow, Victoria, *For Appearance's Sake: The Historical Encyclopedia of Good Looks, Beauty and Grooming* (Westport, CT: Greenwood Publishing Group, 2001)

Stonor, Julia Camoys, *Sherman's Wife* (Abingdon, Oxon: Desert Hearts, 2006)

Summer, Julie, *Stranger in the House: Women's Stories of Men Returning from the Second World War* (London: Simon and Schuster, 2009)

Sweeny, Charles, *Sweeny* (Canterbury: Harrop Press, 1990)

Waugh, Evelyn, *Vile Bodies* (London: Penguin Classics, 2000)

Weideger, Paula, *Gilding the Acorn: Behind the Facade of the National Trust* (London: Simon and Schuster, 1994)

Wells, Gully, *The House in France: A Memoir* (London: Bloomsbury, 2012)

Index